TO BE QUEEN OF SCORCHED ASHES

Madison L. Bailey

SANCTANIA
USTARIA
CARLISLE
ACLOS
APLIL
ADRAIN
THE CAPITAL
VERMUSE
BAYTOWN
MOUNT JAMES
ST. MARIE'S
ISLES DES MORTUES
COAST CROWLEY
FOOTHILL
MOLISAN

Dedication

To those who believed in me.

A dream is just that until you act upon it.

Author's Note

This book contains foul language, talks of sexual and physical assault, violence, murder, anxiety, PTSD and depression.

While this is a character in a fantasy novel, all of her experiences and emotions are real life issues that many of us have experienced.

Please don't hesitate to reach out, your mental health matters.

My tongue is stuck to the roof of my mouth as I woke from a dreamless sleep. Trying to swallow, I bring my hands up and rub my face. Bright lights hurt my eyes as I attempt to pry them open. Wait, bright lights?

Where the Hell am I?

I shoot upright in a bed I quickly knew wasn't my own. My vision slowly crept back to me, and I took in my surroundings as quickly as I could. It looked somewhat like the small infirmary in Foothill, the capital of Molisan, where we had to take Rose when she had a horrible fever, but I knew it wasn't the right place. The small room I sat in had pristine white walls, multiple small empty beds besides the one I currently occupied, a small desk to the front of the room and double doors leading somewhere. It smelled of salt water, but not the comforting kind of the ocean, this was a sterile sort of smell that immediately made me uncomfortable. This definitely wasn't in Foothill. My heart began to pound just as much as my head was from sitting up so fast.

Wait, where is everyone?

Why am I alone?

It became hard to breathe as panic settled into my chest. I looked down at myself and the bed I sat on. I was wearing a papery white gown, and from what I could feel, nothing underneath as the cold crept through the thin material.

I feel dizzy.

I touched my head, realizing my usually tangly, unruly, thick hair had been put into two braids like Mother used to do. Something yanked on my arm, and I realized I was hooked up to wires and tubes, which were hooked up to monitor screens and bags of Gods know what. An alarm began to sound on the monitor to my left, flashing red numbers across the screen.

I need to get out of here.

I pull at the wires attached to my body, and I try standing up to the edge of my bed. I winced as I ripped the tube, injecting me with some sort of substance, out of my left arm and blood began squirting everywhere. That's when I hear a rush of someone's footsteps and a small door next to the desk open. Looking up, the world starts tilting, and I fight my consciousness and my legs to stay underneath me. A short and slim woman appeared in front of me wearing a long, starched white jacket and glasses that took up half her small face.

"Ryenn, you need to get back in bed now, you're too weak to get up yet," she said in a calm, quiet voice.

Reaching for my arms, she began to guide me back to the stretcher. I tried to say something, to ask questions or to fight, but my mouth wouldn't open.

Gods, what is happening right now?

The small woman turned to the side to press something on the monitor and grabbed a small bandage for my arm that is still bleeding. That's when I notice something *off* about her. Her ears are pointed. Like a Fairy. Wait, was she a Fairy?

Oh my Gods, I really am not in Molisan anymore.

My vision went completely, and I collapsed on the bed.

~

"Ryenn...Ryenn, you need to wake up now."

Startled, my eyes flew open. It only took a matter of seconds for me to remember what had just happened. The woman standing before me was *not* a human, she was a Fairy. Humans and Fairies had been at odds for… well, for centuries, I guess. They didn't really teach us much about them in school, the only thing being that they were not trustworthy and what to look for in the general appearance of them. Pointed ears, fangs, unnaturally beautiful and manipulative. And that's exactly who stood before me. Well, I don't exactly know about the manipulative part, but I was obviously kidnapped and being held hostage, so I think it's safe to assume.

"Oh good, you're awake. There's no need to be afraid. My name is Sara, I am your healer who has been looking after you since you've arrived in Sanctania. You must have many questions," said Sara in that same hushed voice.

It kind of made it hard to be afraid of her when she sounded so nice, but I know better.

Also, what the hell is Sanctania?

"Where the hell am I?" I said, my voice wobbly and scratchy. I cleared my throat. "How did I get here? What do you want from me?"

"You're in safe hands, dear." The small woman smiled, sitting on the end of my bed. "You were found by a Scouting troop from the kingdom only 20 miles from The Wall. I can't answer all of your questions unfortunately. However, the King has requested to see you when you woke and are well enough."

The King. *The Fairy King?* Good Gods I think I may faint again.

Sara glanced up at the monitor as it began flashing.

"I can see you're a bit nervous. That's entirely reasonable. You're in a place you've never been, and likely have never heard of, and are being asked to speak with people you have never met. I know I may be asking a lot right now, but I want you to trust that we are not going to hurt you. You are safe. I *promise.*" She reached for my hand, and I flinched. Her hands were cool to touch but soft.

Trust her? I'm not so sure about that, but clearly, I don't really have a choice right now. As she said, I am somewhere I have never been and have never heard of before. There's no way in hell I could escape even if I tried. Gods, I don't even think I could run out those doors across the room without passing out again as soon as I stood up. I needed to speak to this King, understand where I am and make a plan on how to get out. *Not that I have anywhere to go.* I shut that thought out. Now is not the time. I need to be strong and figure this out.

"When can I see the King," I said, a little less gremlin-like this time.

"Well, since you're awake and seem to be in good spirits, I can take you to see him right now. You will have to sit in a wheelchair so I can bring you up since you're still pretty weak right now." I nodded, and she left to grab a chair with wheels.

Still very unsteady on my feet, Sara helped guide me into the chair. I was now hyper-aware that my entire backside was completely exposed in this paper-gown. Seeing the redness spread across my face, Sara grabbed a blanket from the bed to wrap around my shoulders and one to lay on my lap. *How did she know what I was feeling?*

"Before we leave, I just want to warn you that things you see may be overwhelming for you. If at any point you want to leave and come back here, just say the word, okay?"

Well, that was nice of her.

What things is she warning me about, though?

Despite my anxiety, I nod my head, and she begins to wheel me through the double doors of the small, empty, infirmary-style room.

Chapter 2

So, if I had any doubts about this being a Fairy kingdom and *not* Molisan, they were gone in a matter of a few minutes of leaving the infirmary. Knights or guards, I'm not sure what they are called here, met us outside the doors and escorted us through winding halls. There were floor-to-ceiling windows all along the way, and I looked out to see beautiful buildings, gardens, houses, fountains, and people. Everyone that I saw had the general appearance of a Fairy; mainly noticeable were their pointed ears or their exceptionally beautiful features. I felt like I was sticking out like a sore thumb, honestly. I'm a pretty ordinary-looking 16-year-old *human* girl, maybe even a bit less than ordinary. My wavy, thick and light brown hair is neither bouncy with curls or straight and silky. My eyes are a seasick sort of gray color, and my face is peppered in freckles. I'm also a bit underdeveloped for my age, I guess. I mean, I have no curves or womanly features as of yet. I picture my mother and how perfect she was in my eyes. How comforting her features were, how beautiful and bouncy her red locks were and her kind bright blue eyes. And my little sister Rose, who looked like a spitting image of our mother, would be just as beautiful as she grows up. *Would have been.*

My train of thought is interrupted as we come to a stop in front of two large emerald-green doors.

"This is the Main Auditorium," states Sara. "This is where King Emmet has most of his meetings and where all the important people meet with him. Today is a bit different, though. You'll be meeting with the King and Queen by yourself, well, I'll be here, of course, and so will the Scouts, but the small council was asked to sit this one out to give you some time to adjust."

I let out a deep breath. King and Queen. Cool, okay, I can do this. I just need to get on their good side, learn about this place and then get the hell out of here any chance I get. I can do that. *Maybe.*

"Are you ready, Ryenn?" Sara asks, brushing her soft hands on my shoulder. A shiver goes through me, but despite it, I nod. *I can do this.*

The guards, or Scouts as Sara called them, open the large doors, which must weigh like hundreds of pounds. Sara slowly advances me into the large room. In the room, there are two long, large tables to the right and left with 6 seats at each. Everything is polished and in the same shade of the main doors; an emerald green. The middle of the room is left open, but at the head of the room is a much smaller table with only two seats. In the seats are sitting who I can assume to be the Fairy King and Queen of Sanctania.

I am not sure exactly what I was expecting, but they look different than what I imagined. The King looks young, maybe even younger than Father. He is very handsome and *very* tall. Even though he is sitting right now, I imagine he may be taller than me if I were standing. He has a clean look to him, no beard or stubble to be seen, and his light brown hair is short and slicked back. He is wearing a suit with what I imagine to be the kingdom's crest on his left breast. Next to him is a stunning woman, the Queen. She is also tall, not as tall as her partner, but tall no less. Her beautiful blonde hair is swept into a low hairstyle, and her blue eyes are glistening in the sun that is peaking through the curtains. The dress she wears, a pale blue with her shoulders exposed, fits her beautifully and makes her eyes even more breathtaking. Both wear crowns on top of their heads.

Sara stops my chair about 10 feet away from the table, and a Scout brings a chair for her to sit on next to me. The rest of the Scouts stand by the walls and by the entrance. The King and Queen stand, and everyone in the room either bows or curtsies.

There really is no chance of escaping now.

"Hello, Ryenn," the King announces, his voice deep but kind. It echoes through the auditorium. "Welcome to the Kingdom of Sanctania. My name is Emmet Embers, King of Sanctania and my wife, the Queen, is Celeste Embers."

I swallow deep, and Sara places a hand on my shoulder, which instantly calms me for some reason.

"I understand that you must be incredibly confused and

perhaps somewhat curious of how you ended up in this kingdom and why you are here. I'm hoping that after this talk with you, you will feel a bit better about everything." He smiles at me as he finishes his sentence, and I can see the elongated canines; his *fangs*.

I am unable to speak. I fear if I open my mouth, I'll just vomit everywhere, if I'm being honest.

Turn it off.

"I see you have met Sara," the King continues. "She is one of our best and most prized healers here in the castle, and we wanted to make sure she tended to you individually to ensure your comfort. I hope she has treated you well."

I nod in response to that statement. Sara smiles at me and the King.

"Well then, would you like me to just start from the top, or do you have any specific questions first? I guess I should probably ask how you are feeling. You made us very worried. You have been in a coma for 10 days now," the King states, looking over me in a way that makes me feel even more vulnerable in this stupid gown.

I've been here for 10 days? Shock courses through my veins.

"I'm okay. You can start from the beginning," I say, more meekly than I intend and clear my throat. *Toughen up.*

"Alright then, dear. If at any point you have questions or need a break, just let us know," he says and glances at his wife, the Queen, who is quite literally staring at me, unblinking.

My cheeks warm. One of my greatest flaws is my ability to blush at everything and anything. I'm usually pretty good at keeping my emotions in check, but my face betrays me the moment I feel somewhat embarrassed. It's quite annoying.

"I suppose I will start with how we found you." King Emmet begins, "The Kingdom has Royal Scouts; their duty is to first and foremost protect the citizens of Sanctania. We also have Scouting teams whose job is to monitor the perimeter for 50 miles outside the Wall to ensure there are no mortal civilians that may need help or attacks from that side as well. They rarely find anything, but we learned of the attack on Baytown, which was not our doing, by the way, but I will get into that more later. I had more troops scouting the perimeter since the attack, and one of the main troops ended up finding you under a pine tree, wearing no clothes, with all of the snow melted around you, and merely 20 miles from *our* side of the Wall. Ryenn that means you had to travel over *80 miles*, naked, in the snow-covered dense forest of the mountainside."

All I could do was stare at this man as he told me about this, my body still, fearing if I moved, I'd miss something *or faint again.*

Don't let them see you're weak.

"The Scouts feared you were long dead when they first came upon you, but then you moved, and they hurried to wrap you up and ran as fast as they could, on horseback, back to the kingdom with you. They brought you straight to the infirmary as you were clearly very sick, and I was then alerted of your presence. Myself and Celeste went down to the infirmary, not really knowing to expect, but there you were, and you truly looked nearly dead. It was horrible. I called to have the Septor brought to the infirmary to see if your conscience was still intact and to get a story as to where you came from and who you were." The King looked to one of the Scouts, and they brought in the large, golden-stick-looking thing with a clear globe sitting atop it.

"The Septor is an instrument passed down through centuries in the kingdom for the appointed King or Queen to use only when deemed necessary. It is made with incredibly old magic. It basically allows the beholder to see the memories of someone. All of their memories, even ones the person may not remember that are hidden in the back of your mind, can be viewed." The King passes the Septor between his hands as he explains. "It is a way we keep crime down here as well as we can see the truth of all events. It is difficult to manipulate and, once used, needs to recharge in a way. Anyways, we used the Septor to see if we could get an understanding as to how you ended up where you did, where you came from, and who you were. What we saw, however… well, it shocked all of us."

Wearily, I looked as the King and Queen gave each other a glance.

"What shocked you?" I gulped.

"Ryenn…" The King looked at me intently. "You are the rightful heir to the Emerald Throne of Sanctania."

Chapter 3

"I'm sorry, but *what*?" I exclaim, nearly choking on my surprise of his ludicrous statement. "How could I be an heir to a Fairy Kingdom when I'm not even a Fairy?"

"That is exactly my point… you *are* a Fae," the King leaned forward across his desk. "When looking at your memories through the Septor, we saw your earliest memories. We saw how you were brought into this world. My older sister, Elanore, was your biological mother. She was the Queen before myself. I was never meant to be King, actually, she was the eldest, and she was promised it and to her kin after her. *You.* You see, my sister cared for the mortal lands very deeply. She wanted to fix the divide that our ancestors had caused, and she used to go to the different towns of the Molisan, disguised as a mortal, whenever they were attacked by the Dark King or his rebels. During one of these attacks, Elanore had been visiting Baytown, where you've grown up, to help clean up from a previous massacre. She had been pregnant with you during this. We originally believed she had been killed with you still in her womb and that you died along with her. After seeing your memories, though, we saw Endra, your mortal/adoptive mother, had helped to deliver you after Elanore had been injured. She died very shortly after your birth but had told Endra to take care of you for her. She didn't have the chance to tell her she had been a Fae. We don't say

'Fairies' here, by the way, as it's a somewhat insolent term adapted by mortals. Anyway, Endra raised you as her own, up until… well, her death as you know."

I felt sick again. Like all the blood had drained from my body, and like I was starting to sway a bit.

Gods, I felt foolish.

This had to be real, though, hadn't it? I mean, this Septor thing could see my own memories using *magic*? My chest became tight with panic.

"Your Highness, I believe Ryenn needs a break," Sara stated gently. How could she tell I was losing it? Was *she* magic, too? Wait, was *everyone* magic?

Gods, I need a minute.

Get ahold of yourself.

"Absolutely. Ser Davis, can you get Ryenn some water, please?"

A few moments later, a Scout brings me ice-cold water. I drink it fast, probably too fast, since my stomach churns after.

"I am just confused. If I can't remember this, then how can you see it? How do I know this is *real*? I don't look like a *Fae*, I look ordinarily *human*."

"I can assure you what I say is the truth. We even did a paternity test while you were in a coma to confirm Elanore was your mother, and it came back positive."

He slides forward a piece of paper with the results of the test. At the top of the page is written 'Paternity Test For Ryenn Caslee'. A large positive sign was next to the name Elanore Embers halfway down the page. A question mark was next to the word 'Father.'

"As for not looking like a Fae, you have not yet gone through the Transitioning. This occurs when all Fae come of age, usually the same time a female gets her first cycle. They get the physical aspects of being a Fae, such as the ears pointing, improved hearing, elongated canines, better taste, better sense of smell, feature heightening and they get their powers among a few other things."

"Powers? Do you mean like magic?" I blurt out before really realizing I'm speaking.

"Somewhat yes, for example, Sara is a Healer, meaning she does things that mortals do to heal people, but she also has the ability to heal people with her powers alone; it's how we got you back from the edge of death. She also has abilities to sense how someone is feeling and how to make them feel better. That is probably why you have found her touch to be comforting. There are plenty of different powers, which is something we can discuss in the future. Magic is something far different and much more ancient. Right now, I want to get you settled in and everything in order."

"I don't want to get things in *order*, I can't stay here. *I need to go home*." My chest tightens as I say this.

"My sweet child, we have seen *all* your memories. You and I both know there is no home for you to go back to, as well as no family-"

"Do *not* speak about my family!" I yell, and tears begin to sting my eyes.

Stop, you can't let them see you weak.

Turn it off.

"My apologies for the insensitivity, dear," the King paused. "But you must understand where I am coming from. You are still a minor, meaning you won't be able to survive out there alone. Not only are you heir to the Emerald Throne, you are eventually going to go through the Transitioning. You know you cannot go back to the mortal lands as a Fae."

I did understand where he was coming from. Doesn't mean I liked it, though. I didn't know this world, let alone the Fae or how to *be* one.

The Queen spoke for the first time since I entered the room, "We are here to guide you in all the right directions. You will get schooling, learn how to be a Fae, make friends, and overall be *safe*.

We aren't going to let you fend for yourself anymore. It's going to be okay. Just give us a chance, okay?" I looked at the Queen, staring at me with her piercing blue eyes. Her expression was difficult to read.

"Alright," I said, swallowing my pride.

I know there's nowhere else for me to go. The King had been right when he said that, still, it didn't hurt any less. Let alone having to stay here in this strange world with these strange beings that I apparently was a part of. I still had so many questions, but my head was pounding.

"Good. Sara will see you to your chambers. They are just down the hall and to the left of mine and Celeste's chambers. Someone will come get you for dinner this evening, and we can talk more then," the King states as he begins to stand.

Sara begins to wheel me out of the auditorium.

"Oh, and Ryenn, if it makes you feel remotely any better, troops have been aiding the recourse of Baytown for the last two weeks. There were survivors, albeit not many, but we are looking into the cause of the attack."

Chapter 4

After Sara led me through the halls and to my new chambers, she stated she would be by to visit me three times a day for my new medications and to ensure I was doing okay. I thanked her, and she left briefly after. Since then, I have been sitting on my bed, looking around the chambers. The bed was huge with canopy-style posts like out of the fairytales I used to read to Rose. I had a large walk-in wardrobe filled with dresses and other types of clothing that were not familiar styles to me. On the same wall as the main entrance, there was a washroom that had a large porcelain white tub, a toilet and a basin. All of which had running water, which was not very common in Molisan unless you were wealthy and lived in the capital- Foothill.

Everything felt surreal like I was dreaming. Standing up slowly, I walked to the washroom and looked in the mirror above the basin. I could hardly recognize myself. My face was slimmer, probably due to a lack of proper nutrients, as Sara had stated, and there were dark circles beneath my eyes. I took the braids out of my hair that Sara must have done while I was in the coma. It left my hair in a wavy mess.

After an hour or so of trying to take everything in and wrap my head around things, there was a light knock on the door.

"Uh, come in?" I stated.

Who the hell was here?

"Hello, Princess, my name is Evie, and I am your personal handmaiden. I have come to help you bathe and get ready for dinner," the little female said. She was short in stature, and her features reminded me of a little mouse. She was pretty young-looking, maybe only a few years older than myself.

"Oh, um, I can bathe myself, thank you," I dismiss, feeling a rush of heat come to my face. I don't know how I feel about this person seeing me naked. Even though clearly Sara has. And that group of Scouts that found me in the Forbidden Forest. And probably the King and Queen if they have seen *all* my memories.

Good Gods.

"Are you sure? All the ladies have a handmaiden to get them ready for things." She tilts her head.

"Well, I suppose you can get everything ready, but I'd rather bathe myself," I say, flustered.

Evie looked somewhat disappointed to hear this. I suppose this was her job after all, and now I was denying her from doing it.

"You can style my hair when I am finished if you'd like," I offered, and her face lit up.

"Sure! I'll get all of the things ready." She scurried off.

~

Although I wasn't visibly dirty, it felt good to wash away what felt like layers of grime on my skin. Evie had just finished pulling my hair back into a low knot. I used to do the same style around the house while watching Rose, doing chores and gardening. I found it to be the most effective at keeping the usual tangly mess from getting in my face. Those memories stung when they reached the surface. *I'll never be able to go back to that.*

Shaking the thought from my head, I looked in the mirror. I let Evie pick out the gown I was wearing as I didn't know what to wear for what occasion. The gown I wore was a deep blue color and plain looking, which I liked. It had a scooped modest neckline and long sleeves trimmed with white lace. I looked sickly thin in it, Evie even had to hem in the sides so I wasn't drowning in the material. I stood, still taking my time to do as such since I tended to get lightheaded when standing so quickly. Evie led me out into the hall so the Scouts could escort me to dinner.

"Where exactly are we going?" I asked.

"To the Familial Dining Hall," the Scout, who I remembered as Ser Davis, said. "It is located on the same side of the castle as the chambers and all familial personal affairs are. There is a more public dining hall in the central part of the castle where dinners with the council or other important Fae are held, but the King has requested no audience for tonight's dinner and feels as though you'd be more comfortable staying in the familial quarters of the castle."

It didn't take very long for us to get there. The whole time, I had been enthralled by the sunset outside of the windows. The sky was a beautiful, purply-pink color. Rose would have loved it so much. Pink was her favorite color, but purple came in a close second. Father had once brought her home some pink ribbon that she wore religiously in her hair. *That ribbon is nothing but ashes now.*

Entering the dining hall, I was smacked in the face by all the delicious smells. I can't honestly remember the last time I sat down and had a meal. The King and Queen sat in their chairs. There were about six chairs at the table, but only three places were set. I hastily sat in the last chair.

"You clean up nicely," the Queen says, trying to be sweet, I could tell, but there was a nervousness behind her gesture that almost made me giggle.

"Thank you, uh, your Highness?" *Was I supposed to call them that?*

"No need for formalities when you're in the immediate family, dear," the King said, smiling.

What I assume to be servants come from the adjacent kitchen and begin to serve the food. A large chicken, potatoes, pies, vegetables, more things than I can count really, are being placed on the table. Then servants come and start asking me what I like and adding things to my plate. It's quite overwhelming, and I say I like it all, even though I have no idea if that's true. By the end of it, my plate is stacked. I realize then that I'm not very hungry, but I begin to pick at my food anyway, so I don't seem ungrateful. No matter who these Fae-people were, they still saved my life and are offering me shelter and food, so I should use my manners.

The King clears his throat, "Did you like your chambers, Ryenn?"

"Oh, yes, it's beautiful, thank you," I say, my mouth full.

"It was actually your mother's old room when she was a teenager. Mostly left untouched, really. All the clothes and everything were hers."

That makes me feel a little uncomfortable for some reason.

"So, now that you've had a few hours to decompress from our conversation earlier, Celeste and would like to speak to you regarding what your life is going to be like for the foreseeable future," he states while glancing at the Queen. Panic sets into my chest again, and I struggle to swallow what's in my mouth.

Gods, I hate this feeling.

"So, Fae children and teenagers attend a schooling-type scenario all across the kingdom. The Lords and Ladies of each district send their children to the capital to be schooled together since they will be the future of the kingdom. This way, the children make allies, and all become familiar with each other," the Queen states, taking a sip of her wine briefly and setting it back down ever so gently. "You will be attending this school as well to make some friends and learn the history of the Kingdom and how our world essentially works."

"I, um, haven't gone to school since I was 11 years old." I had to stay home and take care of Rose after that. Not that I missed school anyway, plus Father always brought me home books to read.

"Yes, but from what we can tell, you have basic reading and writing knowledge, which is all you really need. Plus, for an hour after school every day, you will be seeing a tutor in the castle's library to help catch you up to speed with the other children."

"Every morning, we will meet you here for breakfast, then you will attend school for 5 hours, tutoring for 1 hour, then you will meet Celeste for other 'royal' training stuff, then dinner similar to this one or in the larger dining hall," the King said.

Okay, so I guess everything was already planned out for me. Taking a deep breath, I looked at my plate. Hardly anything had been eaten, but I couldn't take another bite without getting sick.

"Okay," I responded, not sure of what else to say and somewhat afraid to push the issue. I could go along with this plan for the time being.

"Good. Oh, and Sara will be meeting with you three times a day to ensure you're regaining your health as you should be." Celeste glances at my body and my plate. I blush.

"Ryenn, do you have any more questions for us? Are you alright?" the King asked. Now, they were both staring at me.

"Yes, I mean no. No, I don't believe I have questions right now; I'm sure some will come up later, but, uh, may I be excused? I'd like to go back to my chambers." My hands were shaking and I felt a cold sweat break out across my forehead.

They looked at each other, worry and concern seemed to take root in their facial expressions.

It was the Queen who answered shortly after, "Sure, Ser Davis, escort Ryenn to her room, please."

Chapter 5

Back in my room, alone finally, I undress from the ill-fitting gown and put on a night dress that must have been laid out by Evie. I felt *numb*. Like I was on the outside of my body looking in.

Laying down in my bed, I watched the candle burn. I knew I wasn't going to sleep. I hardly did on a normal day, let alone after *everything* that had happened.

I don't think I've really wrapped my head around all of this. I'm still not entirely sure I remembered what had happened that night. All I knew is that they were gone. *Dead*. Everyone I cared about. I have nobody left. I think that's why I'm not putting up such a fight about this whole ordeal. I have *nothing* to lose at this point.

Not that I *want* to sit idly by while the King and Queen of this foreign land tell me what it is that I have to do. How did they truly expect me to accept all of this in one day? I can't even wrap my head around being one of them. A Fae. And not just any Fae, the heir of their kingdom. Gods, I was always taught to believe they were *evil* creatures, a little more than the bogeyman since they actually existed but just wanted nothing to do with us besides terrorizing us occasionally. Although I suppose it isn't entirely true. They *have* helped in a way. It was the Dark King, whoever the hell that is, that caused the attacks on the Molisan. On my *home*. More than once, apparently.

My mind is swimming with thoughts.

Yeah, there's no way I am sleeping tonight.

~

After staring at the candle all night, my eyes were dry, and it kind of hurt to blink. The thoughts swarming around my head kept me in a constant state of panic all hours of the night until the sun finally began to peek through my curtains.

I decided it was time to get up and get a bath to hopefully wake myself up. I used to take cold baths after rough nights taking care of Rose or dealing with Father after one of his… episodes. I dipped my head under the cold tub water, my hair floating to the surface.

Evie came an hour or so after to get me ready for the day. She picked out the uniform I was meant to wear to my new fancy Fae schooling. The dress was a plain emerald green with long sleeves, and the skirt ended about halfway up my calf. It was comfortable enough and actually fit me half-decently. On my feet, I wore brown half-calf length lace-up boots. I don't know if I have ever had such a nice pair of shoes; most were hand-me-downs from neighbors or charity shops. Over the top of my dress was a spring style cloak, since it was mid-March, with the kingdom crest on the left breast. The crest was the same emerald green of my dress, with a silver dragon-like creature in the middle, breathing silver fire. Evie had pulled my hair into a braided crown, elegant and out of my face.

There was a light knock on the door, and Evie went to open it. It was Sara. Something about her made me feel a bit better and relaxed.

Probably because she is a healer and has to radiate that energy.

That thought made me a little less comfortable.

"Good morning, Ryenn. How did you sleep last night?" She asked in a cheery mood with a kind grin across her face. She was digging around her large bag for something.

"Fine," I lied.

"Oh, good. And how are you feeling overall? Any pain or dizziness? The Queen told me you hardly ate last night, but I assured her it was most likely because you're still adjusting to everything."

"Oh, uh, no, I'm okay. I can walk without feeling like falling over now. And no, no pain, really." Even though there was a constant ache and tightness in my chest.

"Uh huh, and what about that tightness you're feeling in your chest right now?" She said without looking up from rummaging through that bag.

"Oh," I blushed. "I'm okay."

"It's normal to be anxious, dear. You can talk to me about anything you know. What we discuss doesn't have to leave this room."

"I know, but I'm okay, really," I tried to sound convincing.

I hate this kind of confrontation. It made me feel a bit awkward, even though I know it's not her intent. Finally, she found what she was looking for in the bag.

"Okay, well, here are some medications. A vitamin to aid in gaining some much-needed weight, something to keep the infection and fevers away, and something to help with some general anxiety or depression you may be feeling."

I took them all in one gulp to hopefully appease her and hurry this interaction up.

Gathering her things and fixing her glasses, she gave me a brief touch on my shoulder.

"You're going to be fine. I'll see you after schooling, okay?" She headed out the door.

Evie came back in, and the Scouts escorted me to breakfast in the same dining room as last night.

Except this time, the Queen sat alone at the table.

"Good morning," Celeste said, looking up from a book she was reading. The title of the book was in a language I have never seen before.

"Good morning" *Where was the King?*

"Emmet won't be here this morning, he has rounds with the Scouting teams."

Gods, could she read my mind?

I nodded, taking the seat across from her. The servants brought out some orange juice, toasted bread and some sort of sausage and bacon. Man, I haven't had bacon in *years*. One time, Father was able to trade some rabbit pelts for some at the market. It was the best thing ever. I'm not sure who liked it more, me or Rose. I can picture her with her grease-stained smile as she dug in.

Now I'm not hungry.

I had to show Celeste I was fine, though, so I picked up the toast and began to eat it.

"You look very… pretty," she says, "so much like your mother at your age."

Celeste calling my birth mother my mother felt a bit weird. I didn't even know this woman. Had no clue what she even looked like, so how could I take this?

"Were you two friends?" I asked, pushing the sausage around my plate and taking a sip of the juice.

"Best friends, actually. Ela was a year older than I was, but we were tied together at the hip. I miss her very much." There was a very brief look of sadness across her face, and I felt bad. I know what it feels like to miss someone.

"Anyway," Celeste cleared her throat. "How did you sleep last night? Are you finding your chambers okay?"

"Oh yes, everything is fine."

"Good, good. Well, there's someone I want you to meet before you head off to class. My niece, Amalie, is 16 too. She'll be here shortly to walk with you. She has a younger sister, Pippa, who is 5. She just started schooling this year. She'll most likely be joining you as well."

"Oh, okay, cool," I swallowed hard. I actually didn't have many friends back home. I was too busy raising Rose once I stopped going to school.

"My sister is the Lady of the Capital. Basically, the Lord and Lady of the capital are our second hand. They watch the castle when myself and Emmet are not able to for whatever reason. They live in the extended portion on the west end of the castle, it's attached by a bridge."

I have a lot to learn about this place, and that didn't exactly make me feel great. Before I could say anything, the doors opened, and two girls walked.

"Amy, stop, I can do it myself!" The youngest one, who I presumed was Pippa, said hastily towards her older sister, who was attempting to fix the child's braids. My heart squeezed as I thought of Rose. She would have been the same age as Pippa.

"Good morning, girls," said Celeste.

"Good morning, your Highness," both said in sync and curtsied. Then, both their eyes drifted to me.

Amalie looked somewhat like her aunt. Her blonde hair was a nearly identical shade, but her skin was a beautiful tan, and her eyes were a hazel brown. Although she was the same age as me, she looked more mature, and her ears were pointed into the Fae shape. She was quite beautiful. Her little sister looked a lot like her, although her hair was a lighter blonde and her eyes blue like Celeste's. Both are dressed in the same green dress and cloak as I am.

"Girls, this is Ryenn. As your mother already explained, she'll be staying here. I hope you make her feel at home and be kind to her."

"You're a princess," Pippa says matter-of-factly.

"Pippa…" her older sister begins to scold.

I laugh a bit, trying to ease the tension that is making me feel like running out of the room and never turning back.

"Well, we better get going." Amalie straightens her back. I take that as my cue to stand and follow them.

Pippa grabs ahold of my hand and starts skipping along down the hallway.

Chapter 6

The schoolhouse was just outside of the castle. We had to cut across the main garden, which I made a mental note of to come back to as the flowers were absolutely gorgeous, and then take a short path along the edge of the woods. The building was small and made of stone but had windows similar to the castle.

The whole walk out, Pippa held my hand and had babbled on about her friends at school, her little brother, and everything and anything. Amalie didn't say much besides the occasional shake of her head at her younger sister or the smile in my direction.

"The younger children sit towards the front, and we all sit towards the back. There's about 8 younger kids and 6 of us older kids, well 7 now including you," Amalie states. Pippa had already run off to find her friends.

"Okay, cool," I say, trying to shake the nervousness from my voice.

"You can sit next to me if you'd like to. No one sits at my table anyways."

"Sure, I'd like that."

We walked in together, and all heads turned to look at me. Honestly, I had to look down to make sure I was wearing clothes because the way they were all staring, you'd think I was nude.

Amalie touched my elbow gently, leading me to her table. The room was still so silent. My heart was beating so loud I'm sure everyone could probably hear it.

"Don't worry about them, it's not every day we get a new student. Most of us have known each other since we were born," Amalie says quietly.

"Okay," I try to laugh, but it comes out in a sort of strangled sound.

After a few more moments of silence and glares, the door to the classroom opens.

"Good morning, class!" An older woman walks in and stands behind the front desk.

"Good morning, Mrs. Langerfeld," the class chants back to her.

I guess this is the teacher.

"Ah! It seems our new student has joined us!" Mrs. Langerfeld gestures towards me, "Come on up here, dear and introduce yourself."

Oh, Gods, no.

I have to walk up there? By myself with everyone's eyes all over me? I'm not even sure I'll make it to the front of the room without fainting or be able to say anything without being sick.

"Well? Come on, dear, we don't bite," she laughed. *Tell that to your fangs.*

I stood slowly and walked carefully to the front.

Breathe.

"Now, introduce yourself to the class! We have been very excited for you to be joining us."

"Oh, um, I'm Ryenn Caslee, or Ryenn Embers now, I guess."

"Yes, go on, dear."

"Um, my mother was Elanore Embers, but I was raised by mortals. Up until recently, I thought I was a mortal, so there's that." I laughed a little, trying to ease the tension.

"Ryenn is the rightful heir to the Emerald Throne, something we never thought we'd see again! It's very exciting that's she's here, so I hope you all treat her with respect, she is a *princess,* after all, and welcome her as one of your own."

My face flushed, and I felt far too warm. Mrs. Langerfeld nodded in my direction, so I assumed it was safe for me to go sit down again.

Thank the Gods.

~

The school day went by quicker than I anticipated. I have got to say I did learn a bit as well. The kingdom of Sanctania was split into 6 sub-cities that they called districts. All of which I cannot remember off the top of my head. For each district, there was a Lord and a Lady. After class, Amalie offered to walk me back to the castle. Pippa stayed behind to work on some sort of arts and crafts with her friends.

"How are you finding everything so far?" Amalie asked as we crossed the garden pathway.

"To be honest, it's all a bit overwhelming."

"Yeah, I can see that. I feel overwhelmed all the time, and I have lived here all my life, so I can't imagine what it must be like for you."

"So it doesn't get easier," I laughed.

"No, not really," Amalie laughed back. She had a very pretty laugh.

"So, who are all the others our age?" I ask. No one else really talked to me all day.

"Okay, so there's Corbin, the tall one with the dark brown shaggy hair. He's a bit of a nuisance, so don't pay much attention to him. His friend is Greyson. Grey's girlfriend is Autumn, the blonde; she's pretty annoying too, but in a 'I'm too cool to speak to you' sort of way. Autumn's friends are Luna, the one with the black hair, and

Hanna, the brunette; both are bitches."

I pictured all of the people she was talking about. The three girls sat in the table adjacent to us in the classroom, and the two boys sat at the table behind us.

"I don't get a warm fuzzy feeling about either of them, to be honest," I say, looking down at the grass-covered ground.

"Yeah, they're probably just mad that they won't have a chance to be the Heir Champion anymore since you've arrived and will eventually ascend to the throne due to birthright."

"What do you mean?" I glance up at the girl.

"Oh right, I forgot you probably haven't learned much about any of this yet," she says and clears her throat. "Since the current King and Queen have no offspring, a firstborn from all the Ladies and Lords of the Kingdom were being given a chance to train and prove themselves worthy of the crown. The six of us were all the same age and all first-borns, so we were all training for that title essentially. Honestly, I am glad you showed up. I never wanted to be Queen of the Kingdom anyway; it seems *way* too stressful. My parents, on the other hand, wanted me to be Queen and thought it should go to me since we already lived in the capital. It doesn't really matter, though; we all kind of knew Corbin was eventually going to get the title. He's very popular, especially in the capital, extroverted and pretty strong too. To everyone else, he seems like a golden boy, but he's actually a complete asshole and thinks he is the best at everything and deserves everything handed to him."

"Great, so everyone *does* kind of hate my guts then," I say, chewing on my bottom lip.

Amalie laughs. "I certainly don't, but everyone else hates me too, so we can be a club, I guess."

I laugh even though a pit of dread sits in the bottom of my stomach.

Chapter 7

By the time I get to the infirmary and say goodbye to Amalie, I'm feeling a little less stressed. I like Amalie, and I hope we turn out to be friends.

Sara gives me the meds I need and a bottle of cold water so I "don't become dehydrated" and walks me to the library, where I sit for an hour-long lesson with a woman named Nadine. Nadine has beautiful dark brown skin and midnight hair that is woven into fine braids. She is a patient and kind woman as she leads me through some basic history of Sanctania. After the lesson, I am feeling pretty exhausted and wanted to go lay down in my room, but I still have to meet Celeste somewhere afterward.

Ser Davis comes to escort me to what he called the "Throne Room". He wasn't lying when he said that, either. The room we enter is massive, with high peaked ceilings and an upper seating arrangement looking over the room, emerald marble floors and a staircase leading to two thrones. *The Emerald Thrones*. One is slightly taller and larger than the other. Celeste is speaking to a servant as we enter, pointing and instructing him about something.

"Your Highness," Ser Davis announces. His voice echoes off the tile walls, which somewhat startles me.

"Oh, hello, I didn't hear you two come in," Celeste says,

spinning on her heel to face us. "Thank you, Ser Davis you may go back to your duties." With that, he leaves me in the room. "How was school and everything?"

"Good," I say simply.

"Did Amalie treat you well?"

"Yes, she's very nice."

"Good."

"Yep."

There's an awkward silence in the massive room, and I don't really know what to say.

"Well, I was hoping to show you around the throne room and give you some instructions on how to behave as a princess or queen would."

"Oh, okay."

She begins to walk up the stairs to the thrones. I follow close behind.

"As you can probably guess, my seat is the smaller one. We are getting one made for you as well to use while you are training and still a minor. The larger one will be yours when you ascend to the throne." A shiver snakes down my spine.

"The throne room is used for many things. Citizens gather

here when we have news that may pertain to them, we throw balls here, we have ceremonies here, and we hold trials here as well. Go sit on Emmet's chair."

I do as she tells me to.

"When sitting in a throne, I want you to think your head is being pulled up by a string and need to sit tall, also fold your hands in your lap. There you go. Looking like a proper Queen already," she smiles, I don't.

Celeste talks me through a few more lessons, mostly on how to walk, stand and talk, and then begins to give me a tour of the rest of the castle. She leads me through the East Wing of the Castle, known as the Familial Quarters, where all the personal living amenities to the King and Queen are, and myself now, I suppose. She then leads me back to the central part of the castle, where we just were in the Throne Room, then the Main Auditorium that I was in yesterday, to the huge Main Dining Hall, the kitchens, the wine cellar, and finally, the dungeons in the basement, which are luckily not in use at the moment. The whole time we are walking about, she talks about the purposes of each room and the roles of the different types of servants that are scrambling about the hallways. To end things off, seeing I need a break from walking, she leads me back to my chambers.

"I'll have someone bring you dinner in a few hours. The

King and I have a meeting that unfortunately cuts into our schedule, so you'll have to forgive us."

This news was music to my ears. I got to spend the rest of the night alone and not have to pretend I was fine.

The thing that stresses me the most is that I had to do all of this again tomorrow.

~

Rose was crying, and Father was yelling from the other room. I immediately smelled smoke and woke up.

"Ry, what is going on?" Rose said through her sniffles, "I can't see anything, there's too much smoke."

What was going on?

What happened?

How had I slept through this?

"It's okay, Rosie. I'm gonna get out."

I jumped from the bed and headed towards the window, but there were flames on the outside.

Something snaps.

The ceiling was beginning to cave in. I ran for the bedroom door, trying to pry it open, but something must have fallen and blocked it from the other side. I still heard Father yelling from across the hall.

"Father, can you hear me? We're stuck!"

Rose cries louder and begins to cough.

The flames seemed to be getting larger the more I panicked.

Another snapping sound.

Oh Gods. Flames were devouring the walls, and thick smoke covered hung in the air.

"Ry!" Rose squeals.

And then the screaming stops-

~

Lurching forward in a cold sweat, I scan the room desperately. It takes a moment to bring me back to reality, this new reality; a reality where I'm living in a foreign kingdom and where Rose and Father are dead.

I'm going to be sick.

I leap off the bed and barely make it to the toilet in time. I throw up what I managed to eat for dinner. *So much for that effort.*

I lean back and press the nape of my neck against the cool porcelain tub. I must have dozed off somehow. I didn't feel remotely rested, if anything I felt even more exhausted. I wasn't going to even try to go back to sleep, though. *Fuck that.*

The sun was slowly beginning to creep through my blinds in my bedroom. I flushed the toilet and rose slowly to rinse my mouth out at the basin. Then I began filling the tub with ice-cold water.

As the tub filled, I walked over to my bed to sit and gather my thoughts.

Flicking back the blankets, dread smacked me across the face. There were *burned handprints* seared into the fitted sheet through to the mattress.

Chapter 8

Burned *fucking* handprints.

How did this happen?

Did I manage to do that?

Of course, it had to have been me, who else could it have been?

I ripped the sheets from my bed and threw them on the ground. Thinking quickly, I took the candle from its holder and poured some of the hot wax where the handprints were and burned them so they no longer looked like *my* godsdamn handprints. When Evie comes in the morning, I'll just tell her I dropped the candle in the bed on my way to my bath. Perfect. Problem is solved. *Unless it happens again.*

I hear something in the washroom. *Shoot the bath.* I rush in and turn the water off just in time. Stripping my sweat-drenched clothes from my body, I perform the ritual of slowly dipping my feet in, submerging my body, and then dipping my head under. This time, it feels like my whole body *sizzles* in relief.

~

Evie bought the story pretty easily and even asked if I had gotten hurt in the process, to which I denied, of course. After discarding the trashed sheets and making my bed with fresh ones, she begins to do my hair. Sara knocks on the door and lets herself in. The whole routine is repeated from yesterday until I make my way to breakfast. The Queen and King are both there today. I'm suddenly a little more tense than I already was.

"Good morning, Ryenn. I'm sorry I didn't have the chance to see you yesterday. Celeste has told me you had a pretty good first day?"

"Yes, thank you."

"Alright, dear," he clears his throat. "So, this evening, after dinner, there is going to be a meeting with the small council members in the Main Auditorium. Your presence will be expected for this meeting." *Oh great.*

I nod, but my chest is tight. Gods, I can't breathe again.

Turn it off.

I try to keep a straight face and sit as Celeste has taught me. She always looks so put together and formal.

"Good, well, you better hurry up and eat. Amalie should be here any moment."

With that, Pippa bursts through the door with Amalie on her tail. They curtsy to the King and Queen, and we are on our way. Luckily, I didn't have a chance to try and force food down my throat because I am certain it would just get stuck there anyway.

Pippa runs ahead of Amalie and I as we reach the schoolyard. The older Fae children are waiting by the entrance. This causes Amalie to slow down a bit and give me a look.

"Good morning, princess," the tall brunette, Corbin, says in a mocking tone. The girls around him giggle. Of course, my stupid face blushes.

"Leave her alone, Corbin," Amalie chirps in, trying to maneuver our way past the group. Hanna steps directly in front of our path.

"Come on now, Amy, don't be such a mood killer," Hanna spits out. Gods, Amalie wasn't lying; she really is a bitch.

"I was talking to Ryenn, Amalie, not everything is about you." Corbin rolls his eyes. "Right, Ryenn?"

Corbin lays his hand on my shoulder, but I move back.

"Don't touch me," I say, trying my best to use the voice Celeste had been talking about yesterday during our throne room lesson.

"Relax, princess. I'm not gonna hurt ya." The whole group laughs. "I actually wanted to see if you'd like to go on a date with me. I'll take you around the town and show you a few things that the humans back home couldn't or, should I say, *wouldn't*." The group erupts in laughter again. Acid burns my throat.

"Get over yourself, Corbin," I say, looking him up and down. "There's nothing you could show me that's worth my time." That shuts everyone up besides Amalie, who laughs and covers her mouth in surprise. I get the feeling this doesn't sit well with Corbin as he turns red and his eyebrows scrunch, but before he could retaliate, Mrs. Langerfeld calls us inside. Amalie gives me a high five on the way in.

~

The day went by in a blur. I spent the majority of it worrying about dinner this evening and coming down off the high of telling a Fae child lord to basically fuck off. Amalie walked me back to the castle again, and after seeing Sara, I went to tutoring. We picked up where we left off yesterday, going through some more early history of Sanctania. I learned the crest was of a Drakōn, a creature that was a descendant of a dragon, looked similar to them but were much larger and had the ability to breathe silver flames. They were known to be very loyal to the protection of Sanctania and were incredibly hostile towards anyone they perceived to be an enemy. These creatures hadn't been around for the last few centuries when the last one died along with my great-great-*great* Grandfather, the once King Overon Embers.

After tutoring, I met Celeste in one of the many small board rooms this time. She greeted me and invited me to sit across from her at a table.

"I figured you probably have a million questions bubbled in your head right now, and I'd like to give you this opportunity, while I have a moment to sit, to ask away, and I'll answer to the best of my abilities." She started resting her head in her hands. *She didn't know about the fiery handprint incident, right?*

My hands shook a little. I did have a lot of questions, though, and her oddly comfortable *and exhausted-looking* stature made me feel a bit more courageous.

"Can you tell me more about powers? I am still not sure I entirely understand."

"Okay, I can try to give you an overview, as there are many things I do not know myself." She cleared her throat and sat back in her chair. "There are a few lines of powers you should be aware of first. The Primitives are the strongest of which and have been around the longest. When I say Primitive, I mean the ability to control organic elements like air, water, earth and fire. There's also some off-branching like electricity, weather controlling and some others, but they are not a predominant power like the main four. I am an air Fae, meaning I can control wind and add or remove air from the surrounding atmosphere or from another being. I also have a side ability of being able to control the temperature of the air I use and can also occasionally manipulate the scent." A cool breeze floated across my face with a hint of something minty, and my eyes widened.

"Your uncle is an earth Fae, meaning he can manipulate

growth from the earth, understand and communicate to some animals and can manipulate the ground itself." Celeste took a sip from her drink. "Your mother was a water Fae and one of the best of our time. She also had the side ability to alter the weather, which definitely came in handy many times. Fire Fae are the rarest. There actually hasn't been a fire elemental in, well, centuries, really. Fire is said to be difficult to manipulate and is temperamental if you lack the ability to control it. Besides the Primitives Line, there is the Healer Line, which Emmet already told you about, and the Morphs Line, they can alter their physical appearance into other animals or sometimes be completely invisible." I feel like the information she just told me is sitting in my throat, and I can't swallow it. I can't be a fire elemental, *right*? That must have just been a fluke. I mean, I don't have powers yet. I haven't gone through a, what did they call it? A Transitioning?

"What's the Transitioning?" I ask a bit more eagerly than I intended.

"The transitioning is when a young Fae, usually around 13 or 14 years of age, begins the ascent into becoming a Fae. The initial transition takes about 24-72 hours to complete. It's a painful process, both physically and mentally. Mentally, your powers begin to fully develop, which can take a huge toll depending on your abilities and if you are able to control them. You will also take on the physical aspects of becoming a Fae, and your reproductive abilities mature as well. Luckily, female Fae only go through a cycle every three or four months that only lasts a few days, unlike humans that get one every month."

"I'm confused; what is a cycle?"

"Oh, have you never heard of a menstrual cycle before? Your mother never taught you about it?"

"My mother did die when I was 11," I retorted.

"Oh right, um, the menstrual cycle is when your reproductive organs as a woman mature, meaning you'll be able to bear children. Basically, every three months or so, you'll bleed for a few days. It's typically pretty painful for Fae females. Gods, your mother used to be bedridden for a week or so during hers."

Now, I felt silly for *not* knowing this.

"Wait, you said 13 or 14, but I'm 16, and I haven't Transitioned yet or had a cycle clearly."

"Yes, I mean that is pretty late but also not uncommon. It's different for everyone, so it'll come with time."

Great, so again, I'm an odd one out again.

The room filled with silence.

"Any more questions, Ryenn?" Celeste asks, looking me over.

She really did look exhausted. I kind of wanted to ask her if everything was alright, but that felt intrusive, and I didn't want to upset her or for her to get mad that I had pried. I did have millions of questions, but none that I think I really wanted to address as of now.

"Um, no, I don't think so. Thank you, though."

"Alright, dear, I'll escort you to your chambers so you can get cleaned up for dinner."

Celeste seems like the kind of person that's high-strung and controlling, which she is, as I have seen firsthand so far, but something about her was growing on me. Like I was meant to know her or something.

Chapter 9

A few hours later, I was sitting in my chambers, dressed in a gown that Evie had picked out. The dress, again, was a bit too big, but still beautiful. I had tried one on previously, but the top part was too large as I never had anything there to… fill it out. The one I wore now was a light purple color with flowery-style beading across the bodice. My hair was left down, and Evie had somehow managed to use these rod-styled things to add curls to it. Evie had just left when there was a knock at my door.

"Come in," I answered.

King Emmet came in through the door. That was unexpected.

"Sorry to intrude like this, Ryenn. I wanted to come to escort you to the dinner myself and speak to you a bit beforehand if that's alright."

"Sure," I squeezed out.

"The small council is made up of 8 members, including myself and Celeste," he took a seat next to be on my bed, Gods he was so freaking tall. "The first two members are the Lord and Lady of the capital, Garret and Vada Seredi, whom are Amalie and Pippa's, parents. Then there is the Captain of the Scouts, Hunter Vermeil, he basically oversees all operations the scouts are involved in. The fourth member is Bradley St.Croix; he's the head over the water and electricity section of the kingdom and is an incredibly powerful Fae with both water *and* electricity powers. Then we have the Travelling Hand, Normani Dixon. She takes notes during meetings and makes sure all the other Lords and Ladies of the different districts receive the same information. She's also an informant, meaning she is the voice of the Lords and Ladies as well and brings their concerns to the meetings. Finally, we have the Grand Healer, Juno Albatras. She's the most informative and powerful healer in the kingdom. She's quite old, but she's an absolute wealth of knowledge. She educates all of the healers and oversees them as well. All of these people are hand-picked to be on the committee for a variety of reasons, and they are well-trusted. That being said…" Emmet paused, shifting his weight. "Some Fae have not been so accepting, per se, of your new presence in the kingdom. This isn't true for everyone, of course, but I just wanted to warn you that these committee members can occasionally be… harsh. They just want what's best for the kingdom, of course, and I've already spoken to them about you and everything, but I just want to give you a heads up to not be offended by any of their comments or remarks."

Great…

"Okay," I said, looking at his face. I noticed then that his eyes were a deep gray color. Kind of similar to mine, honestly, though he had little specks of silver and green that almost appeared as if they *glowed*.

"Alright then, we better get going," he held out his arm, and I grasped it lightly as we started walking into the hall.

~

We met Celeste just down the hall outside of what I assume to be their chambers. Both of them wore their crowns, silver with emeralds faced on the front. We all walked together to the Main Auditorium I had been in a few days ago. I practice walking with confidence, as Celeste had taught me.

Never let them know your weaknesses or emotions.

You can do this.

As we entered the large room, I first saw there were three seats at the head table instead of one. The twelve seats had already been full.

I thought there were only 6 council members?

The Fae stood as the three of us made our way to the front of the room.

As we reached the table, I went to sit, but Celeste lightly grasped my arm, "Please join me in welcoming my niece, the rightful heir to the Emerald Throne, Daughter of the late Queen Elanore Embers, Princess Ryenn Embers."

The formality of all this almost made me laugh out loud. *Honestly, how did I get myself in this situation?*

Everyone proceeded to bow. *Oh my Gods, you've got to be kidding me.*

"Well, then, I guess we will get started. Ryenn, I'll introduce you to everyone and then the floor will be open for anyone with comments or questions."

The King proceeded to go around the room, introducing me to all 12 people. He started with the main council members that he had mentioned previously and then introduced to trainees who were with them. Sara was among the three Healer trainees and gave me an affectionate smile as we got to her. There were two high-ranking Scout trainees and then one trainee from the electricity/water committee. He explained they could all comment or ask questions but were not allowed to vote, that remained in the hands of the six council members, and the votes of all the Lords and Ladies were taken into account from Normani.

After the introductions of everyone, I was already able to get a vibe of who liked me and who didn't. Fae don't really know how to hide their facial expressions clearly. Then, the questions commenced. Many were along the lines of; "How can we trust she will be able to handle the kingdom when she has no knowledge of anything? Are we certain Eleanore is her mother? She was raised by mortals; she is practically a mortal, are you sure she's 16 she looks much younger? And on and on." Most of these comments came from Lord Garrett, whom I did *not* get good feelings from. Nonetheless, I sat there and tolerated it, keeping my head high. I wasn't going to let these comments break me down even though, deep down, I knew they were all most likely true and thought them myself. Now that I think about it, I'm not entirely sure *why* they even bothered to admit to the truth of me being heir. Like they could have just ignored the Septor and had me sent off to live somewhere else in the kingdom, I guess. I would be less of a threat that way, and Emmet and Celeste's eventual offspring would have gotten the throne anyways. Wait, why *didn't* they have any children? Celeste even told me she was only a year younger than Elenore, so really, shouldn't she have a child near my age? I mean, they seemed to be around the same age as Mother and Father. Amalie had mentioned something along the lines of that the other day, though, saying something about them not having offspring to pass the crown to, which was why there was going to be an eventual Heir Champion.

My train of thought was broken when I realized the room was silent and everyone was looking at me. *Shit,* someone must have asked me something. I looked to Celeste. "Lord Seredi would like to know what your opinion is on being heir," she whispered.

"Oh, um, sorry, my Lord, I must have been in some sort of trance, I guess," I said, blushing. "It's all very new, and I know I have a lot to learn. I'm hoping I won't disappoint and am able to reach your standards, er, the kingdom's standards, I should say." Man, I'm all over the place. So much for not looking like a complete *fool.*

"Yes, well, speaking on behalf of the kingdom, we hope you meet those expectations, too. Clearly, there is much work to be done." Some of the other council members chuckled in agreement.

Wow, what an asshole.

Emmet cleared his throat and stood. "Yes, well, I believe that is the end of the council meeting. Normani, please send the meeting minutes to my office and then to the other Lords and Ladies of the other districts. Thank you, everyone, and have a good night."

Everyone stood and bowed.

Ser Davis, who had been standing guard by the door the whole time, escorted me back to my chambers. Another sleepless night awaits me.

Chapter 10

The next few weeks went by quickly and generally the same. I would get out of bed in the morning when the light began to creep in. Some nights, I managed to get an hour or so of dreamless sleep; other nights, I stayed awake watching the candle, and then other nights, I would wake in that cold sweat dread and end up puking my guts up in the washroom. Luckily no more nightmares of that night and no more burned handprints. After I woke, I'd get my cold bath, Evie would get me ready, Sara would show up with meds asking general health-related questions, and then Ser Davis would escort me to breakfast. Most of the time, it was just me and Celeste, since Emmet seemed to be busy so early in the morning, until Amalie and Pippa would interrupt us.

Amalie and I began to get close, too, always chatting and giggling about stupid things, really. I looked forward to seeing her every day. Schooling was all the same, and I ignored Corbin and his gaggle of friends, even when he seemed to be staring at me. He never did speak to me again afterwards, though, but he made it a point to stare and make me feel as uncomfortable as possible or doing stupid childish shit like knocking my stuff off the table when he walked by.

Tutoring after schooling was going well, too, and I felt like I was maybe starting to catch up to the knowledge of my peers. Sessions with Celeste were interesting, but not in the way you'd think. Some days, she'd be talkative and allow me to ask some questions, but other days, she'd be zoned out and strict. It was hard to get a read on her. I like her, don't get me wrong, but I wasn't really getting close to her. Over the last few days, she has been busy beginning to plan for the Summer Gala, which was going to happen on the Summer solstice next month. She had been letting me help her and showing me the planning process, but I think she could tell I was getting bored and being more underfoot than anything, so today, she decided to send me to the stables to pick out a horse and begin riding lessons.

Apparently, all high Fae are allowed to pick a horse each year and learn to ride when they are young. I'm pretty excited, if I'm being honest. We had a lot of animals at our small house in Baytown, well, I mean, most people did. We had chickens, cows, pigs, and an old draft horse we used for starting some crops. I loved animals, and so did Rose. Every morning, we'd head out and begin our "farm chores," which usually consisted of me doing most of the work while she chased the chickens around.

"This is the stables, your highness," Ser Davis announces. "Braxton Kelten is the stable boy, he'll be able to help you pick out your horse and start teaching you the basics. I'll be back in an hour to bring you back to your chambers". I nodded and he was off. A tall Fae male, maybe only 2 or 3 years older than myself, walked through the stable doors. He was handsome in a sort of rugged way and had muscles you could tell were forged from hard work. His shaggy, sun-kissed brown hair fell into his face, and he blew it back. He had dark green eyes and dimples as he smiled at me. "Hello, your highness," he began to bow.

"Oh, uh, you don't have to do that," I laughed, feeling a bit awkward.

"Okay then, noted," he smiled. "So I'm supposed to help you find a horse, eh? Have you ever ridden one before?"

"No, I don't think I have. We used to own an old draft horse in Baytown, but he was just used for gardening and stuff," I said.

"Okay cool. Well, you can come in, and I'll show you the unclaimed horses that the Fae are allowed to reserve, and then we can see which you fit best." He led me through the doors and down the aisle. Stalls lined either side, and gorgeous black horses popped their heads out to greet me.

"These are all the Scouts' horses. Yeah, I know they all have to be black to be intimidating, I guess, and so they look put together." I was wondering why they were all the same color… *could he read my mind?* I should hope not because I was thinking some things that I definitely did not want him knowing. I could feel the redness creep across the bridge of my nose.

"Right down here, we have all the available horses. There's

five to pick from. These three are mares," he pointed to a brown horse with a white star on her forehead, a black horse similar to the Scout horses, but she had a long white stripe down her head, and a gray dappled horse. "And these two are geldings," he pointed to another dapple gray and a brown horse with little white speckles all over him.

"Any in particular you want to take out and try? They are pretty well all the same height, but their personalities are all different, of course." The horse with the speckles, that kind of looked like freckles covering his nose, poked his head out through the gate and flicked his ears towards me. I reached out and touched the soft fuzz.

"He seems sweet. What's his name?"

"That's Blaze," he pets the horse's nose, his hand lightly brushing against my own. "He's a good boy and very loyal. I think he likes you too, to be honest. I can take him out and let you brush him if you'd like?"

"Alright."

Braxton leaves the room, and I continue stroking Blaze's nose. Gods, this reminds me so much of our old boy. I can help but wonder what happened to all our animals after the attack. It causes unease to build in the pit of my stomach. *Turn it back off.*

"Alright, I'll lead him out for now so you can get used to him," he clasps the line to Blaze and leads him out of the stall and through some side doors to a post where he ties him.

After a good 30 minutes of brushing and talking to Braxton about horses and his job here, I'm laughing and feel at ease.

"Alright, let's see you sit on him so I can make sure he's a good fit. We will do this without a saddle so you can really feel him under you and connect. Um, since you're wearing a dress, I'll help you up; next time, make sure to wear breeches so you'll be more comfortable." I nod, and Braxton comes over, puts his hands on my waist, and gives me a lift onto Blaze's back. I blush as his hands linger there when I'm up. He must notice and pulls them away quickly, still smiling.

"You look great," he says.

"Sorry what?" Now I'm blushing even harder.

He clears his throat, "On Blaze, I mean. You guys look great. I think he's definitely your horse."

"Oh," I laugh awkwardly. "I think so too."

"Perfect, I'll set up the reserve for you, and we will begin lessons once a week." He puts his hands up and helps me down. I turn too quickly, and now our faces are almost touching. Taking a step back and bumping into Blaze, I look down, a bit embarrassed.

Blaze must sense the tension and gives a little shake, which knocks me forward into Braxton's arms. Braxton straightens me back up, and we kind of just stare at each other for a moment. Luckily, the moment is short-lived as Ser Davis walks around the corner of the stables to get me. I thank Braxton and pet Blaze hastily and quickly leave. He is smiling the whole time, like he's proud of himself.

Walking back to my chambers, I'm grinning to myself, and I'm not entirely sure why. What a weird interaction. *Why didn't I mind it?*

~

The next day, on our way to class, I tell Amalie all about the interaction that occurred yesterday evening.

"Oh my Gods, *Braxton Kelten*!? He's actually a high Fae and only 19 years old," she gives me a sultry look, and I laugh. "His father is pretty high up in the Scout troop, and Braxton, I believe, is training for recruitment coming in the fall. His family has been working in the stables for a long time. Gods, I can't believe you have that kind of interaction with him. I mean, he is sweet to everyone, but it sounds like he likes you," that makes me blush again, and she laughs, "Ryenn, you crack me up. You blush so easily."

"Well, now you're making it worse," and truth be told, she was, which made her laugh even harder.

Our conversation is abruptly interrupted when Autumn and her bitch friends Luna and Hanna shove past us.

"Ugh, Amalie, watch where you're going, would you?" Autumn rolls her eyes, and the other girls giggle. "Oh, sorry, your highness. Didn't mean to interrupt," she sneers, doing a mockery-style bow. The three of them walk off, laughing, to catch up to the other two Fae lords who are hanging around the entrance of the schoolhouse.

"Bitches," I mutter.

"Yeah, no kidding. Welcome to my world," Amalie mumbles back.

Just when I thought our morning couldn't get more intrusive than that interaction. Corbin and his friend, Grey, are standing in the godsdamn doorway.

"I don't understand how she's actually a Fae. Like she's 16 but still looks like that," I overhear Grey says to Corbin. The three girls who shoved past us broke out into laughter.

"Yeah, man, she's fucking ugly. A shame, really, considering her mom was like smoking hot from the pictures I have seen," Corbin barks back.

"I bet she's a slut like her mom was, though," Autumn snickers, looking directly at me.

Amalie touched my shoulder, and we try to get past the group to get to our seats. Tears begin to well in my eyes.

Fuck now is not the time to be like this.

I'm not sure why I even care what this kid is saying about me.

All of a sudden, as me and Amalie attempt to squeeze through the entrance, Corbin sticks his foot out, and I end up on my hands and knees.

"Ha! That's where the wannabe Fae bitch belongs. On her fucking knees," he snickers.

Okay that's *enough*.

"Fuck you, Corbin," I say, standing and brushing the dirt from my knees and hands.

"Yeah? You can if you want to," he tilts his head mockingly.

"You are *unbelievable*," I seethe.

Amalie grabs onto my elbow to steady me, and I realize my knees and palms are bleeding from the gravel stone I fell on.

Anger stings my throat like the acidic taste of bile.

"Corbin Sapphic!" I hear in a loud, stern voice. Mrs. Langerfeld comes stomping over, "You ought to be absolutely ashamed of yourself right now."

"No, Mrs. L, it was an accident. Seriously, I mean, Ryenn is clearly just a bit clumsy and tripped," he said in a mockery sort of tone. "Isn't that right, Ryenn? She's still in her mortal form, after all."

I looked at Mrs. Langerfeld, swallowing past the lump of hot tears in my throat.

"Well you highness? Is he being truthful? From my viewpoint, it seemed as though there was some sort of altercation." Mrs. Langerfeld turned to me.

Did I want to snitch on this kid?

Him and the other Fae teenagers would probably never let me live it down.

Screw them.

"No Mrs. Langerfeld. Corbin purposely blocked my path and stuck out his leg to cause me to trip," I said, head held high and looking at Corbin. His face turned red and gave me what can only be described as a vile look.

"Very well, dear. Corbin, you are suspended from attending classes for the rest of the week. Your parents will be notified of this incident immediately, and I'm sure they will be incredibly disappointed. You may go to the library and assist with putting books back on the shelves as your punishment." Mrs. Langerfeld pointed for him to leave and turned her back to us to usher the rest of the students into the schoolhouse.

"Fuck you bitch," Corbin grabbed my face and muttered. "You're going to regret this."

"It's *your highness* to you," I sneered back, ripping my face from his grip, and walked into the classroom.

Chapter 11

Sara cleaned up my scrapes when me and Amalie dropped by after class for the daily routine. I spared the details to her on *what* exactly happened and just told her I tripped on my way to school. I didn't need her going to the King or Queen and telling them this. They weren't that bad anyways. Amalie had gotten a wet cloth right after and cleaned them up to the best of her abilities anyway. I also didn't have to go to my tutoring session because Nadine had to take some sort of class to go towards her librarian schooling or something like that.

I met Celeste early in the kitchen adjacent to the Main Dining Hall to help prepare for dinner this evening. Apparently, towards the end of every month, we were to have dinner with the Seredis. This meant not only would the Lord and Lady of the capital be in attendance, but Amalie, Pippa, and their baby brother would be as well. From what I could gather, Celeste wasn't fond of her sister, but these dinners still happened at the end of every month, if the King wasn't on one of his many business trips. They hadn't had one last month due to that reason. I can't believe it was almost May. It's been over a month since I woke up in Sanctania.

It somehow felt much longer but shorter at the same time.

Celeste was assisting with the place settings and being controlling as per usual. She was definitely stressed out. Showing me how to properly set out the proper utensils, which included 4 types of spoons for some reason, she quickly looks up at the wine placed on the table.

"Gods, no, this won't do." She shakes her head. "Ryenn, do you remember where the wine cellar is?"

"Yes, I believe so," I say, setting down a floral arrangement.

"Okay, great, could you go down and pick out a red wine from the back wall? The back wall is the oldest wine, and we need something good, or I won't get through the dinner alive."

"Sure, I can go grab one," I smile.

"Okay, be careful dear," she said without looking up from the place settings.

~

I finally find the wine cellar after wandering around the bottom floor for what seems like forever. I need to do this quickly and efficiently so that Celeste will see that I'm competent and not a total idiot. She rarely gives me tasks without overseeing that I am doing them correctly the entire time.

Heading to the back of the room, which is actually much larger than I anticipated, I stare at the selection. There were hundreds of bottles lining all the walls, and some kegs were in the centre of the room. Red. I need red wine. Reaching for a bottle mid way up the wall, I pause.

Did I just hear someone?

Something grabs my shoulder, and I drop the bottle. It shatters. *Fuck.*

Laughter erupts, and Corbin appears in front of me. How didn't I know he was a Morph? He could be invisible?

"Godsdamnit Corbin, you made me drop it-" I pause, noticing a smell from his breath and a flask in his hand. "Have you been drinking?"

Suddenly, he grabs my throat, pinning me against the wall of wine bottles and getting close to me.

"Don't fucking speak, princess," he snarls.

Three more bottles fall from the wall and shatter at my feet. The air escapes my lungs, and I can't breathe. I go to move my hands up to grab him, but he's too quick, dropping his flask of some sort of strong-smelling liquid, and pins both my arms down.

Fuck he's stronger than he looks.

"You have no *freaking* idea how bad you messed up today," he spits. "It doesn't matter, though. I told you you were going to regret it."

"Corbin… stop it," I manage to squeak out.

"I told you to *shut up!*" He yells.

Where were all the fucking Scouts?

He takes me by my shoulders and pushes me. I end up flat on my face in a pool of spilled red wine and glass. A piece cuts my lip, and I taste the metallic liquid mixed with the wine. Faster than I can gather my thoughts, he climbs on top of me, and pushes my head down.

"I'm going to make you pay, princess. Thinking you can just push everyone around and run this place when you've been here for a little over a month. *I* was going to be the Heir champion, but then your prissy little ass comes along and ruins everything." Panting and trying to keep my head up, he begins to lift up the skirt of my dress.

"Corbin, stop it, *please*. Listen, I can talk to Mrs. Langerfeld and tell her I was wrong. You don't have to do this," I rasp, trying to catch my breath.

"Too fucking late for that, *your highness*." I hear him jostling something like a belt buckle and then the screech of a knife coming out of a case. I tense up, stifling a sob. "I'm gonna make you regret it, and I'm gonna make you apologize and weep before me. I'm going to make you scream my name bitch."

Before I could say anything, he rips at my undergarments, exposing my bare skin. Then he laughs. I don't think I've ever heard anything as evil in my life.

"Please," I cry, "don't do this."

"Too *fucking* late"

Pinned against the ground, my cries are muffled in Corbin's hand. He takes the knife he unsheathed from his holster and holds it against the side of my neck. I try to reach for a shard of the glass by wiggling my hands out from underneath me, but he catches me and slices my palm with the shard. I scream. Tears are streaming down my face.

"Nice try," he sniggers.

Gods, this can't be happening.

Next, he hikes up the bottom of my dress, exposing me completely, and plunges his fingers inside me. When he's done that, he unzips his trousers and shoves *something else* inside me. I tense up at the realization, feeling as though all blood has drained from my body.

I'm in so much pain.

I feel my consciousness slipping as everything begins to fade to black. The only sounds I hear are my own internal screams for help, that I know are no use at this point, and the sounds of him using me for whatever twisted purpose this is.

"Ryenn?" A weary voice comes from down the hallway.

"Shit," Corbin immediately lets go of me and goes invisible. "You better not say a fucking word about this or *else*."

I slowly sit myself against the wall of wine, bringing my knees to my chest, and try to breathe.

"Ryenn, you have been down here for 30 minutes; it should not have taken this long to find a red-". Celeste turns the corner of the door and stops. I can only imagine what her point of view is right now.

I clasp my hand over my mouth and close my eyes, stifling my silent sobs.

"Oh my Gods, Ryenn, what *happened*?" Celeste rushes over to me, kneeling before me and taking my hands in her hands.

"I-" the word comes out in a strangled gasp, feeling like knives are shearing my throat.

It hurts.

She looks down and sees the pool of blood mixing with the spilled wine and glass on the floor. The skirt of my dress soaked in both, and my undergarments thrown off to the side.

"My Gods, who did this to you?" Concern bunches in her expression, causing me to sob harder. I feel a cool breeze on my face with hints of lavender. "It's okay, honey. It's okay. You're safe now. Just breathe, okay? I'm going to get you out of here." Looking around, the usual cool and straight face Celeste puts her hands in her hair, frazzled and panicked.

"Okay… okay, I'm going to have to carry you. We're going to room jump, okay? I'll explain more later, but you just need to hold onto me, and we'll end up in your chambers without having to walk through the castle, okay?" She runs over and locks the cellar door. Helping me stand, my legs shaking from the pain between them, she proceeds to scoop me up in her arms with little effort. I cling to her shoulder with my sticky hands.

"Okay, close your eyes. It might feel disorienting, but it'll be okay," and with that, we end up in the middle of my chambers.

At this point, my sobs have ceased, and I feel numb. Celeste leads me to the washroom and runs the bath.

"Honey, you need to get in the bath, okay? I can't tell exactly where you're injured and what's blood and what's wine," she looks at me, but I'm frozen in place.

I'm in so much pain.

"It's okay, I'm going to help you, okay?" She helps me slide off my dress slowly, letting it fall to the tile floor in a lump. She sucks in a breath and covers her mouth.

Guess it looks as bad as it feels.

She helps me into the tub, and I bring my knees to my chest, mortified, as I watch the clear water turn a murky red color.

"I'm going to go get help, okay? I'm going to send for someone to get Sara. Just stay there. I'll be right back."

She leaves the room briefly, going to get a Scout to fetch Sara. I just sit there staring at the water. Gods, it's so red. My chest hurts, and the air is thick with the metallic smell of blood and the wine. I can't breathe.

Celeste comes back a moment later, and so does the lavender cool breeze as she notices my struggling breath. Grabbing the jug from the shelf, she fills it with clean water from the sink and pours it carefully over my hair. The water falls smoothly over my shoulder, and I shiver.

"Sara will be here shortly, okay? She'll need to see your wounds and take some samples. We need to figure out who did this..."

I stop hyperventilating and look up at her. Her eyebrows are knitted, and there's worry marks across her porcelain skin.

I think I might be sick.

"Ryenn... Honey, do you know who did this to you?" Her blue eyes searched my face.

Nodding, I start crying. Gods, this is humiliating.

She lays a hand on my bare back, but before she can say

anything, there is a knock on the chamber door.

"That must be Sara," she states, standing. "I'll be right back, okay?"

Leaving me in the tub, shivering, she goes out into the chamber, sliding the washroom door behind her.

"I came as soon as I could. What's wrong?" I heard Sara in a calm but ushered voice.

"Sara, she's hurt badly. Someone attacked her in the wine cellar. She's hardly said a word…"

"Oh my Gods"

"Sara. I think someone may have raped her."

I don't think they knew I could hear them speaking. *Rape.* I've heard of the term before. There was a news article a few years ago about a young woman who was raped and killed. The man who did it was hung in the town square.

Now, I really might be sick.

Missing the last part of their hushed conversation, I swallowed the urge to throw up, and Celeste comes back into the washroom with towels and a robe and begins to help me out of the tub.

Chapter 12

After carefully drying off, I follow Celeste into the chambers and sit on the bed. The water had left a red ring around the tub. It looked like a murder scene.

Sara was setting up some different instruments on the nearby table and turned to look at me as we came through the door.

"Hi, Ryenn," she tried to smile, but I could see my appearance took her by surprise. I hadn't looked in the mirror in the washroom. I couldn't bring myself to do it.

"Ryenn, I have to do an assessment of your injuries and gather some samples, okay?" I sat on the edge of the bed, and Celeste sat next to me. "It might be uncomfortable, but I'm going to use some tricks to make it more tolerable. You can lie down on your bed, and we can get this over with if I have your permission."

Glancing at Celeste, face still worried, she nodded.

"Okay," I breathed out. Laying back on the bed.

~

Sara went through a bunch of assessments and tests and tended to the obvious wounds on my body. My top lip had been sliced open. There was a deep cut on my hand from the shard of glass, bruises on my neck, arms, and back, and some other scraps over my body. The whole time, she spoke to me, letting me know what she was doing next and when it was going to sting. I didn't mind the stinging from the cleaner. It kept me conscious and my mind from wandering to dark places. Celeste held the hand that hadn't been cut.

"Ryenn, we need to examine your pelvic area now, okay? Celeste mentioned there had been some… *trauma* down there. It's going to be uncomfortable, but we need to get the samples. If you need a break, let me know at any point." She turned towards the table of things.

I clenched my teeth, and breathing became a task again. Celeste had been helping with the cool breeze she provided, and the lavender scent helped calm me a bit, but my chest felt tight at the thought of what was coming. Celeste shifted to the head of the bed, sensing I was uncomfortable, but kept holding my hand.

"Alright, dear, I'm giving you fair warning this is not going to feel good," she begins the assessment.

My entire body tenses as the cool metal instrument is inserted inside me. The cellar events come back to me; tears spring to my eyes, and I gasp.

"I'm so sorry, Ryenn. Try to relax, okay? I'm going as quick as I can."

Celeste moves my head into her lap, and she strokes my wet hair.

"You're doing good. It's almost over. Just keep breathing," she repeats in a calm voice as cool as the ocean.

Sara finishes up and pulls the blankets up over me since I'm shivering.

"You did so good," she states. "Ryenn, you do have some damage, and it is clear that you were hurt severely. While the test results will give us some answers as to who did this to you, if you have any idea who your attacker was, it would help immensely."

Sucking in a breath, I closed my eyes, seeing that smirk across Corbin's face as he pinned me against the wall.

"You can tell us, Ryenn. No matter what this person said to you, you are safe now. This assault needs to be reported, and severe actions must be taken to ensure nothing ever happens like this to anyone again," Celeste explains.

Opening my eyes, I realize she's right. This can never happen again. There needs to be consequences. I attempt to clear my throat.

"Corbin Sapphic"

~

I laid there, staring at the ceiling, as Sara and Celeste were moving around the room. Celeste had gotten a scroll of paper from the desk and began writing something out while Sara was packing up all her medical things. She gave me some sort of medicine that tasted gross, like pine needles, but she said it would both calm me down and ease the pain. I didn't fight taking it.

Handing the rolled note to Sara, Celeste asks, "Can you drop this off to Emmet on your way down? They are all most likely in the dining hall and wondering where we are. I'm going to stay here to make sure she's alright."

Sara nods, giving me a friendly wave, and leaves the chambers.

Turning towards me and wiping her hands down her gown, Celeste begins to tidy up some of the mess around the room.

"Are you feeling okay?" she asks.

I wasn't really feeling anything. There was a heaviness that laid over me.

Damn, what had Sara given me?

I'm exhausted, but I know there's no way in hell I'm getting to sleep.

"Tired." My voice is raspy and sounds gross.

I feel bad. Celeste was so stressed about the dinner, and now she didn't get to attend because of this whole situation because of me. I really did mess up everything.

"I'm sorry," I say quietly.

"What are you sorry about?" She says looking up with a confused expression.

"You missed the dinner that you were trying to make perfect, and I broke a few wine bottles. I can't do anything right."

"Ryenn," she moved to the foot of the bed, touching my leg. "Don't apologize. I couldn't care less about that stupid dinner and wine. I'm sorry that you had to experience what you did. You should have been more protected, and Scouts should have been guarding the basement. I should have been more aware of your safety."

"It's not your fault." Our gazes meet. Tears are welled in her eyes, and she wipes them quickly with her hand. "Thank you for staying…"

"Don't worry about it. Would you like me to stay for a bit longer?"

"Please."

I didn't want to be alone, as pathetic as it sounded. But I did feel pathetic. I felt like a little kid again and wanted my mother to stay with me when I was sick or injured. Celeste isn't my mother, and she can be strict sometimes, but there's no one else I'd rather have with me right now.

"Okay, I'll sit here and read-"

There's a loud knock on the door, and I shoot upright in the bed, breathing heavily. Celeste goes to answer it.

Emmet walks in, looking like he ran here with what I assume was Celeste's letter balled in his fist. He stares at me, eyes wide in horror, which makes me feel sick to my stomach again.

"Let's speak in the hall, dear." Celeste touches his arm, and he follows her out.

Gods, I really do feel like I'm going to be sick.

Taking deep breaths to pass the nausea, I listen closely to see if I can hear what they are saying. No luck. The walls are thick stones, so it's hard to hear anything on the outside of them unless you're right by the door.

I kick my blankets off and stand up, feeling sore everywhere, and shuffle to get a closer listen.

Do you know who did this?

She said it was Corbin Sapphic.

The firstborn of Keaton and Carolina? I always thought he was a good kid. He was training for the role of Heir.

Yeah, well, apparently, he isn't such a good kid now, is he?

Are you sure it was him?

Why the fuck would she lie about something like this, Emmet?

I'm not saying she would. I'm just trying to be certain, Celeste. You know this means we have to have a trial with the Septor, right?

Yes, I know. Gods, Emmet, she's going to have to go through those memories again. I don't know if she'll be able to handle it. It's a fucking sin. She is only a child, for god's sake.

The last sentence sounded like she was crying. My stomach roiled.

What did she mean by having to go through the memories again?

Bile started rising in my throat. I try to sprint for the toilet, but I only make it as far as the sliding washroom door before vomiting all over the floor.

Celeste opens the door to the chambers as I'm heaving.

"Shit," Celeste runs over to me, supporting me to stand and rubbing my back. I remember doing the same for Rose when she was stomach sick one time. It was the only thing that stopped her from crying every time she had to throw up. The thought of Rose makes me heave again.

"It's okay, get it out," Celeste says soothingly.

I take some deep breaths, and I'm finally able to look up. My legs are weak underneath me, but I'm able to get back to my bed with the help of Celeste.

"I'm sorry."

"Stop apologizing, Ryenn honey. It's no big deal. I'll have Evie called to come clean it up. Are you feeling okay now?"

I didn't feel nauseous anymore. Just embarrassed.

"I'm fine I think."

"Okay. Listen, it's getting pretty late. Why don't you roll over and try to get some sleep, okay? We can talk more after you get some rest."

"Don't leave." Now, I really sounded like a child.

"I'll stay right here," she smiles, sitting in a chaise next to the window.

~

Sleep devours me relatively quickly, whether it was whatever substance Sara gave me to relax or the stress effect on my body. It doesn't last long, though. I wake up, grabbing at my throat, feeling like I'm being choked. I can't get a breath in, and panic swallows me whole.

Celeste jumps off the chair she's sitting on and rushes over. A cool, soothing breeze follows. Still, I can't seem to catch my breath, and I begin making gasping sounds.

"Relax. It's okay. You're safe in your room. No one is going to hurt you."

Celeste tries to calm me, but it's not working. She holds my hands, bringing them away from my neck.

"Try breathing with me," she inhales deeply for three seconds, holds the air for three more, and exhales for three. I try to mimic her and am able to find some relief. We sit like this until my hands stop shaking, and I can get some air down.

I lay back down on my pillow, still following the breathing pattern she set, when my eyes start to well. I try turning off my emotions like I've been able to do before, but the tears come anyway, like a dam has completely ruptured.

Turning to my side, I try looking away from Celeste, putting my hand to my mouth to stifle the sobs I'm unable to stop.

I feel the bed dip.

Celeste crawls in next to me, rubbing my back while I cry the hardest I have ever cried before, and I'm unable to stop myself.

Everything that has happened to me, my whole life up to this point, weighs heavy on my head and I feel like I'm drowning.

Unjudging, Celeste stays next to me the whole time, attempting to soothe me by tracing small circles on my back, to let me know that I'm not alone.

Even though, right now, I feel more alone now than I ever have before.

Chapter 13

I managed to doze off in the early morning, my eyes feeling like a ton of bricks was weighing on them from crying for so long. Celeste had stayed there, soothing me, the entire night. I felt somewhat embarrassed that she had, I mean, she didn't really know me, yet she felt like it was her duty to make sure I was okay. I don't know, I just feel *heavy* about the whole situation.

I laid there staring at the ceiling. Celeste must have fallen asleep too. I could hear her snoring quietly, which made me giggle a bit. Such a gorgeous woman, yet she snores when she sleeps. I tried to sit up against the back of the headboard.

Gods, I really have to pee.

My whole body is tense and incredibly sore. I'm not sure I can support my own legs from underneath me. Using my hands to push myself up a bit, I wince, forgetting I had a pretty big cut on my left hand. I look at the bandage Sara had wrapped around it yesterday, and there was old blood soaked through to the other side.

I *really* need to get out of this bed.

Carefully, I tried swinging my legs off the side, attempting not to hurt myself in the process but also to not wake Celeste. She was probably exhausted after having to stay up all night with me. It didn't work, though, because she rolled over as I was scooting to the side nearest to the bathroom.

"Are you okay?" She sat up, rubbing her eyes and smoothing her hair.

"Oh, uh yeah… I just really need to go to the washroom." I blush.

"Would you like some help?" She said, getting off the bed and walking around to the side to help me up.

"Yes, please," I mumble.

Celeste takes my arms gently, guiding me slowly to my feet. It was like a shock went through my body as I initially stood, attempting to get my muscles and body together to walk so I wouldn't pee on the floor.

After a few moments of shuffling, we made it to the washroom, and Celeste said she would stay outside the door to give me some privacy to attend to my needs.

It hurt.

Badly.

Although Sara said she was able to repair the internal damage done to me, the pain was still there, and significantly more so now I was able to relieve myself. I carefully dry off and slowly, like a little old lady, make my way to the basin to wash my good hand.

That's when I see my reflection for the first time since the attack.

Holy shit.

It took all my strength to keep myself standing as I held on to the counter. My face was gaunt looking, and I had a scar on the left side of my top lip. Although it wasn't bleeding due to Sara's quick healing abilities, the scar was dark and was most likely going to end up staying. I also had tiny cuts made from glass shards, I assume, on my left temple and eyebrow. My left eye also had a purple-green shadow. I took a deep breath, and my chest hurt. I untied the robe I had fallen asleep in to look at my body. There was bruising on both sides of my chest, most likely broken ribs, I can remember Sara saying. There was also a cut on my neck; though it wasn't deep, I knew it had been from the knife he had held there. It accompanied the hand-shaped strangle marks. Besides the gash on my hand, I only had some superficial bruises and small cuts to both arms and legs. My lower abdomen hurt the most. Most likely because of what he had used me for. I felt dirty even though I bathed right after yesterday.

"Everything okay?" Celeste asks, sliding the door open a crack.

I quickly tie up my robe and wipe a stray tear that had run down my cheek.

"Yes, I'm done."

She came back in and helped me to a chair next to the windows, stating that Evie had to come change the sheets. She looked concerned, and something about her facial expression sat like a rock in my gut.

"How are you feeling?" She asks wearily, poking a strand of stray hair behind my ear and then sitting across from me.

"A bit better… sore though."

"I can imagine you are, my dear," she says, swallowing a sigh.

"Thank you… for last night. I don't know what came over me, and to be honest, I'm quite embarrassed over it," I decided to admit.

"Don't worry about it. And don't be embarrassed. It's okay to have emotions, Ryenn. You don't need to put on a facade around me."

Hearing that had taken off a little bit of pressure. I always learned to hide my emotions, even the ones I felt very strongly. I could turn them off whenever I needed to, especially in the eye of the public, and I had gotten good at it. If I were to guess, I would say it mainly stemmed from raising Rose after Mother had died during her birth. I wasn't allowed to feel that loss as I probably should have. I was too busy trying to keep a baby alive and happy and also pick up the pieces of my heartbroken father. Showing emotion meant admitting to weakness, and although I knew deep down I was, I had to make sure I kept strong for those around me. The few times I had shown my emotion had led me to trouble anyways.

Usually, the belt across the backside for being a brat.

I'm pulled away from these thoughts as a light knock on the door.

Celeste walks over to answer. And Sara walks in, with her large bag in tow.

"Good morning, your Highness," she curtsies briefly and then looks up to where I'm sitting. "Good morning, Ryenn."

"Hello, Sara," Celeste responds. I give her a grin. Or at least I try my best.

"My Queen, would you like to go get refreshed while I am here with Ryenn?"

Celeste looks at me. "Are you alright with that, Ryenn?"

I worried a bit, like a child when their parents leave them on their first day of school, but that was foolish, so I nodded. "Yes, go ahead."

"Okay dear. I won't be long, okay? While I'm out, I need to

speak to Emmet briefly. He's worried sick. Then I'll come back, and we can… talk."

I had a feeling I knew what the conversation would entail since my eavesdropping yesterday.

I nod anyway, and Celeste thanks Sara and heads out of the room.

Sara turns her attention back to me.

"How are you feeling?" She asks. Her tone is hushed, and she has genuine concern on her face. She takes a seat in front of me. To make this easier for myself, I feel like I should probably tell the truth.

"I'm pretty sore. Everything hurts a lot."

"I've bought something that will help with the aches and pains. Could you tell me a bit more about the pain you're feeling?"

"Well, what hurts the most is my stomach, I guess," I mumble.

"Uh-huh, and what does the pain feel like? Where exactly is it?" her glasses fall down to the tip of her nose, and she pushes them back up.

"It's *aching*. All around here," I smooth over my lower abdomen, "… it hurts when I use the washroom too."

"Ah okay. Unfortunately, even though I was able to repair a lot of damage, some things just can't be undone. The pain you feel is normal, well, normal for this circumstance. Do you understand what happened to you? I know you haven't started your cycle yet, and Celeste mentioned you didn't even know what it meant."

My face blushes, and I look away from her.

"I heard Celeste say the word 'rape' yesterday. I remember reading about it in a news article back home about a year ago, that a woman was raped and killed. I assumed rape meant that he pinned me down and… hurt me."

"The whole thing that happened to you was an *assault*. Being raped was one part of that assault, and it was the part where he had thrust something inside of you against your will. Based on your assessment, I could gather that he used his fingers and also his… *'manhood'*, for lack of a better term. Is that right?"

Heat flushed my face, and tears began to pool in my eyes.

Gods, this was *mortifying*.

Hearing it all out loud when I really didn't want to believe it.

"Yeah… he did," a soft sob escaped me.

Sara gave me a tight hug, and I breathed in her scent deeply.

"I know this is a hard conversation. I know it must have been even worse to have to go through that. No one should ever have to." She wiped a tear from my cheek. "Besides that pain and the cuts and bruises, is there anything else? Like mentally?"

"It's hard to think about. It kept me up last night and made me sick to my stomach."

"Okay dear. I can give you something to help with the emotional trauma this whole thing has caused, too, okay?"

Sara began tending to me, changing bandages, cleaning wounds, applying ointment to bruises to ease the pain, giving me medicine to take, and then using some of her powers to try and heal more internal damage. After that, she waited with me, as promised, for Celeste to return.

Chapter 14

Celeste returned in less than an hour. In the time she had been gone, Evie had come and changed the sheets and brought me some breakfast. She didn't say much but did look worried. I am not sure if she knew exactly what had happened, just that I didn't look good clearly. As I said, Sara had been there the whole time. She tried coaxing me to eat the warm porridge they brought me and I managed a few mouthfuls and some of the juice. I couldn't do much more after that and she hadn't pried too much on it. When Celeste returned, she was wearing a comfortable looking dress, less extravagant than her norm. It was an off-white color had short sleeves and a smooth fabric. Over the top, she wore a matching off-white shawl that was trimmed with gold. Her hair was braided into a crown around her head. She was truly beautiful and I wished I had her features. I felt a little silly sitting here in my robe. I was *definitely* in need of a wash and my hair had dried into a wavy mess overnight.

Seeming as though she sensed my unease, Celeste headed for the closet, pulling out another comfortable-looking robe that was soft and light green with little pink flowers on the collar.

"I figured you'd like to get out of that robe. It would be comfortable to keep a robe on, though, just for healing purposes. I think it's best if you rest here for the day at least, if not longer, depending on Sara's opinions."

"Okay," I said. My voice was starting to sound a bit more like me again, with less scratchiness. I guess Sara healed some of the vocal cord damage she had mentioned from the strangling. *Strangling.* I had been *strangled.* He had used his hands to pin me against the wall and choke me before pushing me to the ground and raping me.

Breathe.

I'm not choking now. I can still breathe.

Trying to do what Celeste had done to calm me yesterday, I took deep breaths in a slow sequence. They were shaky, but at least I was trying. A summer breeze and the smell of flowers and fresh-cut grass filled my lungs. I turned to Celeste, who had come closer and was now standing right beside me, as she touched the broad of my back gently.

"You're okay. You can do this," she said.

I nodded and stood shakily, but I managed without support. I went to the washroom and changed into the new robe, using a cloth and warm water to wash my face. I didn't look in the mirror this time.

When I came out, I sat on the bed. I knew now was the time to have that talk she had warned me about just by looking at her standing there, biting her lip as if deciding whether or not this would break me altogether. The sad thing was I wasn't sure it wouldn't.

"Ryenn, I spoke to Emmett earlier. I told him that you're doing okay but still a bit shaken up. I need to talk to you about the next steps now, though, okay?"

"Okay," I swallow.

"Do you remember when you first got here and we told you what the Septor was used for?" I nodded, knowing where this was going already. "Okay, well, we told you that the Septor is used for trials to keep crime down in the kingdom. This practice hasn't been used very often, probably only two times the entire time I have been Queen, mainly for petty crimes. What happened to you, though, is a *serious* crime. One that cannot go without reprimand. We need to do a trial with the Septor to be able to provide that punishment."

"What would the trial look like?" I asked.

"The thing is, since you knew who the attacker was, a warrant would go to Corbin, stating he must appear in front of the throne or be considered automatically guilty. The trial would have to occur within two days after the initial crime, meaning it is going to happen tomorrow morning. It needs to be a fresh event and we need to have *all* the lords and ladies available for it. They were informed of their needed presence late last night, so they left this morning from their districts and will arrive sometime this evening. You need to be there too. Both of you will sit at the front and the

Septor will be used first on the victim, you, and then on the attacker," she inhaled but continued.

"The only thing is, instead of just the king or small council seeing it and being biased off the memories that come to the surface, your memories of the event will be broadcasted for everyone who attends the trial to see. It is also a rule that *anyone* is allowed to attend the trial; basically, this is used as a strategy to keep the crime down. Anyone can ask questions or make statements, but only the small council, including the lords and ladies of the five other districts, will be allowed to make the final vote on a punishment. The King is the one who deems the Fae guilty or not guilty, then based on the votes, a punishment is put in order."

There was so much to process. Everyone was going to be able to see what had happened to me. How I'd been pinned to the ground and-

What if they don't believe me?

Oh Gods, I might be sick.

Air trapped in my lungs again.

Fuck I'm sick of this.

How am I going to keep it together?

"Ryenn, are you okay?" She rubbed my back again.

"No…no, not really. Celeste, what if they don't believe me?

Has the Septor ever been proven wrong or shown the wrong thing? They could just vote against me anyway. I know some people aren't as welcoming of my presence here. I don't know if I- can - do - this." The last few words came out in gasps.

"Relax. It's okay. Catch your breath, honey."

It took a few minutes, but the crashing noises in my head quieted and I stopped hyperventilating.

"To answer your question regarding the Septor, it has only been wrong once, a very long time ago. And that was because it had been used on a very powerful Fae who had the ability to somehow manipulate what the viewer was seeing. Corbin isn't going to be able to do that. The difference with this type of trial is not only will we be able to see the crime committed from the point of view of the attacker, but there is also a direct victim involved, so there is double evidence. People will see the *truth;* that you were hurt. People may be stupid and try to come to his defense, but there's too much evidence there to deny. I will not let anything happen to you and I'm going to make sure Corbin gets what's coming to him. Emmet wanted me to tell you the same thing. He's unable to come speak to you himself because he's busy arranging the Trial as we speak and making arrangements for the arrival of the other Lords and Ladies. He also wanted to give you space out of respect that you're not well right now."

"What consequences could there be?"

"It's for the council to decide based on the findings. Don't worry yourself about the consequences, though, okay? The main thing is you're not going to have to deal with him ever again after this."

I wasn't worried about what was going to happen to him. I just wanted revenge. I wanted him to pay for what he did and I was hoping the consequences are going to equate to that. I also want to prove to the council and to the kingdom that I'm *not* weak and that, whether they like it or not, I will eventually be their Queen one day.

Chapter 15

I ended up falling asleep in the chair by the window for the afternoon. I hadn't really realized how long I'd been asleep until Evie had come in with a tray for my dinner. Before I had fallen asleep, Celeste had left to attend meetings regarding the trial, promising to return this evening. In the meantime, she let me know there were four Scouts outside my door and that if I should need her for anything, to just tell them and they'd get her immediately. Evie had been in and out all day doing tidying and whatnot. She even brushed my hair and put it in a comfortable braid. I must have fallen asleep while she was doing that.

I was able to eat some soup for my lunch, but I couldn't touch the sandwich. I feel like if I tried to eat something like that, I'd choke on it in the process. I know that sounds stupid, though. Now that I have my dinner in front of me, I really am going to try to eat more. I know it's going to make me feel better and less like a corpse.

An hour passes, all alone in my room and so far, I have eaten the bread roll and a slice of cheese. That's all I could manage. I was starting to get a little bit anxious. It was getting dark outside now.

I decided I should get up and move around a bit and, in the process, make my way to the washroom. It was painful, but I managed. I caught a glimpse of my reflection in the mirror again and my stomach did a flip-flop. I hear my bedroom door open and close, so I finish up what I was doing and creep slowly into my room.

Please be Celeste.

Thankfully, it was her and I let out a sigh of relief and walked to my bed. She looks like she's been crying and is exhausted.

"Are you okay?" I ask meekly.

She sniffles, wiping her eyes again. "Yes honey, I'm alright. It's just been a long day. Don't worry about me."

I give her a concerned look.

"The trial is coming together. It's just getting everything ready and everyone's accommodations and everything. Nothing bad. The reason I look upset has nothing to do with you, though it's okay."

"Okay. Are you sure?"

"Yes, dear. Emmet and I just had a little disagreement, that is all. Everything is okay now, though. Anyways, how are *you* doing? Did you rest at all?"

"I ended up falling asleep in the chair all afternoon."

"That's good, I'm glad. What about lunch and dinner?"

"I ate." I didn't feel like elaborating.

She sized me up a little with disbelief.

"Okay, dear."

"Celeste…"

"Yes."

I'm embarrassed, but I continue. "I really hate to ask, but would you mind staying for a while tonight? I know the Scouts are there and that I'm technically safe, but I just- I don't know. I'm being foolish. It's okay. You don't actually have to. I know you're tired and-"

"Ryenn, I'll stay. As long as you want me to. I do not mind at all."

"You sure? I mean, you don't have to stay all night, but maybe until I fall asleep?"

"Would you feel safer if I stayed all night?"

"Yeah… Yes, I would. I know it's unlikely, but… I'm afraid he'll get in. He's a *morph*. He used his invisibility to be able to sneak up on me in the wine cellar…"

"Oh honey," she said, sitting down on the bed. "I'm so sorry. I'll stay. I promise you're not in any danger, but I don't mind staying. Evie can bring up a cot that I'll sleep on. I usually don't fall asleep until late anyway, so it's completely okay."

"Thank you."

~

Smoke fills my nose and I'm awake.

"Ry, what is going on?" Rose said through her sniffles, "I can't see anything; there's too much smoke."

Fire.

Fire was climbing up the walls.

The ceiling is starting to cave in.

"It's okay, Rosie. I'm gonna get us out."

The fire swallowed up the windows.

The bedroom door is stuck.

Father was yelling.

The ceiling is going to collapse.

Rose cries louder and begins to cough.

I'm panicking.

SNAP.

Oh shit.

"Ry!" Rose squeals.

And then the screaming stops-

I'm screaming.

She's gone.

She's gone.

She's dead.

The fire killed her and my father.

But I'm still here.

I'm here, in my bed in Sanctania, screaming at the top of my lungs.

"Ryenn! Ryenn, it's *okay*. It was just a dream."

My vision becomes clearer. Celeste is standing in front of me. It *was* a dream, but it *has* actually happened. I stop screaming, trying to catch my breath. I breathe through my nose and smell smoke.

Looking down, I see my sheets; they are singed.

I burnt them.

Not just my hand prints this time. The blanket was completely destroyed.

Wide-eyed, me and Celeste stare at the blankets and then at each other.

"Shit," Celeste says after what seems like an eternity, sitting there and just staring.

"I-" fuck I don't even have words right now.

I turn my hands over and look at the palms. There is no difference. No burns. No evidence that I had even done this. I bring them to cover my mouth. I'm going to vomit.

"Ryenn-" Celeste begins.

"I'm gonna be sick."

Celeste grabs the trash bucket next to the table by my bed and holds it underneath me just as I start urging. I throw up about four times before I can look up and breathe. The taste of sick still in my throat.

"Ryenn, honey, it's okay. Just let me take the blanket off." She takes it off and looks over me. I'm completely untouched by the fire that must have charred my blankets.

"Celeste, I don't understand how this happened. I- I keep having this nightmare and I guess I caused this fire somehow? But like, it can't be me, right? I haven't transitioned, *plus* you know fire fae are rare, so there's no way I could've done this. Maybe the candle flame somehow jumped over and caught the blanket on fire? *Fuck* what are we going to do?" I throw up again. A cool breeze finds its way to my face to replace the smell of ash and bile.

"We're going to pretend it didn't happen," she states.

"What?" I say, swallowing and looking up.

"This never happened. There's so much on your plate with the trial being tomorrow, so you're stressed. You just knocked the candle in your sleep after waking up from a dream. That's all. Plus, this is the only time this has ever happened anyway, so it's probably nothing."

"Celeste," I say quietly, now looking her in the eyes, "this *has* happened before."

"What?" Her stare goes blank.

"A few weeks ago. I had the same nightmare. When I woke, there were handprints burned into my sheet. *My* handprints."

"What did you do with the sheets?"

"I spilled candle wax on them and burned them a bit more and told Evie I dropped the candle in the middle of the night."

"Good. I'm not going to tell anyone. It's going to be our secret. We need to get through this tomorrow, okay? I mean, powers don't usually manifest until the transitioning, but sometimes some Fae have spurts of them when it gets close to that time. Not saying you *have* fire powers. This could all be a fluke due to stress."

"If anyone were to know, could they use this against me in the trial?" I was shaking violently.

"No, because no one but me is going to know. We are only going to be looking at memories from the attack itself and not what came after. It's going to be fine."

Celeste moves the bucket to the floor and takes the blankets from the bed, laying them next to the washroom. Turning, she makes her way to the wardrobe and grabs a new blanket, smoothing it across me gingerly.

"I'm scared," I admitted.

"I know, honey," She takes me into an embrace. "I know."

~

The night was long. I was restless, worried about what was to come next. I tried to keep the whole potential-fire-powers thing out of my mind, but it kept creeping back in. Same with the dream I kept having. And when I wasn't thinking about those two things, I was thinking about the trial that was about to happen in less than eight hours.

I flip over to my side and look down at Celeste on her cot. She was awake, too.

"Can't sleep?" She whispered.

"No."

"Me neither." She gets up and sits on the bed, "Scooch over."

I move over and she climbs in next to me.

"Do you want to talk about anything?" She asks, propping her head up on one arm.

"I don't know."

"Okay. Would you like me to do the talking?"

I nod.

"You really do remind me so much of your mother, you know that? She was just as beautiful and strong as you are."

"Beautiful?" I ask, stunned a bit by her statement.

"Yes, Ryenn, *gorgeous*. You see that, don't you? She has freckles just like yours, peppering her face. I was always a bit jealous of them, honestly, I thought it made her look like she had been kissed by the sun. Her hair was like yours, too, thick and wavy. Gods, the only thing that is really different about you, too, is your eyes. Hers was a deep emerald green, fitting since she was Queen of the Emerald Throne. Yours are similar to Emmet's, though, but still different. *Unique*. Almost silver."

I blushed a little. I never thought I was pretty. I never was really impressed by what I saw in the mirror. *Especially not now.* But hearing that from Celeste made me feel, I don't know, nice, I guess, since it was coming from such a beautiful woman.

"She blushed just as easily as you do, too," she laughs,

making me even more red. "She was always so good at hiding how she felt from others, except when it came to blushing. It always made me laugh."

"I don't find it funny." I rub my cheeks, willing the red away.

"Ha, well, I suppose not, but you'll grow out of that."

"Were you and Emmet always in love? He is my mother's younger brother, right? Did you guys always know each other well?"

Celeste clears her throat. "I'm going to be honest with you, Ryenn. My relationship with Emmet has always been…different. I was best friends with your mom. I mean, I lived in the castle my entire life since my parents were the Lord and Lady of the capital, which is why my eldest sister is now. Anyways, Emmet and I are the same age. Your mom was only a year or so older than the both of us. We were always kind of set up to eventually marry each other, which is something I never totally agreed with. While I love Emmet, he's a very hardworking and great guy and incredibly understanding and supportive. I was never *in* love with him. He knows that and is okay with it. Our marriage was set up from birth; we grew up together and while we became incredibly close, we never had the chance to even think about loving someone else. It wouldn't be fair to them, honestly, because we were technically already betrothed to one another."

"Oh wow. That kind of sounds awful. I mean, you never had

any boyfriends or anything?"

"No, I never had boyfriends, but that doesn't mean I didn't have fun in secret." She winks.

I realize what she meant by fun and, again, I blush and she laughs.

"Is that why you guys never had any children?"

The warmth drains from Celeste's face and I instantly feel bad.

"No, Emmet and I have tried having children multiple times. Unfortunately, after trying really hard and losing a couple of my pregnancies, the healers deemed me unable to have children. It's just how my body is and there's nothing I can do about it."

"I'm sorry."

Celeste brushes a piece of hair behind my ear

"Don't apologize. I've come to terms with it and it's okay. I think I always knew deep down that I could never bear children. I still had to try anyway, though. When the king and queen reach 100 years old, they have to try and have a child that will be able to take over reign by the time they are 121."

"Wait, what!?" I say much louder than I intend to.

"Yes, you heard me right. I'm 114 years old now. Once you

transition, your aging slows significantly. Fae have very long lifespans, like up to hundreds of years. Your mother was Queen from the time she was 21 until she was 100 when she got pregnant with you. Myself and Emmet only had to take over when she died, so we've only been in reign for almost 16 years, which is nothing really. The reign of a King and Queen is only to be about a hundred years and then the offspring take over and the old king and queen are able to retire. Once they retire, they usually partake in the small council and whatnot, but unfortunately, both your grandparents passed before your mother did."

Holy shit.

It's just one thing after the other, isn't it?

Now I can live to be hundreds of years old?

"Celeste, when I first came and Emmet showed me the paternity test results, it said my father was unknown. Do you know who it was? Was there not a king to my mother?"

"Your mother, being stubborn, which is a quality I loved about her, refused to marry until she found someone she loved. She served as Queen alone and did a damn good job at it. As for your father, I figured this conversation was coming. Ela was under a lot of pressure to produce an heir and to marry once she reached 100 years old. Out of spite, during one of her conferences or travels across the kingdom, she became pregnant with you. She never told me who it was, only that she had to do it for the kingdom. She was incredibly nervous about having to raise you alone, but I assured her I was going to be there and help. I was kind of shocked by the paternity results myself, though, that no one was found in our system, which has the DNA of every Fae across the kingdom. But it wasn't a mortal either because it would've told us that too. Plus, Fae can't really produce offspring with mortals. Your father never came forward either when the pregnancy was announced to the kingdom, so I'm not entirely sure who it is."

"Oh, alright then."

I'm not sure how I felt about all that. That my real father wanted nothing to do with me. Then again, my mother wanted nothing to do with him, so maybe it wasn't so bad.

"You should know Ryenn; despite her worries and uncertainties, she loved you unconditionally. She was so excited to be a mother to you. I felt the same. Knowing that your father wasn't in the picture and your grandparents were dead, Ela trusted that I would be your 'secondary parent,' along with Emmet, of course, especially if she had to be away for whatever reason. You had a support system set up for you despite the circumstances."

An overwhelming sense to hug Celeste had come over me. So I did just that. I hugged her, taking her a bit by surprise at first until she hugged me back.

"Thank you," I said, my voice muffled in her hair.

"I am just happy to have you back. When I lost her, it was like I lost both of you even if I hadn't met you yet," she said back, stroking my hair.

For the first time in a long time, since the fire and since my mortal mother's death, I felt like I belonged. I didn't feel alone. I *did* have a family and they had been waiting for me since the moment I was born. It didn't make up for my losses by any means, but it at least made me feel not completely and utterly alone.

Chapter 16

The sun came through the curtains quicker than I anticipated. Celeste and I had stayed awake the rest of the night. The whole time, she told me stories of my mother and her from her childhood. I knew she was trying to distract me and keep the bad thoughts about today and what had happened at bay, and I appreciated her for it. Evie wasn't allowed to see me this morning. No one was supposed to tend to me on the day of the trial. Celeste, being Queen, felt as though she overruled that and made an exception to help me get ready. My body was locked up in fear.

I took a bath, a warm one this time, and Celeste washed my hair. She picked out a dark green, nearly black, dress for me to wear that was a velvety sort of material. It was modest and comfortable, which made me feel a bit better. My whole body was about to be on display through memories in front of the entire kingdom, so I'm not sure why modesty was something on my mind. She also braided my hair back into a low knot. The scar on my lip was still visible and quite the eye sore, but luckily, the bruising had faded enough for her to use some cosmetics to cover it up. The entire time I was getting ready, she spoke in a calm tone, talking me through the trial again and again, making sure I was ready and trying to ease my nerves. She even had her own handmaid bring her dress and other things so she could get ready in my chambers so that I wouldn't have to be alone longer than necessary.

I could hardly say anything, fearing if I did, tears would start, or I'd vomit again. I was also mentally preparing myself for this day. I needed to look put together and not like I was on the verge of breaking. I wanted to look professional and not let the events that took place bother me. So that's what I did. I practiced while waiting for the Scouts to come and retrieve me.

A knock sounded at the door and my stomach dropped. It's time.

Celeste, wearing a long black dress with silver and gold beading, turned to me before answering.

"You know I have to go ahead of you. Ser Davis will be bringing you down shortly after I leave. When you are led down the halls and into the throne room, all eyes will be on you. You're going to be fine and walk like I taught you, okay?"

I nodded; my teeth were chattering.

"Ryenn, you can do this. You are so strong. I'll meet you back here afterward, okay? It may take me longer due to duties, but I'll be back as soon as I can. You're going to be okay."

She answers the door and slips out with a Scout.

Now I'm alone.

Waiting.

I practice breathing. In for three, then hold for three, and then out for three. This is what Celeste had taught me the other night. It helped occasionally and I tried to focus on it besides thinking about what was about to happen.

Ten minutes or so pass when another knock sounds on the door.

I feel frozen on the bed.

Get up.

I do and walk to the door, my hand on the handle.

Turn it off.

I open the door and Ser Davis is there.

"Ready, princess?"

I nod and we walk out.

~

Hundreds and hundreds of Fae line the halls as we reach the central portion of the castle. I keep my head held high, my hands clasped behind my back and focus my attention on the back of the Scout's head that's leading the way. There are 5 scouts surrounding me. Ser Davis is to my right, one leads in front of me, another is to my left and then two flank me. We reach the Emerald doors and I take a deep breath.

I can do this.

It's going to be over soon.

The doors open and everyone in the throne room flicks their heads in my direction.

Emmet and Celeste are up the stairs, seated upon their thrones. The entire space is filled with Fae. The small council and, who I assume to be the other Lords and Ladies, are positioned to the front of the crowd. Lining the ceiling where there is extra seating, hundreds more look down. Everyone is standing, waiting for my advancement. I have to walk to my chair, positioned at the front of the room, with one of the same style positioned across from it.

Let's do this.

I make my way down the narrow aisle, keeping my attention to the thrones and my aunt and uncle who occupy them. I make my way to my seat and wait.

The doors open again.

Corbin Sapphic makes his way down the aisle.

I feel like the earth is shifting beneath my feet. I will Emmet to dismiss the crowd so we can all sit before I topple over.

Corbin takes his place in front of me.

His eye has a purple/gray shadow.

Had he been hit?

He smiles an evil grin.

I'm going to be sick.

Everything about the attack feels like it hits me all at once. I feel like running out of here, running out of the stupid castle and never turning back. But I can't. I have to do this.

Turn it off.

"You may be seated," the King's voice booms through the room.

As I sit, I give myself the opportunity to glance around the room.

I see Amalie sitting behind her parents. The other teenage Fae are in the crowd, too. I see Sara towards the side of the room along with other healers in their starch white jackets. Scouts are scattered amongst the room. I catch a glimpse of Braxton towards the back. *Great.* My attention is brought back by the sound of Emmet's voice.

"As you all know by now, we are brought together today due to a crime committed by a citizen of Sanctania." He begins, "Corbin Sapphic, eldest child of Lord Keaton and Lady Carolina Sapphic of district Vermuse, is accused of the aggravated assault on Princess Ryenn Embers, child of the late Queen Elanore Embers of

Sanctania, and rightful heir to the Emerald Throne."

The statement is followed by whispers throughout the crowd.

What is everyone saying?

You can do this.

It doesn't matter what they say. It's going to be fine.

"Due to the alleged crime, a trial with the Septor is in order. Corbin, please rise."

Corbin does as he says.

"Do you agree with the terms presented and allow the kingdom to view your memories through that of the Septor, knowing that if you should refuse, you will automatically be found guilty?"

"I agree," Corbin said in a tone that made me seasick and he takes his seat.

"Ryenn, please rise."

I do as he says, trying to make it look as though my legs are solid under me and not like they are made of jelly.

"Do you agree with the terms presented and allow the kingdom to view your memories through that of the Septor, knowing that what we are going to see may not be comfortable for you?"

I scrounge up the courage to use my voice.

"I agree," I say, sounding clear and confident.

Taking my seat, I glance at Corbin. He is staring at me.

I look away.

It's okay, you can do this.

"Since we have the agreement of both parties, we will begin with the victim."

The golden Septor is brought to the king as he makes his descent down the stairs. Celeste has to stay behind.

"The Septor will be able to read the memories from the events of the alleged attack and, using magic as by the conjuring of a member from the electricity powers, it will be displayed to the screen above the thrones." I glance up, seeing a white sheet draped across the wall.

"I ask that all questions and comments from everyone in attendance wait until both parties memories have been broadcasted. That way, we have the best evidence tangible before jumping to conclusions."

King Emmet finally reaches the end of the staircase and stands next to me. I sense sorrow in his eyes as he looks at me. He isn't allowed to address me separately from the trial; thus, no words of wisdom are imparted to me.

"We are going to begin. Ryenn, please place your hand on

the globe of the Septor."

I do as he says and I am sucked back to the wine cell.

~

Reaching for a bottle of wine, I pause, sensing someone's presence.

Someone grabs my shoulder and Corbin appears in front of me.

I drop a wine bottle and it shatters.

I get mad at Corbin for making me drop it, but I notice something isn't right. She smells odd and is carrying a flask of some sort of strong liquid.

I try to ask about it, but he drops the flask to the floor and pins me to the wall by my throat, strangling me.

I can't breathe.

He tells me off, saying that I shouldn't have tattled on him earlier that day before class and that since my arrival, I was ruining everything.

I try to speak, but he yells at me, then takes me by my shoulder and shoves me to the wet ground.

My face meets the floor and the broken glass cuts my face.

He holds a knife to my throat.

I try to wiggle my hands out to grab a chunk of glass to defend myself, but I am too late as he grabs the glass and sticks it through my hand.

Pain is searing through me.

I am screaming but make no noise is able to leave due to this hand covering my mouth.

He hikes up the skirt of my dress and rips off my undergarments.

The entire time, I am sobbing.

I can't move, or he'll slit my throat.

I can't scream for help.

No one will hear me anyway.

I feel him as he shoves his fingers inside me first, then his dick.

Everything begins to fade until I hear Celeste calling for me down the hall.

Corbin goes invisible and threatens me to keep my mouth shut about what just happens.

I crawl to my knees and sit against the wall, taking in my surroundings with silent sobs as Celeste rounds the corner.

The memory fades to black.

Chapter 17

I am gasping as my vision comes back to me and I am back in the Throne Room.

I am not in the wine cellar.

I am okay.

I am here, taking part in a trial for revenge for my assault.

Biting my tongue and easing my breath, I sit back down, willing the red heat to evaporate from my face.

Turn it off.

I look around the room at horrified faces. Celeste is on the throne, attempting to look put together, but I can see her swallowing her disgust. A woman in the audience, one of the Ladies, who I assume to be Corbin's mother due to her features, is sobbing. Amalie is looking directly at me and I catch her stare. Tears are welled in her eyes. I look up to the King next, realizing he has not yet spoken. He is looking at me with a wide-eyed expression and clenching his jaw. Corbin looks unbothered.

Emmet clears his throat, willing himself to speak. I am trying to focus on my breathing to attempt my heart, which I am sure is going to explode from beating so hard.

"Corbin, please place your hand on the globe of the Septor," he says in a flat tone.

Corbin does as he is told.

I look at the screen stationed above the thrones.

I am not sure I want to see what is about to happen, but I sure as hell don't want to see all the reactions, either.

~

Ryenn is walking down the halls of the basement, looking for the wine cellar. Corbin follows her, tracking her movements since she left the dining hall.

She reaches the cellar, makes her way to the back wall and goes on her tippy toes to reach the wine she's looking for.

Corbin sneaks up behind her, still in his invisible morph form, his favorite of his powers, and grabs her shoulder.

The only thing going through Corbins drunk mind is revenge. This girl has to pay for ruining not only his chance at becoming an heir but now is bossing her way around and got him in trouble today.

He decides he knows just the way to put her in her place.

She's trying to say something, but disgust is written all over her face.

He grabs her neck, strangling her. It's almost like she turns blue from lack of oxygen.

More wine bottles break in the background.

She attempts to speak again, clearly not getting it through her head that he had told her not to speak.

She was really getting on his last nerve.

He pushes her to the ground and her face smashes into the pool of wine and glass.

Before she even attempts to get up, Corbin gets on top of her and holds his knife, the one his father got him for his birthday, against her carotid, making sure she wasn't going to move.

The bitch tries to reach for the glass but is too slow and Corbin pierces it through her hand.

Before she can scream, he wraps his sticky hand around her mouth.

Time to make her take back everything she said.

Ryenn's backside is completely exposed as Corbin pulls up her dress and rips off her panties.

This was definitely a site to see; the princess so weak and frail. Nothing more than a child, really, not even Transitioned. So innocent and pure. Yeah right.

Corbin laughs as he thinks about what he's about to do,

Ryenn is wiggling beneath him but is not able to get anywhere.

Quickly, without warning, he shoves his fingers deep inside her, breaking that little film along with her spirits. He wanted to make sure that every time she sought pleasure, her mind went to him and that she should've kept in line and stayed the hell away from Sanctania.

He forces his cock next, thrusting into her.

He doesn't find relief, though, as he hears someone coming up the hall too quickly.

Fuck.

Corbin goes invisible, threatening the princess that if she tells anyone, she will wish she didn't.

Corbin leaves the room, as the Queen of Sanctania is left to pick up the pieces of the mess he left behind.

He doesn't feel one ounce of remorse.

~

I tasted the metallic essence of blood fill my mouth as I sat there, watching the screen before me. I had bitten my tongue so hard, trying not to show emotion, that it was now bleeding and coating my throat.

I don't know what was worse; feeling that memory again from my own perspective or seeing myself be treated that way from his perspective.

Everyone had been able to see me, pretty well naked and vulnerable, lying on that stupid wine-covered floor.

I felt *dirty*.

Even more so, I felt sick and the blood pooling in my mouth definitely wasn't helping.

When Corbin takes his hand off the Septor, he looks directly at my eyes, not a single morsel of regret in his features. He then has the audacity to grin.

I look away before I vomit.

In three.

Hold three.

Out three.

Repeat.

Turn it off.

You can do this. It's almost over.

A cool, minty breeze caresses my face and I glance up at Celeste, who nods ever-so-slightly.

The king makes his way back to the throne without saying a word.

The room is completely silent.

I fear everyone may be able to hear my heart beating out of my chest.

~

"The questions and comments from the audience may begin. You have 30 minutes to say your piece and then the council will vote on a punishment and a decision will be made," the King states. His voice is tense.

The room is silent for a moment and then I see someone standing in the audience.

It's Sara.

"Yes, go ahead, Sara."

"Thank you, your highness," she bows. "Council members, I would like to make it known that although the Fae you see before you today looks remotely unscathed by the assault, besides the gash to her lip, the injuries were extensive. I was Ryenn's appointed healer after the incident and was able to heal her quickly, yet she was badly hurt." Sara swallows and reaches into her pocket. I am feeling numb and hope I look at it on the outside as well.

"I have a list of all the injuries the Princess acquired from the attack and I would like to read them to you," she starts. "Mild concussion, glass abrasions to left forehead and temple, left black eye, left lip gash, glass shards stuck in hair, bruising to the head, strangle marks to the throat, shallow knife incision to throat near the carotid artery, three broken ribs on the left, one broke a rib on the right, bruising to chest, bruising to the abdomen, penetrating wound to left hand, in which glass shards had to be removed, glass abrasions to both arms, bruising to both arms, bruising to both legs, blunt pelvis trauma, ruptured hymen, blunt force trauma to the vaginal canal, bleeding from the pelvic area, ripping to the external pelvic area, and emotional trauma consisting of severe anxiety and PTSD."

I am dizzy.

The room is spinning.

Get ahold of yourself.

"As you can see, Ryenn sustained multiple severe injuries from this assault, which should *not* be taken lightly. Thank you." Sara sits back down, giving me a quick, calming glance.

"Thank you, Sara," Emmet proceeds, moving his jaw. "Any other comments?"

A man from the council stands, the one that was next to the crying woman. Corbin's father.

"I would just like the audience and the rest of the council to know that my son is a *good* man. He always has been. He spends much of his time volunteering and is very popular in both Vermuse and the capital. That being said, it is clear he has made a mistake. From my understanding, there had been an altercation at the school earlier that day in which some choice words were exchanged between my son and the princess," he looks at me briefly and I go stiff. "It was clear from both perspectives that Corbin had been drinking, which is not something we condone, but it was clear he was not in the right mind. I believe he would have never done such a thing if he were not intoxicated. What he did was clearly horrible, but I believe it was all a mistake. He's a good boy. I would just like everyone to keep that in mind as we proceed."

Acid burned my throat.

How could he truly believe something like that?

Amalie's father stood next.

"I agree with Keaton, Corbin is a good kid. I oversaw a lot of his training to be heir champion. The children have all been a little… upset with Ryenn's arrival. I mean, they were all promised a shot at the throne until she randomly showed up and her birthright usurped all of that. I can see why he would be mad and feel like he had to take his anger out one way or another. I'm not agreeing with what he did, simply, I could see where he's coming from."

Anger blinded my vision.

He assaulted me.

He took a piece of me that I was *never* going to get back.

Turn it off.

Celeste had said some Fae would attempt to defend him. I just need to let it bounce off of me.

Mrs. Langerfeld stood next.

"With all due respect, my Lords, Ryenn never asked for any of this. Had she been born in the kingdom and raised here, there would be no question of her birthright to the throne. It is not a good enough reason to violently assault a *child* over. There had been a disagreement between Corbin and Ryenn earlier that day and Ryenn had been truthful even in the face of the peers who had not been so accepting of her. Despite knowing Corbin since he was a child and teaching him since then, what he did is truly unacceptable."

A Lady from the council stood next. I didn't know what her name was….

"Based on the evidence shown by both memories from both parties, how can you, Lords, truly stand to defend him like that? I'm sorry, but this assault was aggravated and whether or not he was drunk shouldn't even be in the question. Not only did this boy assault a child violently, but he also assaulted the future Queen of the Kingdom. It's shameful that you even came to the defense of someone like that. Also, where were the Scouts? Why hadn't they been guarding the princess and why hadn't there been any in the basement of the castle at all? Hunter, do you have anything to say about this?"

Hunter Vermeil, the Captain of the Scouts, rose next.

"The fact there were no Scouts available for the aid of the princess does not excuse the fact that it still happened. The Scouts that were meant to be in the basement during this time have been reprimanded for not reporting to their duty. Forces have since been increased in guarding the castle itself if you would like to know Lady Juniper. This assault has opened our eyes to the fact that perhaps the team have become too comfortable and needs to be more alert."

More people started arguing and the audience erupted into a frenzy of voices.

My head was swarming and I was still dizzy.

I'm not sure how much longer I can manage sitting here like this.

"That's enough!" the King exclaimed and the room went quiet.

"Based on the evidence provided, Corbin Sapphic is guilty of the assault on Princess Ryenn Embers. Council, you have 10 minutes to come up with the consequences for the crime committed; you may use the adjacent board room to discuss. In the meantime, we ask the rest of the audience to remain quiet."

All blood left my body and it's like my heart stopped.

He was guilty.

Thank Gods.

The council members quickly left the room together and two healers were allowed to come over to myself and Corbin, offering water.

I drank mine, the cold helping get rid of the after-taste of blood.

A bit of blood rimmed the glass, but I wiped it off quickly before the healer noticed.

Looking up, I see his stare.

His jaw is clenched like his fists in his lap. His blue eyes pierced through my own, making me lose my breath.

I swallow....

The council members make their way back into the room and find their seats.

~

"Normani, you may do us the favor of announcing the decided consequences and sentencing of the guilty."

Normani stands and lifts a piece of paper.

"Corbin Sapphic is to be exiled from the kingdom. A spell will be placed so that he may not enter the realm again without experiencing immediate death. His title of the next lord of Vermuse is to be passed to his younger sister. The Scouts will leave with him immediately after this trial and bring him to the east border, where he will be left to fend for himself. Juno Albatras will be performing the binding spell. He will not be permitted to say goodbye to his family members."

Holy shit.

He is going to be gone.

Forever.

"Thank you, Normani. I, King Emmet Embers of the Kingdom of Sanctania, deem this sentence to be acceptable for the committed crimes. Thank you for coming, everyone and let this serve as a reminder that crimes are not taken lightly in the kingdom. We operate off of trust in each other and any threat to such shall be eradicated. We may clue up now and the princess may be escorted to her chambers." He motions his head for Ser Davis to come forward to retrieve me.

"May I say one last thing, Your Highness?" Corbin spits out all of a sudden and everyone's attention flies to him.

"I'm not sure that's wise, Corbin," Emmet returns back.

Corbin's attention falls upon me in an instant.

"I should've slit your *fucking* throat when I had the chance," he lurches at me but not fast enough.

Scouts grab him and push me back out of the way. I stumble and fall on my ass.

He fights them, trying to get to me, fury built in his face, fangs glistening in the light.

Screams that I'm not sure *aren't* from me fill the room.

Ser Davis lifts me up and ushers me out of the Throne Room quickly.

Chapter 18

Ser Davis safely gets me back to the familial quarters of the castle. My mind is swimming.

I'm going to be sick.

"Your safe now, princess," Ser Davis states, "He'll be out of the kingdom shortly, no need to worry."

I hardly hear him.

The day sits heavily in my head.

So much had just happened, and my mind can't process it all at once.

I take off in a sprint down the hall to my chambers.

I make it through the door, slamming it behind me, rush to the bathroom, and throw up in the toilet. The only thing that comes up is blood and watery bile.

He was going to kill me.

He wanted me dead.

Dead.

Like the rest of my family.

Maybe I'd be better off that way.

The rest of those Lords seem to think he was innocent anyways.

I don't realize how quickly I am breathing and how fast my heart rate is.

Fuck.

I can't do this anymore.

Where is Celeste?

I am going to die.

I *am* dying.

Fuck.

My vision narrows, the bad thoughts are creeping in and taking over. All that pent-up emotion I felt the whole godsdamn day makes it to the surface, and I feel like I may explode.

I'm heaving again, but nothing is coming up. It's just making it harder to breathe.

Strangled sobs make their way out of my throat as I am hyperventilating.

I bring my knees to my chest and my hands to the collar of my dress.

It's *choking* me.

I'm choking.

I can't do this anymore.

Maybe I should just end it here and now, do what everyone wants from me.

"Everything was fine before you existed" I hear in his fucking voice.

Shaking, I reach for the cupboard under the basin and find scissors.

"I should've slit your throat when I had the chance."

I hear the loud crash of the chamber door I slammed, and someone rush in.

"Ryenn?!" Celeste rushes into the washroom, and I drop the scissors.

I start sobbing uncontrollably and irrevocably.

Maybe I'll just drown in my tears.

~

Celeste kicked the scissors out of the way when she came in.

She got down on her knees and held me in her arms, fearing if she let go, she was going to lose me.

That's where I've been for the past 30 minutes, screeching in Celeste's lap like a child as she rocked me back and forth.

The tears finally seem to cease, probably because I no longer have any water left in my body, and I take shuddering breaths.

"You did such a good job," Celeste says, smoothing my hair back out of my tear-stained face. "You looked professional and put together. You're so *so* strong, Ryenn. It's all over now."

The cool, minty breeze had been helping me get air into my lungs.

"He's gone now, okay? You're not in anymore danger. You're safe. It's just me and you right now."

I swallow. My throat is raw and dry.

"You were right," I managed to squeak out.

"About what?" she caresses my cheek.

"People tried to defend him. They didn't care about the fact that he hurt me. Nobody wants me here."

"And those people were wrong for saying those things and should be ashamed. It didn't matter in the end, though. He got what was coming to him."

I take a shivery inhale.

"He was going to *kill me.*"

Celeste sighs and closes her eyes, bringing my head closer to her chest.

"Ryenn, honey, what were you doing with the scissors when I walked in?"

Tears, that I apparently still had left, started streaming down my face again.

"I'm sorry. I just. I couldn't take it anymore."

Celeste wipes tears from her own face and then mine.

"I'm sorry. I'm sorry. I'm sorry," I keep repeating in between sobs.

"I'm sorry too," Celeste says. "I never ever want you to feel that way again, okay? We're going to get through this. It's going to be okay."

We stay on the floor for what seems like forever.

~

I wake up in my bed. How I got here, I'm not exactly sure. I must have fallen asleep from exhaustion, and Celeste must have carried me. I sit up, blinking at the sun through my curtains.

How long had I slept?

Celeste is sitting in the chaise by the window. In a different dress than before.

"How long was I asleep?" I ask, my voice groggy and gross.

"You slept all night. It's about 10 am the next morning. Would you like something to eat?"

I don't think I could even swallow a pea right now if I tried.

The memories and everything hit me like a ton of bricks. He was gone. *I had tried to kill myself.* Fuck.

"Ryenn?"

"Oh, uh, no, I'm not hungry." I stand up and begin walking to the washroom, Celeste closes in behind me.

"I'm just going to pee," I say, blushing.

"Okay, I'm going to stand outside the door, okay?"

I nod, do my business, and walk back to my bed.

That's where I stay for the rest of the day.

Lying there, looking at nothing except the walls or the ceiling. I don't dare sleep out of fear. Celeste tries having a conversation with me a few times, but I don't give much of an answer, so she stops trying. She doesn't leave me, though. She let me know that the group who exiled Corbin were successful and were already on the way back to the capital, for some reason, that news made me feel nothing at all.

Sara had also been by at one point to give me some medications and to check up on me. I didn't say much to her either but took the medicine with a small sip of water. Both Celeste and Sara had stepped just outside the door to have a conversation. I could assume it was about my attempt at suicide or that now I was hardly moving or speaking, but I didn't really care. Honestly, I don't think

I care about anything right now.

I stayed the way I was for the rest of the night into the next morning. I refused to eat anything even though Celeste had tried multiple times. The only time I got up was to relieve myself, and then it was only when I thought my bladder was going to burst if I didn't. Last thing I wanted was to wet the bed I was staying in for the foreseeable future. It still hurts to go to use the toilet. Every time I did, it reminded me of *him*.

There were a few times where the thoughts would get too much, and my numbness would be quickly overtaken by agonizing sorrow. I would cry, Celeste would crawl into bed, soothe me quietly, give me some of the medication Sara must have given her to relax me, and then I would return to my shell.

I don't think I'll ever be able to move on from this. I thought it would be easier once he was gone, but it wasn't. I don't think it ever will be.

Chapter 19

The night comes and goes. I don't sleep much. I think I doze for maybe an hour, but I'm awoken without air in my lungs. It takes me a minute but I get it under control without waking Celeste.

It's now afternoon, Evie just came and brought my tray for lunch.

"Ryenn, you really have to try and eat. It's going to make you feel better."

"I'm not hungry."

"Can you at least try? Please? Honey, you are wasting away. If you don't start eating, you're going to need to be hooked up to supplemental nutrition again."

"I can't." I look at her, tears in the corners of my eyes.

"Okay," she sighs, "okay. We can try again at dinner, okay?"

I turn over just as a knock sounds on the door.

Celeste gets up from her chair, smoothing her blue dress that was brought to her this morning, and opens the door.

"Hello, your highness," I hear Ser Davis say, "There is someone who has been requesting to see the Princess and has been quite persistent. We told them the Princess didn't want visitors. However, she has been relentless."

Now, my attention turns towards the door.

Celeste peaks her head around the corner and smiles.

"You can let her in, Ser Davis."

Who the fuck was here?

With that thought, Amalie turns the corner.

"Ryenn, are you alright with Amalie keeping you company for a bit? I have some meetings I must attend regarding the ball, okay? I'll be back in a few hours, plus it wouldn't hurt for you to socialize."

I don't have a chance to respond before she slides out the door, leaving Amalie standing awkwardly at the front of my chambers.

She's wearing her school uniform. I suppose school was just finishing up for the day now. She's carrying a bag in her hand.

I sat up in bed, smoothing my hair down. I knew I must look like a sewer rat, but I don't think I really care all that much.

"Hi," Amalie says, her bottom lip is quivering.

"Hey?-"

"Ryenn, I'm so sorry," she starts, tears now streaming down her face. "I'm sorry for what happened, and I'm even more sorry for what my father said during the trial. He can be a horrible man; trust me, I know better than anyone. My parents are controlling and have made me lose all my friends over the years, and now it's going to happen to us, and I don't know if I can take it. I'm sorry. You're just so nice, and I really do enjoy hanging out with you and. I was hoping we were starting to become close, and then all this happened. And now I'm making everything about me, which isn't fair to you. Fuck I'm so sorry."

Amalie drops her bag and drops to her knees. I've never seen her like this. She's usually a lot like her aunt in a put-together sort of way. I feel bad and get off my bed, pushing back the covers and kneeling in front of her.

"Amalie."

She looks up, her hazel eyes watery.

"I'm not mad at you. What your father said is by no means your fault and I know that. We are friends, in fact, I consider you my best friend."

"Really?" She sniffles, wiping her nose with the sleeve of her dress.

"*Yes*. I'm sorry I haven't wanted visitors… it has nothing to do with you I just haven't been in a good headspace."

"I know. I just… Gods, I've been so worried about you. I *hate* Corbin, and I'm glad he's gone for good. What he did- it's unforgivable."

"Yeah, I'm glad he's gone too," I admit.

I feel a small weight lift from my chest. I *was* glad he was gone. He may have taken something from me that I'll never get back, but at least he'd never be able to hurt me or anyone ever again.

"Can I hug you?" Amalie asks, looking me in the eyes.

"Yes," I laugh, and she leaps, nearly knocks me over.

We sat there for a moment, laughing and crying, taking each other in. It feels *good.*

"Ryenn?" Amalie says, pulling back a bit to face me.

"Yeah?"

"Since we're *best* friends, that means I can tell you anything right?"

"Sure."

"Okay. When was the last time you took a bath? Because girl, you are a complete mess."

I crack up. I can't remember the last time I laughed like this.

"I don't know if I'm being honest," I admit, still laughing.

"Okay, well, we're gonna change that. You go get in the bath, I'll get a dress and stuff picked out for you and then I'll show you what I brought. Gods, I have *so much* to tell you."

We both get off the floor, and I head to the washroom. I fill up the tub using lavender soap and try to wash away the past few days of depression, anxiety, guilt, and anger.

~

When I'm finished, I do admit I feel much better. I look at myself in the mirror; all the visible injuries have nearly completely faded besides the lip scar, which was actually kind of growing on me because it made me look a bit badass. When I'm finished, I walk out to the wardrobe, where Amalie has picked out a simple pink cotton spring-style dress.

"You have the coolest wardrobe *ever*. I can't believe I've never come over to see it. Maybe we'll be the same size soon, and then I can 'borrow' some things." We both laugh.

After I get dressed, she talks me into letting her do my hair. I eat a lemon danish she bought from the bakery in town. She had told me she bought half a dozen but ended up eating three, so now I *had* to try it. Lemon is my favorite, anyway, and this *was* really good.

"Pippa never sits still long enough for me to do her hair nicely."

"I can see why," I say as she pulls it back. "Ouch!"

"Oh, don't be a baby."

Something about the interaction warms me, and I feel a little more normal.

"Rose had very curly hair. It was always wild and all over the place. I could hardly ever get a brush through it, and she always wanted a silly pink ribbon that our father had given her tied in it somehow."

"She sounds like she was a funny kid," Amalie finished up the braids that twist around my head and fall down the length of my back. "Tell me more about her."

I close my eyes as I picture my baby sister.

"She was beautiful. She looked a lot like our mother, and had the same bright orange hair and blue eyes. Her skin was so fair that she couldn't be out in the sun long or burn up. She was such a smart girl and was excited to start school in the fall. In Molisan, children start school in the fall until the spring, and they have the summers off. Rose had just turned 5, so she'd be going in September. Her favorite thing in the world was animals, especially our chickens, that she had named each individually. When she found out father killed the chickens so we could actually eat, she refused and cried and cried," tears sting my eyes, but I will them away. "I miss her very much. I pretty well raised her by myself. My mother, or my mortal mother, I should say, died giving birth to her in our small cottage home. My father was never the same after and spent most the time hunting or in the off seasons at the bar in town. So, me and Rosie were left to our own devices. I wouldn't have had it any other way."

"That's beautiful," Amalie said, wiping a tear from my cheek. "Ryenn, I'm sorry you lost all of them. I'm sorry for a lot of things that have happened to you. You're the strongest person I know. You're my hero."

I laugh at the last word.

"What! It's true," Amalie laughs with me.

"What was it that you wanted to tell me about?" I ask after a few moments.

"Oh, right! I nearly forgot," she clears her throat and sits across from me. "So you know how at the trial Corbin had a black eye, right?"

His face comes back to me, and I stifle a shudder. "Yes…"

"Grey was the one who gave it to him."

"What? As in his best friend, Grey?" I ask, caught by surprise.

"Yes! The morning after the attack, before word had gone out to the city, Corbin came to class and was bragging about what happened. Grey took him by the collar of his shirt, pinned him up against the school wall, and punched him in the face, saying that he was an asshole and should be ashamed. It was *insane*. I'm shocked he came to your defense. Autumn wasn't very happy about it, though."

"Holy shit. What happened after?"

"Well, Mrs. Langerfeld showed up and told us all to go back to the castle and that more would be explained later. I went back home, and my mother and father were talking about the upcoming trial and what happened. It made me sick to my stomach Ry, *Gods,* what a fucking tool. I had just thought you had gotten sick, and that's why dinner was canceled, but when I found out the truth, I could've hunted him down and killed him."

"Wow!" I was at a loss for words.

Why did Greyson defend me?

I thought he hated me, too.

Weird.

"I know. So that's pretty well all the exciting things that you missed out on. I've been in my room, 'forbidden to leave' because my stupid parents didn't want me coming to see you, but I've been bugging Ser Davis ever since, and I finally made it out of the castle's west side and came to see you. I missed you, you know. A lot. I was really, really worried."

"I missed you too, Amy."

"You're gonna get through this, you know? Despite all the shit talk of people thinking you're broken for good, you're going to bounce back even stronger. Hell, you're going to be a force to be reckoned with when you transition."

She had no idea.

Keeping the whole fire thing quiet felt wrong. Like I was keeping a secret. But I wasn't even sure it was real yet, so it didn't matter.

Chapter 20

Celeste was only gone for a couple of hours. After those couple of hours with Amalie, I felt much better than I had in my shell this morning. We talked about lots of things, laughing and sometimes crying, but it felt *good*. Celeste walks in the room and has a slightly shocked expression to her face, probably expecting to find me still in bed.

"Oh! You look good!"

I blush.

"Amalie dear, your mother came looking for you, I told her you were helping me with planning something for the ball and not that you're up here. I know she didn't want you too, but I appreciate that you did."

"Oh my... Thanks, aunt Celeste. Well, I better get going." Amalie turns and hugs me. "Oh! I brought some of my favorite books for you to read. I figured you're probably a bit bored. Hopefully, you come back to class soon?"

"Um, yeah, maybe soon. Thanks for coming, Amy."

Amalie walks over to the door, and Celeste stops her, taking her in an embrace.

"Thanks for coming, dear."

"Oh, uh, no worries?" She turns and gives me a bit of a confused expression.

I guess Celeste has never been the affectionate type from Amalie's reaction. When I first met her, I got those vibes too.

"How are you feeling, Ryenn?" Celeste turns to me as the chamber door shuts behind Amalie.

"A bit better." I stand and walk over to her. "I'm sorry for how I've been... acting."

Celeste takes me in her arms. She's warm and smells like a pretty perfume.

"Don't apologize. I know this has been hard on you. I'm just happy you're feeling a bit better."

"I do. I felt *numb* these past few days. But since getting up, bathing, and dressing, and eating something, and talking to my friend, I do feel a bit better. All the thoughts just... paused for a few hours, I guess."

"Good," she takes my face in her hands. "I know you can do this."

Using her thumb, she brushes the stray tear that escapes me. It wasn't a sad tear, though. I don't know what kind of tear it was.

"Would you like to hear about some of the plans for the Summer Ball?"

"Sure," I say, smiling.

I'd never been to a ball before, clearly, so I'm not exactly sure what to expect. I know it's in like three and a half weeks, but Celeste has been busy at it planning.

"The theme this year is decided to be pastels and floral," she says, grinning. "The gardeners have been working super hard in floral arrangements."

"That's exciting," I say, intrigued. "Do many people come to the ball?"

"Oh my Gods, yes. From all over the kingdom. It's open to the public, and most high Fae will be there. We have a ball with each turn of the season. Summer is probably my favorite; it was your mother's birthday too, so I like to take charge as a way to sort of remember her, I guess."

"Oh wow, that's really nice."

"I don't necessarily love all the people and crowds, but I do enjoy the ambiance."

I was a bit nervous about the ball, too, honestly. This would be the first with my attendance, and given the recent… events, I'm not sure how it'll pan out.

"Sometime in the following weeks, I'll take you to town so you can get fitted for a dress and choose the colors and everything."

"Really?" I hadn't been to town yet and haven't really had a chance to pick out my own dresses. They were just already here when I got here.

"Yes, dear, that's the best part!"

~

We talked a bit more about the ball, and then my dinner tray came. Emmet brought it to me.

"Hi, Ryenn," he said after I allowed him in.

Butterflies swarmed in my belly.

"Hello, Emmet," I squeaked out.

Celeste was sitting in her usual chaise. The King looked nervously at her.

"How are you doing?" he asks.

"Better than I have been…"

"Good," a few moments of awkward silence later, "Ryenn, I wanted to speak to you sooner, but I've been incredibly busy. Celeste assures me you're in good hands, though." he winks at his wife. "Listen, I just want to commemorate how brave you are. That trial was incredibly difficult. You sat there and took it all in stride. You're going to make a great queen one day. Your mom would've been incredibly proud, hell I know I am."

His kind words flooded me with emotion. I wasn't close to

Emmet like Celeste. He had a good presence to him, though, and I did like him, he was just always busy.

"Thank you," I say grinning.

"Okay dear, well I hope you enjoy your dinner. I have to get going, I'll be taking off for Vermuse to do some upkeep for the next few days."

"Emmet, before you go, can I ask something?"

"Sure," he says, smiling.

"Can you teach me how to fight?"

"You want to learn to *fight*?" he asks, his smile turns into a shock.

"Yes."

"Ryenn, I don't know if that's a good idea…"

"Why not? I haven't seen any females in the Scouts. Plus, I *never* want to be weak again. I couldn't have fought back even if I tried. I don't ever want to be in that sort of position again, Emmet. I need to learn how to defend myself."

I try calming my emotions, making their way to the surface.

"Okay, I can see where you're coming from. It's just that females aren't usually interested in fighting."

"I feel as though that's pretty sexist." I cross my arms.

He laughs. "Gods, you sound just like her." Shaking his

head, he looks at me. "Look, I'll make you a deal, okay?"

I nod, not really knowing where this is going.

"I will have someone train you in self-defense and maybe combat. But before that happens, you need to put on some weight and focus on getting *healthy*. You can't train in your current condition, it's far too dangerous, and you'd just cause injuries which would do more harm than good. I'll give you a month to prove to me that this is something you want, and then we can speak more about it."

His conditions were fair, but still made me a bit irritated. I just wanted to start now, screw food and everything. But I also knew I wouldn't make it very far without probably fainting. Hell, I get winded walking from my bed to the washroom.

"Okay, fine. One month. You won't be sorry."

I reach out my hand, and he shakes it, grinning.

"You better get to your dinner then," he says, glancing at my tray he laid down on the table by Celeste.

I walk over, scoop a spoonful of potatoes into my mouth, and give him a sarcastic grin. He laughs and leaves the chambers. Celeste shakes her head with a grin across her face.

I can do this.

I am going to get strong, learn to fight, and *never* be in the position I was before.

Chapter 21

After eating my dinner, I felt like I was going to burst. I hadn't eaten that much in… well, I can't remember exactly. I haven't really been eating much since arriving here nearly two months ago, and then this whole thing has made it even worse.

"Ryenn," Celeste said, coming out of the washroom, "when do you think you should go back to school?"

Panic rose a little, threatening the dinner in my stomach.

"Not saying you have to go back tomorrow or anything," she quickly adds, "but it won't hurt to get back on track, plus, Amalie is going to be there, so it's not like you're alone."

"I don't know." Heat rises up to my face, just thinking about leaving the room.

Celeste comes over, a breeze following.

"He's gone, honey. He's not going to be there. You're safe."

I take a deep breath. "I know."

"Scouts are more present in the capital now as well."

"I think I need another day just to… recuperate."

"Okay. That's reasonable. You need to try and sleep a bit tonight, too. I'm here, so nothing bad will happen."

"What about the …. fire thing."

"It hasn't happened again since, so don't even worry about it."

"Okay," I breathe.

I get ready for bed, and Evie brings the cot in for Celeste, which I still feel bad about, but I just don't trust myself to be entirely alone yet. Plus, she assures me she doesn't care, but it doesn't help my guilt. I take some of the pine-needle-tasting medicine that Sara left for me in hopes it will help me sleep soundly.

I decided to pick up a book that Amalie bought for me and read it. It's a romance about a female and male who grew up together since infancy and eventually fell in love. I'm a fast reader, so I'm nearly halfway through the book in two hours. Some scenes are…. Indecent, to say the least, and I end up blushing at the section I'm reading now. It involves them swimming in a private lake and lots of kissing, among *other* things. I hear Celeste laughing from across the room and look up, red still spread across my face and shut the book quickly.

"Good book?" She smirks.

"Mhmm," I say.

"I've read just about every book in this castle. Let me guess; chapter 14, the lake scene."

My face gets even hotter, which makes her laugh harder.

"Don't be embarrassed, Ryenn." She's still laughing, but I don't find this interaction remotely amusing. "It's natural. Sexuality is nothing to be ashamed over. One day, you'll find someone like the prince you read about."

I wonder if I will. Every Fae in the kingdom has seen what occurred a few days ago. I'm not sure anyone will want me. Plus, I'm not that desirable, considering I still look like a child. My mind drifts to Braxton and our encounter, which makes butterflies swarm low in my belly. I remember him being at the trial, towards the back of the crowd. Gods, I don't even know if he'll look at me ever again.

I go back to reading, a little sorrowful, but I don't even finish the chapter when I fall asleep.

I don't even dream all night. I wake early, though, before Celeste does. I sneak out of bed and begin to fill the tub without waking her. I need a cold bath, hoping it'll make me feel something. Moments like these, when everything is quiet, and I'm left to my own thoughts, my mind tends to wander in many directions. I don't like it. It usually ends up with panic attacks.

I drop my robe and look in the mirror as the tub fills. Emmet and Celeste were right to worry. I still looked sickly thin, my hip bones pointy and ribs visible. I do notice that my breasts seem to be filling a bit more than I previously remembered, and maybe I have more curves to my stature. *Interesting.* I'm still not overly impressed by what I see in the mirror.

The bath is full, and I dip my toes into the frigid water.

Perfect.

Easing my way in, I slip all the way under and hold my breath, bringing my head under the iciness. Something about the cool is calming, like it shocks the system, and the only thing you can think about is how cold it is; nothing else. I pull my head up out of the water, taking a big breath. I can hold it for nearly a whole minute now. Celeste bursts in the bathroom, startling me.

"Good Gods, Ryenn, you scared me half to death," she pants. "You weren't in the bed, and then the bathroom door was shut, and I didn't hear anything. I called out your name, and there was no answer. Fuck I thought-" she breathes deeply and grasps her hand to her chest. She was *crying*.

"I'm sorry. I didn't hear you. I was just taking a bath, and I must have been under the water when you said my name. I didn't want to wake you."

She's still crying, and I begin to panic. I grab the robe on the floor and slip it around me.

"I'm sorry, Celeste. I'm okay. I'm sorry." I wrap my arms around her, and she wraps hers around me.

"It's okay. It's okay. I just got worried. Gods, I just thought something bad happened, and it was my fault again for not being there."

I pull back and look at her tear-stained face.

"What do you mean your fault? What happened to me wasn't your fault."

"I know I just… I don't know. I just blame myself for your mother leaving, which caused me to lose you *and* her for the first time. Then I was the one who sent you to the cellar to get wine, and then I thought you had done something while I was asleep just now."

"I'm sorry, Celeste." Tears burn my throat. "I don't blame you. None of that was your fault. I should've told you I was getting a bath, but I thought you needed the rest."

"Okay, honey. It's okay. I'm alright, I'm just glad you are," she takes a deep breath and holds me for a little longer.

I had no idea she blamed herself for all of that. Gods, if it hadn't been for her, I wouldn't have gotten through any of this. She never meant for any of it to happen, yet she was the sole person who had been able to pick up some of the pieces.

"You're freezing," she states all of a sudden and reaches her hand into the bath water. "Ryenn! Oh my Gods, this is ice cold!"

"I know it's just something I like to do to wake me up. It

feels good and calms me. I do it all the time."

She looks me up and down with scrunched eyebrows.

"Alright then… let's get you warm now. I'll get you something to change into." She skeptically leaves the washroom and quickly returns with a deep yellow dress.

~

Celeste and I sit by the window and eat our breakfast together. I'm not hungry, but I force it down, knowing my deal with Emmet.

Celeste isn't saying much of anything, which makes me feel bad.

"Celeste?" I ask, placing a piece of a peach into my mouth

"Mhmm?" she looks up from her mug of coffee.

"Thank you," I say.

"For what, dear?"

"Just for everything. You and Emmet didn't have to keep me here. You easily could have just passed me off for a mortal and sent me back to Molisan, but you didn't. You kept your promise to my mother and took me in as your own. You taught me so much and still are about how to act as a princess and everything. I also wouldn't have made it past this last week if you hadn't been here."

I cleared my throat. "When I first got here, I won't lie, you intimidated me a bit. You're gorgeous and just are so in control of everything. I just didn't think I'd ever amount to you or that you'd really care about me, but you *do*. I know you said you blame yourself for my mother, but I know deep down it wasn't your fault. You kept your promise to her and are definitely making up for lost time. I just wanted to thank you for that. You're someone I look up to, and I don't care if other people think you're too uptight. I think you are perfect, and I wouldn't want anyone else to be my 'second mom.'"

Tears silently stream down her cheeks as she brings her hand to her mouth.

"Oh honey," she sobs lightly, "thank you."

"You're welcome." I grin and grab her hand. "I love you."

"I love you too, Ryenn."

Chapter 22

I spent the rest of the morning finishing the book I was reading last night. And then I started reading the second one she bought for me. I will admit I was getting kind of bored in this room.

I sighed, looking out the window at the late-spring sun shining through.

Celeste noticed my stare.

"Would you like to go for a walk? I could use a break from paperwork." She had been sitting at my desk all morning working on something for the ball.

The thought of leaving the safety of my room after spending the last 4 days here made me a bit nervous. But the sun looked so nice, and I had wanted to go see the gardens, plus I needed to push myself.

"Yes, I think I do. Can we go see the gardens? I haven't been yet."

"You haven't been to the gardens yet?! Well, that's exactly where we're going."

I laid my book on the stand next to my bed and walked out of the chamber with Celeste.

~

Three Scouts guarded us from 10 feet behind. They were quiet, and I hardly realized they were there. The sun was warm on my skin, and the wind was lightly blowing my hair. We walked together through the arched hedges that I always passed on my way to school.

Flowers, trees, and other greenery surrounded us. It was nothing like I've ever seen before.

"This is *insane!*" I exclaimed.

"Isn't it? I love it here. I try to come every day just to stroll through."

"I had a small garden in Baytown. It was mostly for growing vegetables, but I had some flowers planted there as well. It's *nothing* compared to this, though."

"Oh, I don't have a green thumb at all. But I appreciate the garden that much more because of my inability to keep a plant alive," Celeste laughs. "Come, I want to show you something."

Celeste leads me down a narrow path past a large fountain to a huge cherry weeping willow tree. The petals were a bright pink, looking like they had just sprouted for the season.

"Oh, it's beautiful!" I say, touching the flowers.

"Me and your mom used to come and sit under this tree to talk. We've had quite a few conversations here, from boy troubles when we were young to kingdom troubles when we got older. Sometimes we laughed, and sometimes we cried. It was our favorite spot, though not many people know about it because it's hidden behind the fountain." She lifts up a branch and ducks under. I follow close behind.

The willow is even prettier from underneath. The sun peeks through its branches, casting a pink hue over the trunk and soft mossy ground beneath it. We sit down together, and I look at the plaque that has been placed on the trunk:

"In memory of Elanore Embers. May you always seek comfort under the willow."

Celeste brushes the plaque with her fingers.

"It's been hard for me to come back here, but I still do occasionally for a good cry," she laughs but has an undertone of sadness.

I put my hand on hers.

"This is beautiful."

"I know. Feel free to use the willow to your advantage. It's a pretty good listener."

"Thank you," I whisper.

"Don't mention it. Come on, let's finish our walk."

We end up walking all the way around the garden, which is much larger than I anticipated. It links the castle grounds to the main town. The main entrance to the castle also leads to the town, so this is a sort of secret way, which I keep in the back of my mind for safekeeping. We decide to walk just on the outskirts of town so we can get back to the front part of the castle. There are lots of Fae walking around doing their daily routines. Some notice the Queen and bow or curtsy, but others are simply too busy with what they're doing to notice the queen, Princess, and three Scout escorts walking around. Celeste explains she doesn't mind. In fact, she likes it when people treat her normally. She hates being the center of attention, which I find kind of redundant, considering she's always on some sort of display. I suppose I kind of was now, too, which made me feel a little uneasy as I straightened my posture.

The front portion of the stone castle is entered via a large matching stone bridge. Lots of Scouts guard its perimeter. I actually haven't even seen the front face of the castle before, considering I haven't really left the grounds. It looks humongous from the outside, and a river runs underneath the bridge. The windows look daunting, but I realize you can't see through them from the outside. The west side of the castle, separated by an outdoor bridge as well, is like a smaller version of the main thing. The familial quarters are more displaced to the back of the castle, so you're unable to see my room or anything from this side.

"Good day, Your Majesty," a Scout, one wearing red lapels, which I have learned are for sergeants or other higher-ups, says to Celeste.

Then Celeste actually *blushes.*

"Hello, Ser Arry. Lovely weather we're having, isn't it?" she says, a little flustered, which causes me to grin.

Why was she acting like this?

"Indeed. Hello Princess. We haven't been formally introduced. My name is Ser Arington, but many call me Arry. I am the battalion sergeant of the first division of Scouts."

"Arry, er *Ser* Arry, is basically the second hand to the Captain that you've already met. He sees the field much more than Hunter, though, as the Captain is a more paperwork-type job and to train younger recruits."

I shake Ser Arry's hand, and he places a light kiss atop it.

"Nice to meet you. Ser Davis also wears the red lapels, is he a sergeant as well?"

"Yes, Ser Davis is a sergeant in the second division. Different divisions mean different things. The gold stripes on the lapels differentiate between which division they belong to," Celeste explains. "The first division is on guard outside the castle and also scout the wall perimeter. The second division often serves inside the castle. The third division is separated into different groups around the rest of the kingdom. Actually, you met Braxton, his father is one of the five sergeants in the third division."

Realization hits me.

"Wait-"

"Yes, it was Ser Arry's group that found you outside the wall."

That's why he said not formally introduced.

Oh Gods, that means…

"I am glad to see you're doing much better than that night we found you, child."

"Thank you." Knowing this man and his other Scouts found me naked under a pine tree unconscious doesn't sit well in my stomach.

"Just doing my job, dear. Have a good day, ladies."

Ser Arry winks to Celeste, and I get the feeling that is inappropriate for a Scout to do to the queen. Nonetheless, Celeste has a silly grin as we walk inside.

~

"What was all that about?" I ask Celeste when we get back to my chamber, lunch already waiting for us on the small table. She still had a silly grin on her face.

"What?"

"Oh my Gods, you're *blushing.*"

Touching her cheek, she whips her head away from me

"Now I can see why you get irritated when someone points to your blushing habits."

"Do you *like* Ser Arry? He seemed to be a bit smitten with you. I mean, he *winked* at Celeste! I do believe that is quite inappropriate for a sergeant to do to the Queen."

"Ryenn, keep your voice down," she hushes, and I crack up. "Oh, I am glad you're getting a kick out of this."

"What? He is quite handsome."

"Ryenn!" she squeals like a teenage girl, and I laugh again.

"Listen, I told you before that my relationship with Emmet is… different. Let's just say there had been some history between myself and Ser Arry *previously*. That, however, is not something that can leave this room because I could get into a lot of trouble if I were seen to be unfaithful to my husband, who is the King, may I remind you?"

"Don't worry, Celeste. My lips are sealed. What kind of history are we talking about?

"Oh my Gods. I am not going there. Eat your lunch. You have a deal with Emmet, remember?"

I am still laughing as I bite my sandwich.

I feel good, and my body feels light, like I am actually living and not simply existing. Things are starting to feel a bit better, and I hope everything goes up from here on forward.

Chapter 23

After lunch yesterday Sara had come by to do an assessment and to bring more of the medication that had been helping me sleep better. She seemed pleased enough by her findings and cleared me to go to school today. I was pretty nervous about the whole ordeal and didn't sleep as well as the night prior but at least there were no nightmares. I still had Celeste stay, I know I'm being childish at this point but I don't want to chance anything. She did leave in the morning to go get ready in her own chambers and told me we could meet for breakfast in the familial dining room. After I bathed Evie came and did my hair for me in my go-to low knotted style. Ser Davis escorted me to the dining room.

I ate all my breakfast despite the constant gnaw of nerves in my belly. Amalie and Pippa weren't long before showing up to retrieve me.

Pippa bounded in the room like a little puppy and leaped into my lap to give me a tight hug.

"Ryenn, I missed you so much! I am so happy you are feeling better. Amy said you were sick, I was sick one time, too; it was the worstest ever."

"I missed you too munchkin. Have you gotten taller? My Gods you're growing like a weed."

I sized up the girl and she giggled as I poked her ribs.

"I have growed because I always eat my veggies."

"Ah good, maybe I need some of these veggies too."

"Come now Pip, let Ry up so we can get to class. We don't want to be late," Amalie came over tickling her sister and she skipped over to the door.

I swallowed and looked to Celeste.

"You can do it. I know you can." A breeze followed her voice and the smell of her usual perfume came with it. It was comforting and I pushed the nerves back down.

"See you later?" I said.

"Yes dear."

Amalie linked her arm through mine and we headed off on our usual path.

~

Seeing the school house again was a little nerve racking but Amalie kept close and we chatted which kept the bad thoughts and nerves down.

Turn it off.

All eyes were on me when we neared the building.

Autumn, Hanna and Luna were sitting on one of the benches outside. Neither said a word to me, Hanna did roll her eyes though but it didn't bother me at all. Grey was standing against the wall and his expression was unreadable as I neared the door. He watched the entire time. I gave him a quick grin, I guess as a way to thank him for the whole defense-act that Amalie told me about, and he gave a curt nod.

We make our way inside and sit at our table.

"That was weird wasn't it?" I asked Amalie.

"It was but it's been that way since everything went down. Autumn and Grey have been on the outs it seems, so don't mind their moodiness. Plus, Hanna is just always a bitch and Luna is always clueless so, again, not much difference with them."

I laugh at her response and then realize Mrs. Langerfeld is walking towards us.

"Hello Ryenn, I am happy your back," she says in a soft tone.

No one has entered the classroom yet so I don't mind the confrontation as much.

"I am happy to be back too, Mrs. Langerfeld."

"Good! Honey if you need a break at any point just feel free to do so okay? I'm on your team. You'll get through this. I have sent the work you missed to Nadine so she will help you catch up on that but if you have any questions just feel free to ask," she smiles.

Mrs. Langerfeld is a bit of an odd-bird but she's a very nice woman. Plus, she stood for me at the trial, so I owe my gratitude to her.

"Thank you, Mrs. Langerfeld… Not just for that but for your statement at the trial as well," I give her a half smile and she cups her hand gently on my shoulder.

"Don't mention dear, just telling the truth." She walks back to the front of the room and the rest of the class begins to pile in.

~

Class goes by relatively normally. The vibes are definitely different now that *he* isn't there but not necessarily in a bad way. After class Amalie walks me to tutoring, since Sara will be seeing me in the evenings now instead. Scouts are definitely more present; it seems there is always one within a few yards of myself. Amalie has dance class, which she tells me she loathes significantly, so she drops me off at the library door. I find Nadine at our normal table and we begin to go through the stuff I missed. It isn't hard and I make a pretty big dent in the work within the hour. Nadine simply focuses on the task at hand which is nice because I don't have another person asking how I am and everything, even though they probably wouldn't want to hear the truth anyways. Exhaustion is beginning to creep in as Ser Davis escorts me to Celeste in the

Throne Room.

A third throne has been placed next to theirs. *My* throne.

It's similar in shape to that of Celeste's, only a tad bit shorter due to the height difference between the both of us. All three have the same lush emerald green cushions and the polished silver metal that twists into the chair shape reminds me of that of tree branches.

Celeste is standing at the bottom of the stairs that lead up to the throne platform, grinning.

"Well… what do you think?"

"It's beautiful" I say, still a little shocked. This made the whole princess thing feel a little more real.

"Let's go up and have a look."

We walk up the 22 stairs and I sit, properly as Celeste reminds me, in my custom throne. It is very comfortable and was measured perfectly to my size.

"You look stunning."

"Now all I need is a crown I guess," I joke.

"Yes, you'll get one." I give her a confused look. "The Heir to the throne gets a tiara when they Transition; it marks the beginning of their era technically and is to be celebrated. You'll get the real crown, the one passed down through generations, when you ascend to the throne during your coronation on your 21st birthday."

"Oh shit that's crazy."

"Foul language for a princess," she grins.

"Oops," I yawn and cover my mouth realizing that gesture is probably also rude.

"You're tired," Celeste looks at me with concern.

"Yes. The day was good don't get me wrong, I'm just not used to leaving my bed for more than an hour at a time I guess," I laugh.

"Yes I can imagine you're exhausted. Let's go to your chambers, you can rest until dinner. After dinner Braxton has requested to start your riding lessons."

"What?!" I choke on surprise as we walk down the stairs again.

"Yes, he said your horse, Blaze is it? Is getting lonely. Plus, this is a skill everyone needs to learn." She looks at me, "Oh now look who's blushing."

"Nope I am not. Just find it warm, don't you? Gods this room can be suffocating," I fan my hands at my face.

"Uh-huh sure," she shakes her head.

~

When we got to my chambers I flopped on my bed, my legs were exhausted. Apparently, I was so exhausted that I fell asleep in the position I landed in; my legs hanging off the edge of the bed and my arms out in front of me.

Celeste wakes me by gently rubbing my shoulder.

"Ryenn, wake up now, dear."

"Huh?" I roll nearly off the bed before I catch myself. There's literally drool on my face and I wipe it quickly, blushing.

"You really were tired, weren't you? Dinner is here now, and you have to go to the stables after so eat up."

I go to the washroom first and change into the riding breeches and tunic she had laid out for me, fixing my hair into a low braid and wiping the remainder of the spit residue from my chin.

I eat, although I can't finish my plate because I'm just too full. I feel a bit defeated by that as I sit back and stare at the remainder.

"Honey, if you're full, don't force yourself. You don't want to make yourself sick. Your body is still adjusting to the food and everything." Celeste notes without really looking up from her plate.

I'm still not sure she can't read minds…

"Can you read minds?" I decide to ask her.

"What?" She laughs covering her mouth and swallowing her food. "No, Fae can't read minds, but we do have a heightened sense of awareness. We also have a good sense of smell so sometimes others give off certain smells when they feel a certain way I guess. I could just tell you were feeling full because you sat back in your chair and looked like you might yack everywhere."

"Oh…" Well now I'm embarrassed.

"Ah but now I can sense the embarrassment," she laughs which makes it worse.

A knock sounds on the door and I jump to go answer it, Ser Davis is on the other side.

"Ready to go to the stables Princess?"

I look over my shoulder to Celeste who is still reading a book and eating.

"Go on dear I'll be here when you get back. Ser Davis will be standing guard outside the stables so nothing is going to happen."

"Okay," I turn my attention back to the Scout. "Let's go."

~

Once we reach the stables I feel a bit sick to my stomach. I don't know how Braxton is going to act and I'm nervous. I am excited to see Blaze though, I've been thinking about him since I saw him a week or so ago.

Braxton meets us at the entrance of the stables.

"Good evening Princess" he smiles "I'd bow out of courtesy however you told me last time I shouldn't."

"Yeah, that's not necessary," I smile back. Okay not that awkward so far.

"I'll be staying out here until your done Princess," Ser Davis states and I follow Braxton inside.

He already had Blaze on the cross ties. The freckled horse's ears perk when he sees me and he gives me a low whinny.

"He's excited to see you," Braxton says, petting Blaze's neck. I touch his soft velvety nose.

"I'm excited to see him too. And I'm excited to learn to ride." I glance at the Fae. He is *quite* handsome. My mind drifts to the book I read last night and I'm instantly embarrassed. I look away so he doesn't see the red across the bride of my nose.

"You're wearing much more suitable riding clothes this time too. I'll go grab your saddle and everything if you want to start brushing him."

I nod and he leaves the room.

I pick up one of the soft brushes from the box to my left and smooth it over Blaze's coat. He isn't dirty so I assume Braxton already brushed him for me but the act was calming.

"You're a very handsome boy Blaze. And a good boy. You're not going to hurt me right?" His ears move like he's actually listening to me. I used to talk to the animals on my farm all the time. They were the best listeners anyways. Well they were really the only ones who'd listen, I mean I had to choose between a toddler or a drunk if not for them. I remember crying to our old horse a few times after putting Rose down for a nap. He just stood there, letting me pet him and cry into his neck from exhaustion and pent up emotion.

Braxton comes back and begins to tack up the horse, teaching me what goes where and what everything is called. When he's done we lead Blaze outside to a fenced arena.

"Okay for today we're just going to go over some basics like how to go, steer and stop. If you're ready, I can give you a boost up."

Butterflies flap around inside me.

I clear my throat. "Sure."

"Okay, put your hands up there, yes, just like that, then I'm just going to grab your leg like this, and you'll swing your other one over when I lift, okay?"

"Okay."

"Ready? One, two, three! Good! There you go you're a pro already."

Now that I'm up I feel a bit better. The whole interaction wasn't so bad.

We spend the next 30 minutes or so going over how to steer left from right using my hands and legs, how to stop and how to change speeds. By the end of the lesson I'm completely tuckered out.

"You did really, really well! Are you sure you haven't ridden before?"

"Nope I haven't."

"Well, you're a natural," he winks.

"Thanks." I can't help the grin that spreads across my face.

"Let me help you down."

He reaches up and puts his hands on my waist, and I tense up a bit. He removes his hands immediately.

"You okay?"

Some flashbacks hit me.

Fuck now is not the time.

I feel a bit dizzy up here.

"Oh, uh yeah, sorry. Why don't I swing my leg around and you can help me from there?"

"Sure, no worries."

He does as I said.

Gods I feel a bit like an idiot now.

"I'm sorry," he says.

"Oh don't be sorry, it's not your fault. I'm still… adjusting is all," I scramble.

"Ryenn, just so you know, I think you're incredibly brave, and I'm very happy to be working with you."

"Really?" I say blushing.

"Yeah, you're a complete badass. What happened to you is completely fucked up, but you're still here, and I think that takes a ton of strength."

"Thanks," I say smiling. That was sweet of him.

He brushes a strand of hair that fell into my face gently behind my ear.

There's a moment between us where we just look at each other. *Really,* look at each other, and I feel like he understands me somehow. Our moment is interrupted by Ser Davis. *Again.*

Braxton clears his throat. "So, I'll see you in a few days then?"

"Yes, sounds good."

"Good. Can't wait until then," he smiles. "This guy needs the exercise," he pats Blaze on the back.

I laugh. "See ya. And goodnight, Blaze, be a good boy."

Walking back to my chambers I feel giddy. Gods he's so perfect. He's respectful, strong and likes animals. So basically perfect. But why did I feel so weird when he touched my hips? I try to shake off the tight feeling grabbing my muscles. Turn it off Ryenn, you're *fine*. He wasn't trying to hurt you; he was just being nice. Then why do I still feel a little… off?

Chapter 24

I start to get back into the groove of things over the next couple weeks. Celeste stopped staying overnight. Well she stayed in my room until I fell asleep and then she'd go just down the hall to her room but at least she wasn't sleeping on the cot anymore. The medicine that Sara gave me for pain and sleep seemed to work really well and most nights I had a long dreamless sleep. Occasionally I'd wake and feel a bit suffocated but that would pass after doing my breathing exercises. Then I'd repeat the same thing as before, breakfast, school, tutoring, Celeste lessons and sometimes riding lessons with Braxton.

Riding had quickly become a favorite of mine. Not only because I enjoyed talking to Braxton but also because I loved Blaze. Riding kept me grounded and gave me something to focus on. We had been going to trail rides together for the past three lessons I had, Braxton on his own horse Zaraphina. Amalie was always excited to hear about my interactions with Braxton as well. She was convinced he *liked* me but I wasn't so sure because I just can't see how anyone would right now. I was also finally starting to gain a bit more weight thanks to actually eating food and I was feeling much more energized and happy because of it.

I still had moments though. Sometimes it's like the littlest thing would trigger a memory or something and I'd have a bit of a meltdown. I was able to regain control of those emotions pretty quickly especially if I was in class or something but there had been one incident, last night, where I was eating dinner with Celeste and a servant had dropped a wine bottle on the floor. The sound of it and the smell too I guess just brought me right back there. Celeste had to bring me back to my chambers to calm down since I was hyperventilating and near choking on my steak. It had taken nearly 20 minutes for her to get me to relax and even then I threw up twice. That was the only bad time though. I had made her stay with me all night. A bit of a setback, I know, but it scared me a bit. She did leave early this morning so she technically didn't stay the *entire* night.

I was just now getting up to get ready when Evie came in and told me Celeste had summoned me to her chambers.

Weird.

I put on a dress quickly and headed down the hall with a few Scouts. She opens the door and lets me in.

Her chamber is like six times the size of mine. It's literally *insane.* I've never been in here before and it feels like something straight out of a fantasy. She was pinning pins in her hair when I walked in.

"Your room is *beautiful,*" I say, my eyes still wide.

"Oh, thanks," she says, smiling. "I got to design it myself

since Emmet's is the next room over."

I didn't realize that they didn't even stay in the same room as each other. Emmet was still in Vermuse, where he had been for the last two weeks. He was due to leave to come back tomorrow and I was excited to show him my progress. I only have two weeks left until our bargain so I'm hoping it'll be good enough.

"Ryenn, I was wondering if you would like to go pick out a dress style for the ball today? There's only a week and a half left to get something so I figured we could do it today. It would give you a break as well," Celeste asks, still fooling with her hair.

"Yes I would love to! What about school, though?" I ask.

"I'll just have Evie tell Mrs. Langerfeld you're taking a day off. She says you're already caught up on the work anyways, so it's not going to be an issue."

"Alright," I smile. This is exciting. Not only haven't I been to town yet but I'm pretty excited to pick out my own dress and everything.

"Good well go get ready. It's warm out so wear a light dress and leave your cloak, you won't need it. I'll meet you at your door in fifteen minutes."

"Okay!" I rush off down the hall.

I decided to go with my favorite light blue dress. It has

quarter-length sleeves, and a sweetheart neckline. It's also easy to get on and off, which I feel would be good for a fitting. I had a slip-on underneath, too, just in case. As I'm getting ready and doing my hair into a low knot, my head starts hurting a bit. Almost like my *teeth* are hurting, which is weird. I shake it off though, a little bit of pain is probably nothing, plus I really wanted to go into town. I take one of the pain medications Sara left just to see if that will help. Celeste shows up mere seconds later. I don't tell her about it though because I don't want her to cancel or to worry.

~

We take a carriage into town. The whole time, I'm looking out the window at the buildings and Fae we pass. It was such a beautiful day, and Celeste was right; it is very warm. We stopped outside a store called "Bellarose Boutique". Celeste tells me this is where she always comes for party dresses. My head is still pounding a bit and there is a sharp pain in my teeth now, but I shake it off. I've felt worse before. I probably just need to drink more water.

We enter the boutique and there are hundreds of colors of fabrics and different prints. Oh Gods, I may not be able to choose!

"Good morning your highness," a small woman with gray curly hair curtseys to the queen and me.

"Good morning, Mary Louise," Celeste smiles. "I've brought Ryenn to get fitted for her ball dress and pick out a potential design. I already sent you what I wanted, but she'd like to pick out her own today."

"Oh absolutely princess! Come now, we'll get you sized."

Mary Louise makes me strip off into my slip and measures me on a small stand surrounded by mirrors. I find it hard to look at myself while she does this, so I keep my focus on Celeste standing in front of me. After the measuring is done and I put my dress back on, we sit at a desk and go through different styles and different colors. I really wished my head wasn't hurting because it would make this experience far more enjoyable. My stomach was beginning to pain a bit as well but I pushed that off as probably just being a bit hungry where I didn't keep down any of my dinner last night.

Mary Louise sketches the dress as I tell her what I like. The dress is floor length, obviously, with quarter sleeves that bell off. I chose to have the dress tie in the back so it has a corset style to it. There is also a bow that will rest right above my hip. The front will have flower beading to the neckline and will also be two tones in lavender.

Gods, I *really* don't feel the best right now.

"Mary Louise, do you have a washroom I could use?" I ask as Celeste goes over some fabric patterns with her.

"Yes, dear, right down the hall to your left."

"Ser Davis, stand guard to her, please," Celeste states without looking up.

I head down the hall and into the small washroom and look in the mirror. Why is my head hurting so badly? I open my mouth and notice my gums are actually bleeding.

What the fuck?

Maybe I've been clenching my teeth from the pain?

I figure I should pee while I'm here since I don't know how much longer Celeste will be discussing the millions of patterns.

When I go to sit down I notice a stain on the back of my light blue dress. A red stain. I lift my skirt and sit on the toilet and there is *blood* everywhere. All over my undergarments, on my legs, on my slip and on my dress. I'm in a complete mess. A sharp pain stabs through my lower abdomen, and I gasp. Something must be wrong. Something must have happened and Sara's work or something didn't hold up. I could be *dying*. Ser Davis must hear my gasp and knocks lightly.

"Everything alright, Princess?"

"Um, yeah. Can you actually get Celeste for me, Ser Davis? Tell her I need her right away."

"Are you hurt?" He reaches for the doorknob.

"No! No, don't come in. I'm just not feeling well. Just get Celeste, please."

"Okay, I'll be right back."

Pain spears through my abdomen and back. Then through my head and mouth. I bring my hand to my mouth and wipe some of the dripping blood.

Tears spring into my eyes.

Gods, this was the end, wasn't it?

I was going to die in a dress shop from bleeding out. I hear the clack of heels rush down the hall and Celeste jiggles the handle.

"Ryenn are you okay? Ser Davis said you're not feeling well. Can I come in?"

I reach the lock from where I'm sitting, and Celeste comes in.

"Celeste, I'm dying. I'm bleeding out… we need to go back. I think something is really wrong. Gahhh, I'm in so much pain." I clench up, trying to breathe through the pain that is twisting my intestines.

Celeste laughs. *Laughs.*

"I'm glad my death is funny to you?" I glare.

"Oh honey, no, you're not dying. I'm sorry, I shouldn't

laugh. You're starting your *Transition*. This is what I was telling you about, the whole bleeding thing is your cycle. Now your mouth is bleeding and throbbing head is from the fangs and ears starting to change." She starts running the tap and getting wet paper towels for me to clean up.

"I don't think you understand. This is far too much blood," I say. I was not expecting it to be like *this*.

"No, my love, that's normal. Gods, you really are in a mess, though, aren't you?" She holds my chin and cleans my mouth with a cold towel.

I should be more embarrassed than I am but I'm in far too much pain to care about what she's seeing right now.

"I'm going to go tell Mary Louise that we need to head back now, okay? Just tidy yourself up as much as possible and I'll get you something to wrap around yourself so no one can see the stains. I'll explain more in the carriage, okay? You're fine this is all natural, albeit it still sucks, but I promise you are not *dying*."

"Don't tell her we're leaving because I started my cycle, please. Spare me the humiliation," I groan as another wave of pain comes over me.

"Okay," she laughs. "I'll just tell her you have a headache." She leaves me to clean up the bloody mess.

Chapter 25

Celeste returns to the small boutique bathroom minutes later. She has a cloak in tow for me to put on. I am not exactly sure where she got it, considering we both didn't bring one with us, but I am very grateful for it. I cleaned myself up as much as I could, but it didn't seem to cease even slightly.

"Alright, put this on." she wraps the cloak around my shoulders. "The carriage is ready for us, so we'll go straight there. Mary Louise has everything she needs for the dress anyways, so we are good to go."

"I don't know if I can walk." A wave of pain makes me nauseous.

"Here, hold onto my arm, I'll help you out."

I do as she says, and we walk quickly out of the small boutique and to the carriage just outside. It has white seats.

Fuck.

"Okay, hold on, let me lay the cloak on the seats," she takes the cloak off and lays it down. Embarrassment burns through me, and my face is definitely blood red.

We get in the carriage and head back to the castle.

"I didn't believe you when you said this was going to hurt,"

I say as another wave washes over me.

"I know," she laughs, and I look at her with glared eyes. "Oh honey, I am not laughing at you it's just this is something that happens to everyone. Unfortunately, it *is* very painful, and no healers have been able to take away the pain. You're just going to have to bear through it. When we get back, I'll get some supplies for you, and you can go to bed."

The carriage hits a bump, and the pain shoots from the tip of my toes to the top of my head.

"I might be sick," I admit.

Celeste grabs a brown paper bag that had some fabric sample in it, empties it out, and hands it to me just in time for my breakfast to make its way back out of my system.

I lay my head on her shoulder as I attempt to breathe through the agony, a sweet-smelling breeze soothes me.

"How long is this going to last?" I groan.

"Well, it depends on the Fae. The initial transition can take anywhere from 24 hours to 72 hours. Your cycle though can last for up to a week. Luckily, the cycle only happens two to four times a year."

"That's two to four times too many." I throw up again, and Celeste smooths my hair.

"We are almost at the castle. Do you want to room jump to avoid having to walk through the corridors?"

"I forgot about that! How do you do that? Can everyone do it?" I remember when she got to my chambers from the wine cellar. It was a weird feeling but one I must have blocked out because I had forgotten until just now.

"No, it takes a while to master. I can only room-jump from one place in the castle to another room in the castle. Emmet can jump far, though. The real term for it is *Locus*. Not many Fae have the ability to do it, and mainly only Primitives can."

"That's crazy. But yes, please just get me to my room before I *die.*"

"Again, you are not dying," she chuckles.

We arrive at the castle gates shortly after, and Celeste grabs me so I am close, and within seconds, we are in my chambers. It is very disorienting and makes me very dizzy. Which then makes me throw up all over the floor.

"Oh honey, okay, just get into the washroom. I'll get this cleaned up. I will bring you some stuff now in a minute."

I walk, feeling near cripple from pain, to the washroom and slide the door closed behind me. The site I see in the mirror is *not* pleasant. My lips had blood caked on them, and my favorite dress was completely ruined. I smiled to see my teeth; the canines were actually starting to sharpen. That made me a bit excited for some reason. My ears hadn't pointed, but they hurt to touch. I stripped my clothes, throwing my entire outfit in the laundry basket, and decided to sit in the tub with some warm water to see if it would ease the cramping and stabbing. It worked for maybe a minute, and then I had to get out of the bloody water to throw up *again*.

Celeste knocks on the sliding door, handing me my robe to put on before coming in.

"Okay, Sara brought some medication that may help a little, but I can't make any promises. She also brought some cloths for you to put in your undergarments."

She hands me thick strips of fabric that have small slits on either end.

I stared at the supplies and then looked at Celeste, blushing. She could immediately tell I was both confused and embarrassed.

"You lay them in like this," she grabbed my undergarment that she brought in, "and tie them like this in the front and back. It just soaks up some of the blood, so you don't make a mess. They will probably need to be changed every few hours or so, but that's something you'll have to figure out."

This was absolutely mortifying. If the pain doesn't take me

out, maybe the embarrassment will. She hands me the contraption and leaves me to my own devices.

I meet her in the chambers after a few agonizing minutes. The vomit had been cleaned from the floor, and there was a tray with some soup and medicine on the table.

I flopped into my bed and curled into the fetal position, groaning.

"I bought a hot water bottle, it helps ease some of the cramping." she slides it onto my belly, and I hug it like a child gripping a teddy bear. It is nice.

"Here, drink this." She hands me medicine that tastes like dirt, and I gag. "Swallow it I know its gross." I manage to get it down.

"Celeste, this fucking *sucks*," I moan.

She cackles and starts rubbing my back.

"I know, dear. You look just like your mother. Her cycles were always really rough on her, but her transition, Gods, I thought she was going to literally die."

"I feel like I might," I suck in a breath as a stabbing sensation shoots me. She sits next to me.

"Ryenn, once the physical aspects of your transition start to cease, like when your canines finish growing, ears stop pointing, and some other physical changes like your senses and everything clue up their portion of the process, your powers will start to take hold."

I shudder.

"Powers can come on all of a sudden and be tricky to control right away, or they can hardly manifest at all, and then you'll have time to learn how to manipulate them. It all depends on the Fae, what powers manifest, and how strong those powers are…"

"What if it's fire?" Worry consumes me.

"If it's fire, then we will cross that bridge when we get there. I told you fire powers are rare, but that doesn't mean they are inherently bad. It's all how the beholder of said powers use them. Fire powers are said to manifest a lot with emotions, so you *will* be able to control them eventually. It may just be tricky at the start. Not saying you will have fire, but if you do, it will be okay."

"Okay." The pain medicine I took makes me a bit drowsy, and I yawn.

"Have a nap and try to sleep off some of the pain. I won't leave, okay?"

The exhaustion takes hold, and I drift.

~

I woke up sometime that afternoon with a stabbing in my belly. My legs feel *wet.*

I roll from my position, realizing there's a pool of blood beneath me.

That's just *great.*

Celeste looks up from the desk.

"Oh dear. It's alright, I'll call for some new sheets, go clean up yourself."

Maybe I could just jump out of that window instead.

I clean myself *again* in the washroom.

This is so gross.

When I come out, the sheets are stripped off the bed, and Evie is using some sort of cleaner to get the stain off the mattress. She looks up and grins.

"Congratulations Princess! The Transitioning is a very special time."

Yeah, it definitely feels special.

I try to grin back, but my teeth hurt. I touch them, realizing the fangs have taken shape, and prick my finger by accident.

"Ouch!" I yelp.

"Oh yeah, don't do that, they are sharp, honey be careful. It's going to take some getting used to," Celeste comes over, sizing them up. "They came in quite nicely though!"

Evie puts new sheets on, and I get back in the bed.

As soon as I get in a somewhat comfortable position with the heated water bottle on my abdomen and ice on my head, there's a knock on the door. Celeste walks over and opens the door, letting Amalie in.

"Ryenn, my Gods, you had me scared half to death when you didn't come to class today." She rounds the corner. "What's wrong? Are you okay-?" I don't even have a chance to answer when she smiles.

"Oh, you're Transitioning!" She laughs and plops on the bed next to me, I groan and throw my head back.

Celeste laughs. "Amalie dear, would you mind staying with her for a bit? Emmet will be back now shortly, so I need to go meet with him and give him an update on everything. Be careful, though she's been quite moody and now has fangs, so be careful she doesn't bite."

Both laugh, and I give them a side eye. I just don't find this remotely funny.

"Yes, I'll stay," Amalie giggles. "She won't bite me. Right, Ryenn?"

"I make no promises," I grumble, and pain grips me.

Celeste leaves my chambers, and Amalie makes herself comfortable in bed next to me.

"Well. How do you feel?" She asks with a stupid grin on her face.

"How do you *think?*" I mutter.

"Okay yeah, like shit, I gather," she fixes a pillow behind my head, and I squeeze my eyes shut, my head is throbbing. "Gods, I do not miss that feeling at all. Well, tell me how it all started, share the details," she pushes with a wild grin.

"I don't think I can. It's too mortifying," I look at her.

"Don't be dramatic. Gods, it couldn't be any worse than mine."

"Tell me about yours then," I retort.

"Uh, no way. You'll get second hand embarrassment."

"No, I won't. Come on, it'll make me feel better and distract me from the pain that is tearing my intestines apart."

"Fine. But you tell me yours first." She props herself up on one elbow, and I do the same, so we are lying and facing each other.

"*Fine.*" I exhale. "Celeste decided to bring me to get fitted for my dress for the ball and everything today, which is so gorgeous, by the way, you're going to love it. Anyway, off-topic. I had a headache this morning but decided to go anyway because I was excited. Everything was going fine, but when we were sitting at the sketch table with the lady of the boutique, I just got overcome with the pain in my head, and my stomach started hurting too, so I went to the washroom... I realized my mouth had been bleeding, which I thought it was just from clenching my teeth maybe. But then I went to pee, and *oh my Gods* Amalie, there was blood *everywhere.*" She cackles, and I gave her a push.

"It scared me! I thought something was wrong like I had somehow hurt myself again, and Sara's healing job failed or something. Anyway, Ser Davis asked if I was alright, I made him go get Celeste. She came and told me it was the Transitioning, and I was, in fact, not bleeding out and going to die. She got a cloak, wrapped it over my shoulders, and then we went out to the carriage. *Then* she proceeded to lay the cloak on the white seats, so I wouldn't stain them."

"Oh my Gods, *no.*" Amalie was laughing to the point of tears.

"*Yes*! Then I ended up puking in a paper bag, and we room-jumped when we got back to the castle. Then I puked all over my floor. Then I tried to take a bath and puked again. It's not funny. That's not even like the worst part. Celeste had to tie the cloth on my undergarment for me because I had *no fucking clue in the world.*" She was now rolling on the bed, laughing.

"And then I fell asleep, and when I woke up, I was soaked in blood and my handmaiden had to come with new sheets."

"You poor thing," she giggled still, wiping the tears from her cheeks. "I have to admit that's pretty bad."

"Gee, thanks," I groan. "Your turn, meanie."

"No, Ryenn, I think it'll make you feel even worse."

"No! We had a bargain, ma'am."

"Fine… fine, okay. Our stories are similar in a way, though. I was only thirteen when I Transitioned, so picture a much younger and more vulnerable Amalie than you see right now. Anyways, it was the winter ball, and my parents had brought a high Fae who was around my age from one of the other districts to be my date. They're always trying to find me the best suiter since I am going to be *a Lady,*" she said in a mocking tone, making me chuckle.

"This guy was *so* cute, though. He had blonde hair and blue eyes, he also already completed his transition, so he looked stunning. The theme of the ball was silver and gold, so I was wearing a pretty, very light colored-silver dress. The night was going fine, we even danced a few times. At one point, though, we were sitting at a table eating some hors d'oeuvres, and I just felt *off* all of a sudden. My head started hurting, and my stomach was hurting too. I tried playing it off for a little while, but when I wiped my mouth with the serviette and noticed my mouth was bleeding. I covered my mouth and excused myself from the table, and started walking towards the washrooms, which were packed, of course. I caught a glimpse of myself in a tall mirror in the corridor, though, and noticed a massive red stain on the back of my dress. Autumn and her two friends came up from down the hall to also head towards the washroom, and they saw the state I was in and laughed at me. They had all transitioned earlier that year, so I don't know why they were making fun of me but being hormonal, it made me burst into tears, and I ran into a *fucking broom closet*."

Now I was laughing, which was accompanied by stomach pain, so it made it hard to catch my breath.

"Anyways, I swore I was going to stay in the closet for the rest of my life and never leave. I was pretty sick at this point, like vomiting into the mop bucket kind of sick. Celeste was actually the one who found me there. She must have been walking past and heard my sobs coming from the closet, and she opened the door and came in. I cried and cried to her about what happened, and she held me for a few moments. I didn't want my mother to find out because I figured she would get mad that I ruined my dress, and she'd make me go back to my date. She did the whole room-jump thing, and we ended up in my chambers. I didn't puke on the floor, though." I gave her a shove for that, and she laughed.

"Celeste got me the supplies that I already knew how to use because my handmaiden, Yvet, taught me a few months prior, just in case. She tucked me into bed and told me to rest and that Yvet would stay with me."

"Aww, that's such a sin. It doesn't sound too bad, though."

"I'm not finished."

"Oh shit. Okay continue."

"I ended up sleeping the whole night from whatever it was a healer gave me to ease the pain, and I was awoken by Pippa screeching. We shared a room, and she was only three at the time and must have thought I was dying because when I woke up, I was in a pool of blood, there was blood all over my face because of my fangs, and my ears had already pointed. She ended up running out of the room before I could stop her and told my mother. My mother, as you know, is *not* the soft type or the motherly type for that fact. She is pretty strict and ended up coming in and getting mad that I was in a mess and that I wasn't being very ladylike. She sent me to clean myself up and then let Yvet deal with me for the rest of the day. It was mortifying, and I cried to my handmaiden the whole time. The whole process is a normal part of growing up, yet she made me feel like I was dirty and should've been ashamed. Anyways, when my cycle comes, I always just let Yvet know, and she tells my mother that I am not feeling well and can't go to class."

"That's so horrible, Amy." I brushed her hair behind her ear this time. I felt bad. Her mother was definitely not a female I found to be remotely friendly, and I can't imagine what that must have felt like for her.

"I know. It is funny, though, how Celeste came to both of our rescue."

"It is. I love Celeste. She's truly becoming like a second mother to me, well, I guess a third mother in a way. I was intimidated by her when I first got here, but I feel like she warmed up a little."

"I never got close to my aunt, that was the first time we ever had an interaction like that, honestly. My mother is *very* jealous of Celeste, so we never really spent much time with the King and Queen besides for those monthly dinners. Mother always painted her to be high-strung and wanted nothing to do with us, but I know now that isn't exactly true. Yes, she is high-strung in a sense, but she has the right to be. I can see she loves you like her own, Ry, I'm glad you have that. I love you like a sister."

I start crying ugly sobs.

"What's wrong?" Amalie's eyes soften.

"That's just so *nice* of you to say," I sob and lay my head in her lap.

"Aww, your hormones are all out of whack." She pets my head, laughing, and we stay like we are for a while.

Chapter 26

I must have fallen asleep in Amalie's lap because she shakes me gently awake.

"Ry, you're going to bleed through again if you don't get up now."

Shit, she was right.

I roll off the bed, no stain this time, and head to the washroom and do the thing.

When I come out, she's looking at the book I finished.

"How did you find the book? It's one of my favorites."

"Oh my Gods, it was so good. Spicier than I anticipated." I narrow my eyes at her, and she giggles.

"Those are the best kinds of books," she says, fanning the pages.

"Amalie... I don't think you've ever told me what your power is."

"Oh yeah, I don't talk about it much." She frowns, "I have water powers, but they are nearly nonexistent. I have tried so many things to manifest them and everything, and my parents have paid for some of the best water fae in the kingdom to try and teach me, but I can hardly do anything with it. Just another thing to add to the list of things I do that disappoints my parents."

With that, she moves her hand in a way, and a ball of water floats above her palm.

"That's so cool!" I exclaim.

"Glad you think so," she says, and it disappears, "because that's all I can do after nearly three years of practice."

"I'm sure you'll figure it all out. It doesn't really matter all that much, though, does it? Like if you can't wield anything?"

"No, I suppose it doesn't. Almost all Fae who were in high positions have strong powers, though. Both my parents are Earth Primaries and were kind of disappointed when I wasn't, even more so that power I do have is a weak manifestation."

"Well, I think you're perfect. Clearly, there is more to someone than their powers."

"Thanks, Ry…Hey, your ears! They are pointed!"

I touch both of them. They *are* pointed. I rush over to the mirror to have a look at myself. The fangs and the ears were completed and no longer throbbed. My body still hurt, and there was still a pounding in my head, but at least this part was over.

It's only really been twelve hours since the beginning of all of this this morning, though, so I knew I wasn't done.

Celeste comes back in through the door, smiling. A silly grin.

"Hi?" I say, lifting a brow skeptically at her.

Why did she look like that? A little disheveled, too.

She clears her throat and straightens up.

"Hello, girls. Oh, Ryenn! You're starting to really take look, aren't you. No biting incidents, Amalie?"

"Ha, no. She just drooled in my lap for the past hour and a half."

I give her a glare, and both laughed.

"Emmet is back?"

"Oh yes, I let him know what's up, and he said he's going to give you some distance to Transition, so you aren't embarrassed. All is well with them, though."

"Them?"

"Sorry, did I say them? I meant him. Well, the Scout troop that went with him is back too, and I was, uh, talking to them as well."

"Uh huh okay…"

She was hiding something.

A sneeze sneaks up on me, and I feel a gush.

"Oh fuck that's just *great*," I say, looking down, half expecting to see blood all over my robe again.

Celeste and Amalie don't answer, though, and I look up.

The curtain is on fire.

~

Flames are eating up the fabric. *Silver* flames. Amalie and Celeste are both gaping. I stand there, frozen in place.

"Ryenn, you need to put it out," Celeste says. "I'm trying to smother it by removing the oxygen, but it isn't working, you need to will it away."

I'm still frozen, eyes wide at the flames.

Images of my childhood cottage fill my mind as it crumbles to the ground and turns to ashes around me.

I can't breathe.

"Ryenn?" Celeste grabs my shoulder.

"Ry do something!" Amalie urges.

"Just will it away. Think about it, and it *will* happen," Celeste says in a calm tone.

I try to do as she says. I imagine the curtain is *not* on fire. I imagine being able to suffocate the flames I started.

It *works.*

There is nothing but ashes left around the window.

Yet it feels like my lungs are on fire.

I'm gasping for air, but *nothing.*

I can feel the calming breeze provided by Celeste, but it doesn't make its way down my trachea.

I'm suffocating

I grab at my throat.

Pain is flaring everywhere, and I fall to my knees.

"Amalie, grab the ice for me," Celeste ushers, and Amalie jumps off the bed to grab the ice in the bucket on my nightstand.

I still can't breathe.

My vision is going narrow.

Gods oh gods.

Cool ice hits my neck and back, which forces me to take a sharp breath in.

"That's right, in and out. You're okay." Celeste is on her knees in front of me. "You did it. You controlled it, there's nothing wrong, we can get new curtains. *No one is hurt.*"

I was hurt.

My whole body hurt.

Slowly, I am able to breathe shuddering breaths. My lips quiver, and I taste blood. Stupid fangs.

"It's okay, you're alright. Just a panic attack. Ryenn look at me." I do as she says, "Fire powers are not a bad thing. You'll learn them. It's going to be okay. There have been fire Fae before this isn't new it's just rare. You're unique but not in a bad way."

Tears streamed down my cheeks.

"That was so *badass!*" I hear Amalie say, and Celeste and I look up at her. "What? It was. Gods, Ryenn, I told you you were going to be a force to be reckoned with. You were already able to stop the flames."

Celeste laughs gently and helps me to my feet.

"I burned the curtains without even realizing. I fucking sneezed and burned my own curtains to smithereens. *Fuck,* what if I hurt someone by accident? I don't think I can do this like I was fine with all the other Fae shit, but why did I have to get the lethal power that no one can teach me to control?" My heart was beating so loud.

Too loud.

Why is it so *loud*?

"Stop it. The Transition is hard, and there are many accidents that come along with it. When mine manifested, I blew the windows out of my chambers. When your mother's manifested, she flooded the entire familial quarters of the castle. It was just an accident. You didn't mean to burn them, it just happened, and it's okay. No one is hurt. Plus, you were able to stop it yourself before it got worse, which is better than most can do when their powers first manifest. I told you that powers are not inherently good or evil; it's all in the way the beholder uses them. You'll learn. I'll help you. I'll do some reading up on it and see if Juno has any tips."

I was able to breathe a bit easier now, and I sat on my bed. Amalie sat next to me and threw her arm over my shoulder.

"You're not a bad person, Ry. The fire doesn't scare us, so it shouldn't scare you. To hell with what other people think anyways, you're the brand-new bitch who's going to be the *Queen*. You'll end up changing the kingdom as we know it. For *better*."

Okay.

Okay, I can do this.

Just another thing to add to the long list of things I need to master…

Chapter 27

Amalie left shortly after, giving me a hug and promising to return with danishes tomorrow after class. Celeste remained and was now sweeping up the ashes on the window. I sat sheepishly in my bed. My head and lower belly still hurt, but nerves also tangled up my thoughts. Amalie and Celeste had helped calm me down, and I knew I would be able to eventually master it, but… I don't know. Fire just freaked me out. It always had. And my sister and father dying in one didn't help the fact either.

"Why don't you try to sleep a bit, dear?" Celeste said, dumping the curtain remains into the trash pale. "It's quite late out. Plus, sleeping will speed up the painful process."

"Celeste, what if I'm not fit to be a queen?"

"What do you mean?" She asks, sitting on the end of my bed, folding her hands in her lap.

"I just… Maybe it should go to one of the Fae children who grew up here. I don't feel like I'll be remotely good at it. I know it's my birthright, and it's in my blood, but I don't know. This whole fire situation freaks me out, too. What if people don't want a queen with fire powers in fear she'll be emotional one day and turn the kingdom to ashes?"

"Honey, you are more fit to be Queen than I think you

realize. Being able to admit what you just did says everything about the kind of person you are. That you care for the kingdom and don't want it to be put in harm's way. You may have only been here for a few months, but you know just as much as Amalie and the others. You're a fast learner, and Nadine has told me she's quite impressed by your logical thinking and understanding of our history and where we went wrong with things."

There's a pause in between us where I think about what she has told me.

"Did *you* ever feel ready to be Queen?"

"No. And to be entirely honest, I still don't. Me becoming Queen was a bit of a shock and not something myself or Emmet anticipated. Your mother was the best damn Queen the kingdom has ever seen, and she was a tough act to follow. An act that I didn't want to do. The worries of the kingdom still keep me up at night. When it was announced that we were to take the rule to fill the roles, I went into a bit of a spiral. I had just lost my best friend, and now I was expected to take her job even though I was shy and struggled a lot with other mental things. I stopped eating and stopped existing entirely. I stayed in my bed and couldn't move. I mean it like I refused to get up even to go to the washroom. I was terrified and just wanted everything to cease. It was a very dark period of my life. Emmet was the one who got me out of that, and I'll forever be grateful for him and his friendship. We may not love each other in the way that a married couple should, but I do love him and appreciate him very much. I still have loads of insecurities, hence the need to always look perfect and everything to be perfect. Which then leads to the uptight persona, which has caused me some trouble with making friends and being a queen like your mom was. Nonetheless, I try my best, you know why? Because I love this kingdom and its citizens, and deep down, I know that right now, I'm the best chance it has until you are able to take the throne. You're going to be fine. You'll never be alone, and you'll always have supporters no matter what. I'll be the first one there cheering you on."

Stupid tears spilled down my stupid face.

When was I ever going to stop crying?

Celeste was crying, too, though.

Gods, all of this is so emotional.

"Thank you for telling me that," I whisper.

Celeste moved up in bed and gave me a tight squeeze.

I fell asleep shortly after, the exhaustion from pain and crying hitting me like a brick.

~

When I woke the next morning, having a long, dreamless

sleep, Celeste was snoring quietly in the chaise. I felt bad that she had stayed again, but I appreciated that she did.

I get up and head to the washroom. I'm still in pain, but not as much as the initial moments yesterday. Just an aching headache and cramping. There's no mess left behind in the bed, though, so I suppose that's good.

I go clean myself up and take care of my needs and then head to the basin to wash up and have a look at my teeth.

When I look in the mirror, I'm sort of taken back by my reflection.

I'm a little bit taller, my posture much better, my features sharper, and my eyes are lighter. They are actually silver now. My body looks a little different, too, not much, but maybe a bit more mature? I guess it'll all take time to really fill out. But my *hair*. There are two strips of bleached blonde, nearly white, strands on either side of my face. Like the face-framing pieces had completely turned.

No one mentioned this would happen?

It was weird, and I'm not sure if I like it, if I'm being honest.

Everything else feels different, too, like I'm hyper-aware of my surroundings or something. Like even with the door shut tightly, I can still hear Celeste lightly snoring in the far side of the room. I can also smell better too. I smell all my soaps, the lavender, honeysuckle, almond, man, they smell *amazing*. Like they did before, but this is a whole new level.

I have got to show Celeste this is *insane*.

I creep out in the room, hardly making a noise. I move with such ease that the usual floor boards don't even creak. I make my way over and, sit in front of her and tap her gently on the knee, hoping not to startle her.

She wakes with a jump and a snort.

So much for not startling.

"Dear Gods," she mutters and wipes her eyes. "Are you okay? What time is it? Gods, I don't even remember falling asleep here-"

She finally looks at me.

"Oh wow. Look at you! Ryenn, honey, you're even more beautiful! The hair is definitely… different. I've never actually seen that sort of feature change before, but you pull it off."

She's touching my hair, my ears, and lifting my lip to inspect my teeth. I smile. "How are you feeling?"

"Better. Well, my head still hurts, and so does my stomach, but not as badly. But everything feels… *different*. I don't know how to describe it, like I feel more awake to my surroundings or something?"

"I know exactly what you mean. It's all the Fae features and heightens everything. It's definitely going to take getting used to."

"I could hear you snoring when I was in the washroom."

"I do *not* snore." She scrunches her eyebrows, and I laugh.

"Oh yes, you do trust me."

"Not true. Ladies, don't snore." She smoothes her hands down her dress.

"Uh-huh, sure," I laugh.

"Any more fire incidents?"

"Nope."

"Do you want to try and summon it?"

"Nope."

"Ryenn…"

"I don't care if I ever summon it again. I don't particularly want to, and if it stays away, then I have no reason to use it." I crossed my arms. It was true. If it could stop sneaking up on me, and I could keep it from happening, then that's what I was going to do. It's not like I need to use fire for anything anyways, it's useless unless being used for destruction, and that's not something I'm about to do.

"I have to tell you something that you aren't going to like,"

Celeste then states. And I give her a confused look.

"Remember how I said the heir will get a tiara once they transition? Well, it always happens at the next ball closest to the time of the transition, meaning you'll be crowned at the Summer Ball this week. It won't take long, you'll just be asked to stand, and the tiara will be placed atop your head. Basically, it just shows you are the true heir and sets in stone that you will be coronated when you are of age."

Okay, that's not so bad. People will be far too distracted by the evening to really care about me getting a freaking tiara anyways.

"It is custom that the heir display the powers gifted to them during this event."

Well *fuck.*

That's just great now, isn't it?

"Why?" I ask, a bit more saucily than I intended.

"It's just the rules of the kingdom. It doesn't have to be extravagant, just summon your powers to the palm of your hand. Your mother summoned her water powers to simply make water orbs above her palm."

"I don't know if I can't do this," I mutter. Not only did I despise the fire, but the only times it was summoned was when I least expected it. I don't know what will happen if I actually attempt to bring it to the surface or if I'll be able to control it. Also, the fact that I had to show my powers to the whole freaking kingdom was not something I liked the idea of. What if they thought I was dangerous? I already had a bad reputation, and I've been here for less than three freaking months.

"You okay?" She touches my knee, and I shudder.

"I don't want to do it," tears spring to my eyes.

"I know, but unfortunately, its tradition, and there's nothing I can do to stop it. The citizens will be expecting it, and if you refuse, it'll be worse than what you're imagining."

"Fuck."

"Ryenn."

"Sorry, but this just keeps getting better and better." I walk over to my bed and flop like a child. Sure, I'm being dramatic, but I don't care right now.

"We can practice summoning it here, in the comfort of your own room. All you have to do is will the flames to your palms and, keep them there for a minute and then will them away. Most Fae find using their powers makes them feel good. Like they can blow off some steam."

"That's easy for you to say. Your power is gentle and makes people feel good," I grumble into my pillow.

"It doesn't have to be."

"Huh?"

"Get dressed. I'm taking you somewhere."

~

Despite my complaining and groaning about not wanting to leave my chambers, Celeste forces me down the halls and outside. We head towards the back of the castle to the deep forest that guards its northern backside. Me and Amalie walk along the edge every morning on our way to school, but Celeste was taking me deep down a narrow trail. Scouts flanked us yards behind.

"Where are you taking me?"

"You'll see."

We walk for another 15 minutes or so before Celeste tells the Scouts to stay put, and then we make our way into a clearing.

It's a large field with a small creek and waterfall. It's quite beautiful, actually. Wildflowers taint the air with their aroma, bees and butterflies hurry by, and birds chirp from the trees. It's calming.

"This is really beautiful," I say in a less grumpy tone.

"Mhmm," Celeste agrees.

Suddenly, it seems like the wind picks up, and the trees start to sway.

"Oh, the wind is getting strong," I say, looking at the outskirts of the field.

It was getting stronger and stronger. The birds stopped chirping and flew away, flower petals wisped into the sky, and there was a ripple on the small pond.

I glanced at Celeste, half worried that there was a storm brewing or something. That's when I notice her eyes. The blue hue was *glowing,* and there was a calm but focused look on her face. Then everything changed.

Her eyes narrow, making her look *angry.* The wind gets even worse, loosening the braid in my hair and causing strands to fly around wildly. Waves were now lapping in the water; trees were bowing to the strength. *She* was doing this.

"Celeste…" I caution. This was kind of scary. I could hardly hear my own voice over the loudness of the roar of wind in my ears.

She quickly lifts her hands and pushes them away from her. Wind knocks me down onto the soft grassy ground, some branches crack off the trees, and a massive wave skitters across the blue surface.

Then everything calms.

Her expression goes slack, and she takes a deep breath in.

I stare at her, wide-eyed, still sitting on my ass.

"I told you. Powers are how you behold them."

"That was *insane,*" I laugh. Gods I never seen anything like this. She was *powerful.* Much more so than I thought.

"Yes. I come out here occasionally if I'm in a particularly bad mood so I can free up some of my emotional energy. I can easily hurt people, too, Ryenn. Yet, I clearly choose not to. That doesn't mean I don't have that ability, though. What you saw was a tame version of the extent of my abilities, something I have been working on for, well, a century, I guess."

"Okay then. Sorry, but I'm still a bit gob smacked by what just happened. Also, you blew me onto my ass which is kind of rude." She laughs and holds out a hand to lift me up.

"Try to summon it," she says gently.

I give her a weary look.

"There's no one around. The Scouts couldn't even feel the wind I just created. This is a safe place, and I will make sure you're safe. You can do it. You just need to practice and not let it get pent up."

"Okay… I'm not even sure how to start." I rub my hands together.

"Picture it. Close your eyes, hold open your hands, and will it to the surface."

I do as she says. I close my eyes and picture the silver flames in my hands. I picture myself controlling them and not the other way around. It's just a small little flame, it's not going to hurt anyone, and I'm not going to burn anything. I slowly open my eyes and look at my palm.

The fire dances in my hand.

I'm a bit surprised, but I keep my focus on keeping it stable.

It doesn't burn me.

It's actually kind of beautiful now that I look at it.

"You did it!" Celeste is smiling ear to ear. "See! It's not that bad! You're controlling it. That's all you have to do-"

A deer jumps out from the tree line and bounds across the field right in front of us. It startles me, and I lose control.

The flames erupt and shoot towards the sky.

"It's okay! Breathe, it was just a deer!" Celeste yells.

I can hardly hear her in the flames.

I'm trapped.

I'm going to burn down the forest.

Shit.

Shit.

Shit.

"Control it, Ryenn!"

I suck in a breath.

In for three.

Hold for three.

Out for three.

The flames suffocate, and I'm left standing with a circle burned around me at my feet.

Chapter 28

Scouts come running up the trail.

"Is everything alright, your highness? We thought saw flames erupt into the sky," one of them says.

"Yes, everything is fine. Just practicing is all." She smiles as she speaks calmly.

I am not calm.

How could she be calm?

"You can go back to stand guard; we will be done shortly."

The two scouts give each other a look of skepticism, but they decide to obey the Queen's orders.

Celeste turns slowly on her heel towards me.

I'm still just standing there, hands slack at my sides, wondering what the fuck just happened.

"Well, it was going well for the first bit. You just got scared from the deer."

"Yeah, no shit!" I yell and throw my hands up in the air.

"Ryenn, I understand you are frustrated, but do not speak to me that way." She straightens her back, and I instantly feel guilty.

"I'm sorry. I just… Gods, this is all so complicated. It's not your fault. I'm sorry I yelled at you."

"I know, honey, but you know how to remotely control it already. You're strong. More so than you are giving yourself credit for. All you need to do is the same thing at the ball."

"And hope a deer doesn't jump out and scare the daylights out of me."

She laughs, and I dip my chin as I grin.

"Yes, well, luckily, deer aren't invited to the ball. Like I told you, it's all in the emotions. Sometimes, emotions can take over, and your powers can feed on that. Not saying you shouldn't have emotions, quite the opposite really, you shouldn't keep them pent up because it could lead to destruction."

"Okay." that's going to be easier said than done, I think. I don't really like to give into emotions all that much, probably because of what would happen if I did back home. It wasn't always like that, though. Mother was always calm and would hold me and soothe me if I were upset. When she died, that all changed.

"What are you thinking about?" Celeste asks as we walk over to the edge of the pond.

"My mortal mother, Endra. She was a very kind woman and did a very good job of raising me. Whenever I had 'big feelings' as she used to call them, she'd let me scream or cry or whatever I felt necessary without repercussions. That changed when she died, though. I felt *so* much grief, and still do, but my father wasn't emotionally available. Her death destroyed him. I was left to care for my baby sister all by myself and raise her. I wanted to raise her just like how my mother raised me. It was harder than I think anyone realized. I was a child trying to rear a child and also take care of my father. I didn't get a chance to be a kid since I was 11 years old, and I also never got to express those emotions or feelings anymore. If I did, it always ended… badly anyways."

"Badly how?" She asked quietly as we sat on the grassy bank.

I'd never told anyone this before.

"Sometimes, after keeping all my frustrations and grief and loneliness to myself, it would just bubble up and boil over. Only a handful of times, though. Father was not patient like mother and even less so after she died. I loved him, don't get me wrong, but he was broken. If I tried to tell him things, he'd think I was blaming him, or if I was upset, he'd think I was ungrateful. He'd hit me, especially if he was drunk. Usually using his belt across my backside, but the occasional face slap happened, too. The night of the accident had actually been a night where I was frustrated because I had been dealing with Rose all day, and she was upset over something. He came home drunk and smacked her on the hand for being a crybaby, which caused me to yell at him. He gave me six lashings for that, which is the most he'd ever done to me before. It never broke skin, but it still stung. Emotionally more than physically, I think. It's probably why I slept so soundly that night because after I put Rosie to sleep, I cried myself asleep next to her. I'm not sure why I'm telling you all of this, I'm sure you saw it all in the Septor anyways."

"I'm sorry you had to go through that." Celeste looked at me with concern written across her face and took my hand in hers. "Gods, Ryenn, you were just a kid. You still are a kid. Even then, you should never ever feel the need to hide your emotions or feelings in fear of repercussions. Being able to control your emotions versus bottling them up are two entirely different things."

"I think I know that now. Or at least I'm trying to. When I first got here, I kept a lot of things to myself. I was in a pretty dark place, one that I am working on digging myself out of. I didn't eat or sleep hardly at all for the first month I was here. I kept the whole fire thing a secret and didn't want to talk about my family. It's still hard. Incredibly hard. I'm still trying to go through the motions and deal with everything that has happened to me, and sometimes it's very overwhelming. But now I have you. And Emmet. And Amalie. And Sara. That's four more people than I've had to trust in over 5 years."

"You can always trust me. I know I'm not your mom, and I am not trying to be, but I'm always here to help you through anything. I don't care if you think it's embarrassing or inappropriate, I'll do my best to answer your questions and be someone to listen, okay? I owe you that. I owe your mother that. Both of your mothers."

Tears welled up in my eyes. "Now you're making me cry again, and I'm all hormonal, and that's not fair."

Celeste laughed and dragged me into her embrace.

"Let's go back. You still need to rest, your transition isn't done, and I'm sure you're in quite some pain."

"Gods, you have no idea. Why don't males have to go through the whole cycle thing?"

"Because life is cruel sweet child."

~

After returning to the castle, I had a nap for a few hours to pass some of the cramping and throbbing in my head. I didn't dream. I hadn't dreamt of anything in a long while, which I supposed was good. No dreams were better than nightmares. Celeste woke me shortly after, saying that Sara was in her way and that Juno would be coming with her. They wanted to assess my Transition and my powers. I was a bag of nerves and felt a bit sick to my stomach just thinking about it.

A light knock sounds on the door, and both walk in. Juno is an older woman, how old, I'm not entirely sure, considering Celeste is 113 and looks no more than 30. She's short in stature and has gray hair, always tied in a tight knot atop her head. She's a serious-looking woman, and to be honest, I find her to be intimidating.

Sara is the first to speak.

"Hello, your highness," both bow to Celeste. "Hello, Ryenn," Sara smiles at me. I'm already blushing from nerves.

"Hello Sara and Juno, I'm happy you could come," Celeste says in a friendly tone.

"Of course! How are you feeling, Ryenn? Seems like the physical Fae aspects have completed. May I assess you?"

"Sure," I say quietly.

Sara begins to assess me, starting at my ears, then teeth, testing my vision and, hearing and smell. It takes her a few minutes, and she pauses at my hair.

"I've never seen that sort of thing before," twirling the light color strands in her fingers. "Looks pretty, though," she grins at me, and I give her a smile.

"How's your pain, dear?"

"Not as bad now. It was horrible for that first 24 hours, though."

"And your cycle? Are you finding everything okay with that?"

My face warms again.

"It's not very… nice?"

Sara laughs. "No, my dear, it's not. Besides the whole pain and blood thing, there's no other issues, right? Just where you had that trauma, I want to make sure you're doing okay."

"Oh yeah, besides the norm, or what I guess is normal, I think everything is okay."

"Good," she pats my shoulder.

The entire time we are talking, Juno and Celeste are at my desk, discussing something else. Once they hear us stop talking, they turn around.

"Alright, Princess." Juno says, "You need to summon your powers now. The Queen mentioned they are of the fire variety. I'd like to have a look and see what we're working with so I can do some research."

I gulp.

I can do this just don't make a scene.

I close my eyes and picture the flame, small and calm, in my hand.

I'm controlling it.

The flame is mine.

I open my eyes and glance at my palms. A ball of silver flames aglow

I look at the three Fae in my room. Celeste looks me in the eyes and nods, Sara is wide-eyed, staring at the fire with a grin on her face, and Juno is… unreadable. She looks shocked, yes, but also like she's considering something.

"It *is* silver." Juno looks to Celeste.

"Yes, I know."

Looking back at me, Juno sizes me up and meets my stare

"Ryenn…you have the Drakōn Flame"

Chapter 29

"What does that mean?" I ask, glancing between the three in front of me. Nerves tangled in my stomach. Drakōn as in the massive beast that was extinct? I am so confused.

"The Drakōn Flame. It used to run in the Ember bloodline, but the last one was centuries ago; your great-great-great grandfather, the same one that had the last Drakōn. Basically, it's called the Drakōn Flame due to its silver nature. It is also incredibly deadly because, unlike most fires or fire-wielding fae, it can't be put out through suffocation or water. It needs to be willed away by the beholder," Juno explained as she glanced through stacks of papers she brought with her.

"Celeste, did you know this?" I asked.

"I had some suspicions, given the nature of the flame and the fact that I couldn't put it out yesterday, but I had no clue what exactly it was called. I had just remembered reading about it before. It changes nothing, though, Ryenn. It's still just fire powers, just a bit different, I guess." She says and touches my shoulder. My eyes are still wide, and I feel like I can't swallow.

"This changes a lot, actually, your Highness. Ryenn is the first descendant in centuries. Fae may be apprehensive of this, considering the nature of it. Ryenn, you must understand you are going to be incredibly powerful. Learning to control and wield this is essential. We need to approach it all from a safe manner, and when she does her display at the ball, it needs to be explained to the kingdom so she's not perceived as a … *threat*."

A threat?

I feel like I have been perceived as one since arriving at the kingdom. I mean, I was already attacked once and threatened to be killed. What is going to happen now that I have this ancient fire power that no one is going to be able to give me first-hand guidance on? Hell, four months ago, I never knew what Fae were exactly, and now, I was a powerful one with powers from an ancient beast that wields silver-colored fire that can only be put out by myself. I have a funny feeling this is not going to end well for me.

"You okay dear?" Sara asks.

"No… No, I am not okay with this. Juno, will I be able to control this? What happened to my great-great-great grandfather? Was *he* a threat? Why hasn't there been another with the same manner of powers in centuries? Are there any other Fire Fae in this kingdom at all?" All the questions were bubbling out of my mouth like word vomit, and my chest was tight.

"Let's sit down, okay?" Sara motions to the seating area.

"Given proper precautions and training, you should be able

to control it. Your ancestor was the last for many reasons, and I am surprised the trait has come back. He was a king with different values, and having that type of power at his disposal occasionally led to… rash decisions. I did not know him personally, but I have, of course, read the history. He wanted to protect the kingdom but had brutalist ways of doing so. He also had no regard for life besides those of his supporters, something we all know is not the same for you, child. As for other fire Fae, I don't believe we've had many in the kingdom since before your mother's reign. That being said, there *are* fire Fae, just not a part of this kingdom. It seems to be a more common trait among Fae of Aclos, which is something we don't need to worry about at the moment."

Aclos?

Where have I heard that name before…

Wait, that was the opposing kingdom, the rebels, and the Dark King. The ones who terrorized the mortals. There were Fire Fae there? That just confirms my suspicions of Fire being an inherently evil thing. Let alone this Drakōn Flame, which had been last seen in a cruel King.

I just sat there. Staring at my hands, knowing I had the ability to hurt people at sheer will.

"Princess, instead of tutoring with Nadine, you will be meeting with me to help wield your powers. This is integral to learning. I do not think you'll use them for bad, you are good and have given no one reason to not trust you'll be a good queen. Practicing won't hurt though, and it will show the citizens your intentions."

Juno paused and began to gather the papers left about. "Your Highness, I believe it would be wise to call a small council meeting for this evening to discuss our findings. Your presence would be greatly appreciated, Ryenn. You can show the other members the flames you possess so they are not blindsided at the ball."

"Thank you, Juno. I'll send off the invitations for the meeting at once," Celeste said back to the grand healer.

Sarah reached into her bag, leaving some pine needle medication for pain and something purple in color she states is to assist with sleep.

"I'll see you this evening, Ryenn. Do not fret, okay? You'll learn, it's not going to be as bad as you imagine. We all believe in you," Sara says quietly before following Juno out of my chambers.

Again, I am left to digest new information that feels like threatening my ability to breathe.

~

Celeste quickly writes to the other members of the small council and gives them to Ser Davis to deliver, also a note for Emmet to come to my chambers immediately so he can be alerted of the powers before finding out at the meeting.

I still sit there, staring at my hands.

No tears came.

I feel numb again.

Breathing hurts, but I struggle through it.

Celeste takes a seat across from me and wraps her hands around mine. I look up and see her gaze.

"It's going to be okay," she stares deeply with her blue eyes piercing through my own, now silver ones.

"How can you be so sure?" I say in a wobbly voice.

"Have I been wrong yet?" she tilts her head.

I suppose she hasn't, in a sense.

"No, I guess not."

"You arc going to receive training. You'll control them. You already have been controlling them. Right now, the only thing we have to worry about is breaking the news to the kingdom. It may not be well received at first, but you'll not have any reason for them not to trust you have the kingdom's best interest at heart."

I take a deep breath.

I need to stop freaking out about things and stop letting things I can't control get to me as they have been. That's easier said than done with this dark pit growing inside of me.

Emmet arrives shortly after and I show him the flame. Celeste explains to him what Juno has told us. He is surprisingly able to remain calm throughout the whole thing. I missed him, I realize as I look at his clean, kept face. There is just a familiar presence about him that, although used to intimidate me, now feels familial.

"I have no doubts in your ability, Ryenn, so I am not even worried. I am just glad you are feeling better." He smiles, and that piece of confidence warms me. "I have to say I am impressed by the weight you have put on. I think you may have met your end of the bargain. I can see your Transition helped that nicely as well, so you're healing and strength should be good to start learning combat."

"Really?" I smiled wide.

"I think so. Well, you still have a week left, so we will begin after the ball, okay?"

"Sure okay!" I was actually excited about this. Not only am I going to learn to get strong in the physical aspect, but I am also going to learn to control this power in me. I am not going to let anyone down. I am not going to let myself down.

"The hair looks nice by the way."

His compliment makes a pink blush bloom across my face.

"I will see you both tonight, alright?" He looks at Celeste and me, "I have some business I must attend to until then."

Celeste nods and he pats her on the shoulder, leaving swiftly through the door.

That never-leaving panic sits deep within my core. I am going to try and ignore it, though. Maybe taking some of those anxiety medications that Sara left won't be such a bad idea.

~

Celeste remains and is doing work at the desk.

"Celeste, I feel as though since the attack, I have taken up all of your time. You are allowed to leave, you know? You don't have to feel obligated to stay." I decided to say. It's true. I really enjoyed her company and felt quite nervous without her around, but that was something I needed to get over.

"There is nothing I couldn't do from here anyway. I used to just sit in my office and do what I am doing now. I also don't mind spending said time with you, dear. You may tell me to leave whenever, and I won't be hurt. However, if you want me to stay, that is something I don't mind doing anyway. I told you this already, Ryenn, you are not a burden."

That last part felt like it stung a bit in my heart. Not in a bad way, of course, it's just that deep inside, I always felt like I was a burden.

"Thank you," I say. "I will start back at class tomorrow, okay? The pain has become tolerable, and I feel like I can manage it. Plus, the ball is only in 4 days from tomorrow anyways, and I have missed a riding lesson and a few days' worth of classes." I think about Braxton and those stupid butterflies finding their way back. Why am I nervous to show him what I look like after my transition? I don't look that much different than before, I suppose, just a bit… sharper? I don't know if that's the term I am looking for, but it feels right.

"Sure," she says. "Are you alright with me going to my chambers tonight?" she asks.

"Yes, I think so. You're just down the hall anyways. Plus, you'll just keep me awake with your snoring."

She gasps and I cackle.

"Again, I do *not* snore. I have no idea what you're talking about," she furrows her brows.

Chapter 30

If I were to sum up the rest of my day into one word, it would be hectic. Amalie came to my chambers after schooling was finished for the day, bearing the danishes she promised. We sat and ate all six of them while I told her about my fire trial out in the field and the Drakōn flame thing. She thought it was cool and interesting, which made me feel pretty good. At least *she* wasn't afraid of me. She told me about school drama.

Apparently, Grey and Autumn were in a pretty heated argument this morning, and then Autumn had even cried and left early, Hanna and Luna in tow. Grey was flustered and also left, so Amalie was completely by herself. She was too afraid to ditch, because her parents would have her head if she did. I felt bad that I wasn't there. She didn't know exactly what the argument between the two had been, but she heard them talking about the ball or something along those lines.

Celeste had left when Amalie had come and told me to meet her and Emmet in the dining room for supper, which is what I did.

Emmet told me of his travels to Vermuse these past few weeks, nothing out of the ordinary had happened, and there was surprisingly no uprising about the young lord's exile. He also said Scouts have said there have been no reports or rebel attacks on mortals either, which is good and made me feel a bit lighter. The rest of that dinner included some small talk about studies and whatnot. That all felt pretty normal. Like we were actually eating a family dinner together.

After dinner, the three of us walked to the meeting together. The meeting is what made the day hectic. It went exactly how I imagined it would, if I am being honest. The Lord and Lady of the Capital had many questions and comments regarding said powers and accusatory assumptions that I was dangerous, and they didn't think I should be Heir.

Hunter, Bradley, and Normani were also slightly weary but didn't say much. I mean, hardly anyone could get a word in due to Lord Seredi's incessant speaking. Juno had done a really good job at explaining the situation and even brought literature regarding the Drakōn Flame forward. Emmet and Celeste shut down the assumptions from Garret and Vada, causing a tiff between the two sisters.

Gods, I don't know how poor Amalie lives with these two serpents as parents. By the end of it, I was sweating, and my temples hurt. I hardly said anything besides agreeing with whatever the King and Queen said in my favor.

At the end of the three-hour confrontation, Juno suggested I show the controlled flame to the rest of the council, just so they could see I was 'harmless' and wasn't on the brink of bursting into flames and burning down the entire kingdom.

And I did just that. I summoned the flame far easier than I anticipated. It danced through my fingers and made cuffs like bracelets around my wrists. Releasing this bit of energy almost relaxed me and ceased the heat I had been steadily growing in my core all evening. Everyone just sat there in awe.

Well, Emmet, Celeste, and Juno were smiling like they were proud of my abilities. Hunter, Bradley, and Normani looked wide at the flame in surprise, and then the Seredis looked at me with something like fear and disgust combined. When I ceased the flame with little thought, it was like a sigh of relief left everybody in the room, which made me feel a little weird.

The meeting finally ended, although the energy from the beginning and the end still felt the same, like uncertainty tainted the air I breathed. Ser Davis and three other Scouts escorted me to my chambers, where I got ready for sleep. Someone knocked on my door not even thirty minutes afterward. It was Celeste checking on me to most likely ensure I wasn't crumpled like a sobbing mess on the floor. And I wasn't. Which is something I was grateful for. If this had been me three months ago, I probably would have been, given the confrontation I faced, but tonight, I let it all roll off of me. She gave me a tight hug and told me she'd see me in the morning before class, and that was that.

I took the usual pine-needle medicine to help get rid of the cramping that still accompanied my lower abdomen. I really wished the whole cycle thing would be finished by now, but I suppose it's really only been 72 hours, so I have a few more days of bloodshed left. The medication had become a relief as it also ensured I didn't dream, which was good for everyone.

~

I woke up in the morning and had my cold bath. Something about the sheer iciness was a welcoming touch and settled some of the nerves about going back to class. There were now only four days left to the ball, which also made me a tad nervous.

Evie came and pulled my hair into a braided crown. Looking in the mirror, I felt like it made me look quite mature. It also showed off my newly pointed ear, and the white strands weaved through it looked pretty. I actually felt pretty. The dark circles of exhaustion and malnutrition had also lightened, and there seemed to be life back in my eyes. The scar on my lip was still there, it was faded to a light pink coloring now, though. It didn't bother me per se, but every time I stared at it for too long, the twinge of the cellar events pained me, and flashes of memories attempted to crawl to the surface. I shook away the thoughts and took a deep breath, putting on my school gown. As I was pulling it up, it *ripped*. It was too small.

Evie looked over at me, hearing the tear of the fabric.

I started laughing, and a look of confusion sprung across her mousey face.

"It's alright, princess, we have a few other sizes in the wardrobe. Your body has just changed from the transitioning."

I was still laughing. Gods, I was actually becoming healthier. It felt like I had shed the skin that had covered my too-prominent bones and was now lean and happy. This also excited me because I knew next week, I would begin my promised combat training.

Evie came back with a new schooling uniform, a size bigger than the other one, and it fit perfectly. I smiled at her.

"Thank you, Evie. For everything. I appreciate your help as my handmaiden."

She looked a bit taken back and smiled back up at me as she fixed the laces on my boot.

"You are welcome, Princess," she grinned. "Now, let's get you to breakfast."

~

It was just Celeste in the dining room this morning. I wasn't surprised, but a tang of disappointment went through me. I was just hoping Emmet would be there as well, but I was, of course, happy Celeste was.

"Ryenn!" she looked at me with a smile when I entered, and

it kind of startled me.

"What?" I asked, going to take my seat, but she stood and walked over to me, sizing me up.

"You are glowing! Honey, you look so good."

I blush and grin.

"I actually had to go up a size in my uniform. I ripped the other one trying to get it on this morning," I laugh.

"I am so proud of you," she cups her hand under my chin, then walks back to her seat, and I take mine, my face still a hue of pink.

"You better start eating, though." She glances at the large clock on the wall. "You have approximately three minutes before Pippa comes bounding in here."

I do as she says, scarfing down the toasted bread, eggs, and fresh fruits.

"Did you sleep alright last night, dear?" she asks, taking a sip of her almond-scented coffee.

"I actually did," I look up at her. I notice she looks a bit tired, and there are sleepless circles under her eyes. "Did you? You seem tired."

Then she blushes.

"Oh yes, I slept. Maybe I am just a bit stressed about the ball or something," she rambled.

"You are blushing," I grin.

She touches her cheek.

"For someone who makes fun of me blushing, you seem to be doing an awful lot of it." I laugh and then glance at her neck. There's a reddish mark on the side of it. "What happened to your neck?"

She turns bright red and covers the mark with her hand, nearly choking on the coffee she's trying to swallow.

"I must have, uh, hit it getting out of bed this morning. You know me, I can be clumsy. And I am not blushing. I am just quite warm, it is humid this morning," she laughs nervously, causing me to laugh harder.

Celeste was the opposite of clumsy. Then I think of the book I read. The prince had given the maiden a similar mark one evening during their indecent activities. Wait-

"Celeste, is that a hickey?" I blurt out, giggling.

Her eyes go as wide as saucers, still resting the hand on her neck.

My Gods, what had the Queen been up to last night?

Before she could answer, Pippa bursts through the dining room door.

"Oh, thank Gods," I hear Celeste mutter to herself.

The young girl grabs my hand, and Amalie enters the room. I stand to be led out.

"This isn't over," I laugh at Celeste.

"It most certainly is," she grins back. "Have a good day, dear. Meet Juno at the infirmary after class, will you?"

I nod, still smiling, and link arms with my best friend.

"What's all that about?" she whispers into my ear.

"I wouldn't even be able to tell you," I giggle.

~

The air was humid and sticky as we walked to the schoolhouse. Pippa had hounded me to show her my flame along the way, and I did briefly. She squealed like a little pig and jumped up and down.

"That is the coolest power ever! I hope I get that one!" She sees her friends ahead of us and darts off.

"Ry, you look very pretty this morning," Amalie says unexpectedly.

"Oh ha, thank you?"

"Just warning you, be prepared for some stares this morning. Everyone is going to be so jealous."

"Oh, I can't see them being jealous, Amy."

"Seriously? Have you looked in the mirror? Ry, you were gorgeous before, but you are really starting to fill out nicely."

I blush, of course, and she laughs.

"You're so silly."

"Shut up," I laugh and give her a shove.

We round the corner, and the schoolyard comes into view. Everyone is sitting outside, probably due to the heat. As Amalie says, everyone flicks their head in my direction. I don't let it bother me, though. I stand tall like Celeste taught me and continue to walk until we make our way to a vacant bench.

Grey is a few feet across from us, and I catch his slack-jawed stare. He looks away quickly, and I blush. Why was he looking at me like that?

I am not the only one who must notice, though, because Autumn and her friends walk over to me and Amalie.

"Nice of you to show up to class, Princess," she says in a fake-friendly tone. "I forgot that you're better than the rest of us and don't need the same schooling. I mean, how long have you been here? Three months? You must think you know everything there is to know about ruling this kingdom if you've missed nearly three weeks of schooling in that time."

"Why are you so concerned about what I do, Autumn?" I retort, using my 'queen voice' that I was taught, and I tip my head to the side.

"I am simply concerned for the kingdom," she spits back. "Myself and the rest of us have been trained since we were children on how to rule this kingdom, and you simply have *not*. I am not the only one who thinks you'll be an unfit ruler. And now, instead of making up for lost time, you take multiple days off of school to 'rest.'"

Heat settles in my core.

"I don't have to explain myself to you," I say.

"Oh, how very queenly of you," she mocks back. "Is that what you'll say to the rest of the kingdom?"

"Knock it off, Autumn," Grey mutters from the side, and I glance at him.

"Oh, so you're on her side now, are you? Good to know, Greyson." She rolls her eyes, and I see the fury building under her skin.

"Are you done?" Amalie asks her, a bored tone to her voice that I know she was trying really hard to master.

"Butt out bitch" Hanna says.

"Do not speak to her that way," I say as I now stand to face the girls. I am the same height as them now. I feel like fire courses through my veins. Now is not the time.

"Or what?" Hanna retorts, "Will you have me exiled, your highness?"

That hurt.

I am taken back a bit and all feeling drains from my body.

"Oh fuck off, Hanna," Grey now stands. "That was entirely uncalled for."

Amalie is now standing at my back, holding my shoulders.

"That was such a bitch move." She mutters to the girl.

"Gods, no need to be so sensitive," Autumn says in that annoying, fake, sweet tone. "We were just having a conversation. No need to get emotional over it. Well, clearly, you're on your cycle, so I guess the hormones are a bit out of control, aren't they? Nice transition, by the way, the hair is definitely… *something*." All three girls crack up laughing and leave to enter the schoolhouse.

I feel sick to my stomach, and the fire still threatens to make its way to the surface.

"You okay?" Grey asks quietly, staring at me again with his

brilliant green eyes.

"Yeah… thanks," I whisper back.

"Okay…" He turns and heads inside.

"Ry, you look like you're going to be sick…" Amalie is still next to me, touching my elbow softly.

"I can't stay here." I look at her, my eyes filled with tears.

"You can't let them get to you," she says.

I take a shuddering breath.

"Why don't I tell Mrs. Langerfeld that you need a few minutes, and we can go in when you're ready? Ry, you can't leave for the whole day, it'll only get worse if you do."

"Okay," I sigh.

She leaves quickly and I stand there.

My mind was swimming.

So many thoughts swarmed me and I felt like that shell wouldn't leave her bed for days.

Gods, I was doing so well. Why did I let her get to me?

Amalie returns in less than a minute.

"Where do you want to go?" she asks, linking my arm.

"I know a spot."

Chapter 31

Amalie and I sit under the willow tree hidden in the castle gardens. The soft moss is comforting and the pink hues from the sunlight peeking through the flowery branches soothe me. Since we arrived here less than five minutes ago, I have been using my breathing technique to will the burn of flames from my veins. In for three, hold for three, out for three.

"This place is beautiful," Amalie whispers as she reads the plaque. "How did you know about it?"

"Celeste showed me one day. Her and my mother used to come here a lot, apparently."

"How are you holding up?" she asks, turning her attention to me.

I exhale. "I'm okay."

"Be honest, Ry."

"Well, I *was* doing okay. I don't know why, but Hanna's comment really got to me. And I know it shouldn't but fuck, it's like all the blood drained from my body Amy. I could feel the fire pulsing through me, screaming to let it out. Sometimes, it's like the littlest thing brings me back to that… incident. And then my entire mood just flips. I don't want it to, but it just happens."

"Ry, what happened to you was traumatizing. That traumatic

experience is going to affect you longer than I think you'll realize. And that's okay to feel that way. It's okay to feel broken and beaten, there's no shame in admitting that. What Hanna said was mean and, like Grey said, entirely uncalled for. She was just trying to get a rise out of you."

"And I gave into it and let her affect me," I drop my head and look at my lap.

"She got a rise out of me too! Hell, if Autumn hadn't started spewing nonsense again, I was about to attack her. Despite what you think, I was using you to shield myself from her, not to comfort you."

I laugh and she follows suit.

I lean my head over and rest it on her shoulder.

"They're bullies. They always have been. There have been many times when I have run home crying because of them. And then got scolded for leaving class and being a baby." That hurts my heart. "Anyways, beside the point. We're going to go back and you're going to walk in like you don't even remember what happened this morning, okay?"

She's right.

I can't miss any more school anyway. I still had to catch up and I no longer had Nadine to help me with such.

"Okay," I sigh.

"Ry, you can always talk to me, okay? I know the attack was extremely rough on you and you don't like to talk about it, and I think you fear talking about it will make people pity you, but I just want you to know I'm here and will listen. I don't judge. I promise. And I don't pity you, nor do you scare me. I think you're the strongest silver-fire-wielding-Fae-Queen *ever*."

The last comment makes me laugh, but her kindness settles in and helps cool the heat inside me.

"Thanks, Amy. I love you."

"Love you too, Ry-Ry. Let's go back now and show them you aren't going to let them mess with you."

We walked back to the schoolhouse together. I am incredibly thankful for Amalie. I have never really had friends, now that I think about it. Like even when I did go to school in the Molisan, I had classmates, but none of them were really my friends. We played together, but none of them, nor their parents or the teacher, bothered to check up on me once I stopped going to school. Now, I had a friend who would miss out on morning classes, even though her father would most likely punish her for it, just so she could be with me. That thought made me feel warm, but not in the angry and spite way like before, it felt... comfortable and trustworthy.

~

I ignored the sneers and laughs from the three females the rest of the school day. Grey hadn't said anything afterward, either. Not that I wanted him to. It was nice of him to come to my defense again, but I can take care of myself. Amalie walked me to the infirmary so I could meet with Juno for my first fire-wielding lesson. Again, although she wanted to stay, she had dance lessons, so she left in a grump.

I was led to a vacant room, there was a chair, white walls, and white tiles. That was it. This type of lesson was far different from the calming lessons I had with Nadine. Juno was not at all like the sweet-voiced tutor who always gave me reassurance.

Instead, she sat back and read from her research as she made me summon the flame, hold it for five seconds, and then suffocate it. Over and over and over. By the end of it, I was sweating and panting. I had probably done it 50 times in the thirty-minute lesson.

"Are we going to do anything else?" I croak as I will away the fifty-first flame.

"No," Juno states, glancing up from a scroll. "Being able to summon and suffocate is the first step to controlling the flame. We will continue to do as such until you no longer look as though you ran a mile."

I huff and wipe my brow with my sleeve.

"Well? Keep going," she looks back to her page, and I roll my eyes. "Less attitude child."

I blush but will the flame to my hand anyway. It was getting weaker and weaker. The burn I had been feeling inside had all but extinguished me.

Ser Davis knocks on the glass door and lets himself in. "The Princess has riding lessons," he states.

He looks at my hands and my face but says nothing further.

"Alright, put it out, then you're dismissed, Ryenn. I will meet you here tomorrow for the same thing," she says, again not looking up from her papers.

The flame blinks out and I walk with Ser Davis.

"I don't have my riding clothes," I tell him, and he passes me a bag.

"Evie gave me these for you to change into."

"Alright, thank you," I turn into the female washroom down the hall in the infirmary.

I changed into my riding outfit. Evie must have known I would need new ones due to this morning's fiasco with my uniform. I wore light beige breeches and a lightweight green tunic. I also washed up, trying to make myself look like I hadn't been profusely sweating for the past thirty minutes. I fixed my hair into a low braid, the front white pieces of my hair framing my face. It will have to do. I am not sure why I am so concerned about my looks anyway. Well, I *do* know; I just think wanting to look nice for a male is foolish. Yet here I am, worried about what Braxton will think of me.

Meeting Ser Davis back in the hall, we walk together to the stables.

Blaze is already tacked up and Braxton is in the process of tacking Zeraphena.

"Well, how nice of you to join us," he jokes as I near him.

"I'm sorry I am late… *and* that I have missed my last two lessons. I have been quite…busy," I blush stupidly. Gods, he never even said hardly anything, yet why are you being like this?

"Well, I can see that! You Transitioned," he smiles.

"I have." Pink settles on my cheeks.

"You look great… I mean, you did before, but still. Pretty."

Pretty

He thought I was pretty.

A swirl of emotions tugs in my belly.

"Thanks," I say, looking down at my boots.

"Let's go for a ride. We are doing jumps today," he states, and I mount Blaze. I have been getting much better at doing so, and I don't really need Braxton's help, but I don't tell him that. I don't mind his helping hands.

Gods, something is definitely wrong with me.

Braxton leads us down a path behind the stables. We've ridden through these woods previously, but he brings me to a field with some logs lying around. He talks me through how to jump, the proper positioning, and how to count the strides so that I don't mess up Blaze's footing. He gives me examples and takes Zara around the course himself as I watch. I feel like I am drooling as I observe him.

He is gorgeous. His light brown body is lean, his arms glistening in the afternoon sun, and he looks like he was born to ride like this. He rises up slightly when getting to a jump and leans a bit forward to Zara's neck, causing her to sail gently over the fallen logs. My mind goes to very *very* indecent places. Get it together, Ryenn, he is coming back.

"That's how it's done," he says, trotting back over. Zara flicks her golden mane as if being proud of herself, and I grin. "I want you to go try the first one. Just trot him around a big circle, bring him to canter, and go straight for the jump. Blaze is a good boy, so it's not like he'll toss you if you get it wrong at first."

I do as he says and pray Blaze knows what he's doing. The

horse is a saint, and despite my odd positioning, he jumps and lands lightly on the other side.

"There you go! Not bad at all. You need to work a bit more on your position, but it'll come with practice."

"Yeah, I definitely felt like I was doing it wrong. Blaze *is* a good boy, though."

"That he is." he brings Zara close and reaches over and pets Blaze on the neck. Right next to my leg. A shiver goes through me.

"Let's head back. Ser Davis will have my head if I am not back with you…" He looks at the watch on his arm, "shit in 2 minutes. Want to race?"

"Only if you're not afraid to lose," I say back with a confidence I didn't know I had.

"Oh, that's how it's going to be? I am not going easy on ya, princess."

I tap Blaze forward, giving myself a slight head start down the path, and I hear Braxton yell behind me.

I laugh the entire way. I do end up beating him, though. I am not sure if Blaze wanted to show off or if Braxton had, in fact, gone easy on me, but my stomach muscles hurt from laughing and trying to stay on.

"I'll get you next time," he says, and he helps me off of my horse and his touch lingers again.

"When will that be?" I raise a brow at him.

"Well, I have to help with all the horses arriving at the kingdom in the next two days, so it'll have to be after the ball."

"Will you be coming to the ball?" I decided to ask

"Yes. I assume you will be too?" he grins.

"Of course," I roll my eyes.

"Well, I will see you then. Save a dance for me?" he brushes a piece of fallen hair behind my ear.

"Sure," I say, pink once again taking root in my complexion, causing him to have a satisfactory styled grin.

Ser Davis rounds the corner. Gods, he was really good at interrupting, wasn't he? I left without another word to Braxton. This would be something that was definitely going to cause me to panic over the next few days as if I didn't already have enough on my plate. Nonetheless, it made me excited.

Chapter 32

I hadn't met with Celeste that day due to the fact that she was far too busy with ball preparations. I met with her and Emmet for dinner again, and again, it was nice. I looked forward to it. Just to hear them talking, bantering and talking to me as well.

That night, I read another one of the indecent books Amalie had left for me. I devoured the entire thing in one sitting, feeling warm. It was an odd feeling, like being flustered, especially when reading such things on a piece of paper. My mind wouldn't help but drift to Braxton, and I would smile stupidly to myself. Celeste didn't even have to come to my chambers at all, so I felt pretty good about myself, given all that had happened that day.

The next three days before, the ball went rather smoothly and the same. No more confrontations with the Fae at school, but I swear to the Gods, if I had to listen to the three girls speak about their dresses, hair, cosmetics, or anything about the ball, I was going to rip my ears off.

Training with Juno had been the exact same as the first day. Summoning, holding, suffocating.

Repeat. Repeat. Repeat.

It was exhausting, but by the third session, I had done it one hundred times in our thirty minutes. She actually looked somewhat proud of this feat, too, even though I could hardly stand from the sheer exhaustion and sweltering heat, and stated that I was ready for my demonstration at the ball.

The day before the ball, many people started showing up at the kingdom. The central portion had an entire floor for guests to stay, mainly the lords and ladies, and their families would stay in the castle. Other Fae from around the kingdom stayed in motels or hostels around the city. The streets and castle were buzzing with commotion. It was nerve-racking. All of these people were going to see me go through the minor Transition ceremony, getting my tiara and showing them the Drakōn Flame. I was confident I would control it, but I still feared reactions. I tried not to let it get to me, but it did, unfortunately.

I was now sitting in my room, eating dinner alone since the King and Queen were meeting the other important Fae in the main dining hall. I was invited, of course, but Celeste told me it was not expected of me to be there, none of the children would be, and I would likely be bored to death. I was hoping Amalie would come over, but she informed me that her parents had requested she go on a dinner date with some sort of High Fae from one of the districts. She was so annoyed but had to obey. I felt bad for her.

I paced the room for a while after eating. I had far too much energy, but I did not want to go anywhere. There were too many people. It's too dangerous. I look over at my dresser and see the light purple bottle of medicine that Sara had left. It was some sort of sleeping concoction. Made simply to aid with a restful sleep.

The other medicine I usually took, had drowsy effects but it was mainly for pain. I hadn't needed it for a day or so now because my cycle had thankfully stopped. I knew sleep would be good for me this evening. I needed to be well rested for the event tomorrow, and feeling all these emotions were not going to result in that.

I read the instructions she left: *'Take a capful right before going to sleep; works in less than thirty minutes.'* It was starting to get quite late out, so I decided to change into my lightweight nightgown and take the capful. It tasted rancid, and I nearly threw up in my mouth.

I get in my bed after going to the washroom, brushing my hair and brushing my teeth, and pick up my book. I hardly get through a page before drifting off.

~

Smoke fills my nose, and I'm awake.

"Ry, what is going on?" Rose said through her sniffles, "I can't see anything; there's too much smoke."

Fire was climbing up the walls.

The ceiling is starting to cave in.

"It's okay, Rosie. I'm gonna get us out."

Fire swallowed up the windows.

The bedroom door is stuck.

Father was yelling.

The ceiling is going to collapse.

Rose cries louder and begins to cough.

I'm panicking.

SNAP.

"I should've slit your throat when I had the chance."

I whip my head around, no longer in the burning cottage.

I stare into Corbin's eyes.

His hand is around my throat, and the other is around the handle of a knife.

He brings it to my neck, piercing the flesh...

~

I wake up gasping.

I'm choking.

I am dying.

I taste blood.

I smell smoke.

My hands are on fire, the flame snaking up my arms.

Shit.

Breathe.

Breathe.

I am gulping for air at this point.

I will the stupid flames away, and they vanish, leaving me shaking and shuddering for air.

Running my hands through my hair, I look around for damage.

The top blanket is sooty with ashes.

I rip it off, throw it to the ground, and begin pacing.

Anxiety and panic are coursing through me, along with that unseeingly burn taunting me to use the flames.

I can't do this. I am going to hurt someone. I am going to hurt myself.

"I should've slit your throat when I had the chance."

I throw up in the trash bin next to my bed.

Gods, I am a mess.

I need to go get Celeste.

I grab my robe from the hook on the door and head out. There are two Scouts next to my door.

"I just need to get Celeste…" I say as I look at them. "You may stay here and watch me. No need to follow."

Both look at each other as if contemplating my order, but then they nod.

I walk barefoot down the hall to the door on the right. Hugging my arms tight around my still-shaking body, I knock.

No answer.

Maybe she can't hear me?

The door is unlocked as I turn the knob.

I peek my head in.

"Celeste..?"

I see Celeste on her bed.

Arched over a male, hair draped over her shoulders and completely naked aside from a thin sheet draped over her backside.

Shit.

Both look in my direction.

I am frozen in place, eyes wide.

"Ryenn?" Celeste rasps.

I recognize the male; it is Ser Arry, the Scout Sergeant from the other day.

"Shit, I am so sorry" I go to close the door, and another Fae pops up from beside the male. A female. Her hair is the color of a rich red wine, and her gaze shifts from me to Celeste and then to Arry.

Oh Gods, this is bad.

I close the door swiftly before Celeste can get up from whatever position she's in and scurry back down the hall to my room, my face red. The Scouts straighten as they see me coming, clearly flustered.

"Everything alright, princess?" one of them says.

"Yep, all good." I shut my door in his face.

I was shaking even more now. Gods, why did I have to interrupt that? Celeste was going to hate me. I couldn't calm my nerves even slightly.

A soft knock sounds on the door.

"Ryenn, may I come in?" I hear in a soft voice. Celeste's soft voice.

I don't answer because I can hardly form words.

She lets herself in.

She is wearing a cream-colored silk robe, and her golden hair is still down her back. A rosy shade is across the bridge of her nose. She notices me shaking like a leaf sitting on my bed.

"What's wrong, honey?" she comes over and sits next to me.

"I am so sorry." Tears start to blur my vision.

"Oh, don't apologize, dear. I am sorry you had to see what you just did," a nervous laugh escapes her. "But I told you you could come to get me anytime."

I look at her, and she wraps her arms around me.

"You're shaking Ryenn. What happened? It's okay. You can tell me."

I will myself to speak as I breathe in her familiar perfume.

"The stupid nightmare. It changed, though, and I woke up and couldn't breathe." I gasp on my words. "There was fire up my arms, and I ruined a blanket. I also got sick. I know it isn't real, but it really scared me. Gods, I am being so childish right now."

She shushes me, rubbing my back. "You're not being childish. The nightmares may not be real, but the feelings that accompany them are. It's okay."

"I just couldn't be alone. I'm sorry, I didn't know you had… company. I knocked, but you mustn't have heard me."

"It's okay, I really don't care. We were finishing up anyways." She pulls away from me and wipes a tear from my cheek. That statement makes me blush.

"I've told you before sexuality is normal. What you saw is not something I am ashamed of. It does, however, have to remain a secret due to my position as the Queen married to the King, okay? I am not mad at you, sweetheart. Arry and Jess are not mad either, and they were worried about you."

Jess?

I wasn't sure who she was, but now was not the time to hound her with questions regarding those events.

I was still shaking.

"I took some of the medicine for sleep that Sara had left me. It must have caused the nightmare." I point to the bottle, and Celeste clenches her teeth.

"Yeah, that'll put you in a pretty deep sleep. It has nightshade fragments in it, so it puts the consciousness at ease, which occasionally causes weird dreams or nightmares. I know from experience."

She was smoothing my back. Heat still courses through me.

"Take some deep breaths with me," she says.

I follow her chest, rise, hold and fall. We do this multiple times until the tremors cease, and I am able to stand. Celeste gets rid of the blanket that was burned, and I take care of the vomit. Which nearly makes me vomit again.

When I came out, she was lying on the bed, under the new covers she found.

"You don't have to stay…" The truth was I really wanted her to, but I didn't want to take her away from her activities.

"I know I don't have to, but I am. Come. You need to go to sleep. Tomorrow is a big day, and I know that is why you are so stressed, even though you have been taking it like a champ lately. It's okay to admit it and be vulnerable when needed, dear."

I climb into the bed and curl up next to Celeste. She draws calming circles around my back, lulling me to sleep, although I fight against it in fear of what may await me if I close my eyes.

"I'm right here, Ryenn. You aren't alone. Shut your eyes and sleep."

Chapter 33

I woke in the early morning, the sun just now creeping through the open curtains. Celeste had remained, and my head was currently in her lap. I looked up at her face. She was also awake.

"Good morning," she says softly.

I blink away the blurriness of sleep. I didn't dream at all afterward. It was probably only two hours of sleep, but I felt Better. Alive again. Gods, last night felt like the moments right after the attack. My chest still aches from the lasting effects of panic. Then I remember what I found Celeste doing, and embarrassment envelops me whole.

She furrows her brows as she looks at me.

"Why are you embarrassed, child?"

Shit, I forgot she could sense some emotions.

"I just feel bad. About last night."

"What have I told you?"

"That I shouldn't feel bad."

"Exactly."

Her hair is in loose waves down her chest, which makes her look young. Gods, what I wouldn't give to look remotely like her.

I decided to try and lighten the conversation a bit to hopefully dig my way out of the pit I felt.

"So, who's Jess?" I grin.

This causes her face to erupt in red, and I sit up to face her.

"Come on! You told me I could ask you any questions…"

"Yes, well, I didn't think it would involve my sex life, to be fair," she says, rolling her eyes.

"But I have many questions regarding… *that* in general."

"I feel like you're too young to be having this conversation with."

"Not like it hasn't already happened to me," I say before really thinking. Her face goes stone cold.

"No. Ryenn, what happened to you was not at all like sex. You were attacked. It was non-consensual, and there was no pleasure derived from it on your part. It was an act of brutality. Okay? Never *ever* think that again."

There's a pause, but I nod. She was right. What happened to me was not at all like what I read about in the books Amalie brought to me. Those scenes were filled with lust and love.

"I suppose you are 16, though, so… what do you want to ask me?"

"Well, first, I'd like to know who Jess is," I grin. "I won't tell anyone, Celeste, I *promise*."

"Fine," she sighs and begins twirling her hair. I prop myself up on my elbow to listen. "Jess is an old friend of mine. She's a high Fae from Carlisle, and we met some time ago. She comes to any ball she can and every time we meet up. I've always liked the company of both men and women, which is common in the kingdom but not something there is much talk of among royalty and such".

"Anyway, I already told you about Ser Arry and that there is some history there. I met both of them outside of the dining hall after dinner. Arry was keeping guard as usual, but his shift had just finished. Jess had just arrived and was heading to her room. Anyway, somehow, we ended up back in my room, and things escalated. As they usually have between myself and the other two."

Now I was really blushing.

This was… scandalous. Maybe I am too young to be hearing this? No, because if I was too young, then why did I feel this way about Braxton?

"How do you- how do you… do it?" I ask sheepishly.

"Depends on the person involved," she answers simply. "That's for you and whoever you end up with to determine as the event takes place. It's pretty much instinctual. That's something you'll either have to figure out on your own. Gods, I'm not sure how your mother would feel about me telling you any of this." She rubs her brows.

"How old were you when you first… did it?"

"Sixteen. It doesn't have to be, though, and you should only do it when you are truly ready. I regret a lot of things, and doing that at sixteen is one of them. Your mother was eighteen. Jess, however, I believe, was twenty three, and I was her first. It's different for everyone, okay?"

I look away.

"Ryenn, can you promise me something though?" She asks, and I nod. "Let me know when it happens, okay? You'll need a form of contraceptive to prevent pregnancy. Well, that's if it's with a male. If you're attracted to females, then it doesn't matter. I don't have to worry about it because I cannot bear children anyways, but still, it's better to be safe than sorry."

"*That's* how babies are made?" I ask. Why hadn't I realized this before? My Gods, I may truly be stupid.

Celeste laughs lightly. "Yes. It's much easier if you're a mortal, but still, it does happen to Fae, obviously."

I looked out the window to the sun cresting the hills of the city.

"We should probably get up now," I sigh.

"Yes, you're right. I'm going to head back, make sure my company has left and begin to get ready for the day. Next time I have visitors, I'll tie a scarf to the door handle, okay?"

I laugh but nod. "Okay, sounds good."

"Evie will be bringing your dress shortly. See you soon, okay? If you need anything, just come down to my chambers."

"Thanks again, Celeste."

"Don't worry about it, love. It's okay."

~

Evie had brought some of her friends with her to help in getting me ready for the ball. My nerves had calmed down since last night, but the handmaidens were buzzing around my room like bees. I had bathed then they had waxed and plucked just about every inch of my body. The sting hurt but kept my mind from drifting. Evie was now starting with my hair when another handmaiden came in with the dress I ordered.

Grinning from ear to ear, the young Fae females opens the dress and hangs it on the hook outside of my wardrobe. All the handmaidens ooh and ahh...

"That is such a pretty dress, Princess," Evie says. "You're going to look so beautiful."

I grin, my canines peeking through my lips as I glance at my reflection. I was pretty excited, not going to lie. This was the first time I ever had a dress like this. I know it's foolish and girly, but I don't care.

After pinning back curls so that my hair is half in a braided crown and half in loose pin curls, it looks really nice. Evie truly outdid herself. There are about a million pins holding it together, but I'd bear through it. The hairstyle she chose would fit perfectly once the tiara had been placed as well, which is probably why she decided on it. I let the five of the handmaidens do what they pleased and saw fit. I certainly didn't know what looked good and what didn't, but they were trained to serve royalty and such, so they had to know a thing or two about style.

"I think you should put the dress on prior to finishing up cosmetics," Evie states. "It'll be less likely to ruin the look, plus we can see the colors and match them well."

I nod, eating the triangle of a sandwich that had been brought to me for lunch. The ball was to begin in three hours, and there would be food then, but I was actually hungry, and this had been sent to tie me over.

Standing up, I step into my dress as two of the girls hold it on either side. It snags at my waist.

"Hold on, let me loosen the corset," one of them says.

She does just that, and I manage to get it up all the way, but it is clearly far too small. And too short.

Shit, I had been sized before I transitioned.

Had I really changed that much?

"Shit," I mumble, still chewing my sandwich.

Embarrassment threatens, but I actually find it kind of funny. I'm also a little proud of myself, if I'm truly being honest. But now I had nothing to fucking wear.

"Ryenn, you were sized before you transitioned." Evie's eyes were wide, and her mouth gaping. "What are we going to do?!"

"I have no clue," I swallow. "Can… Can you go get Celeste? I hate to interrupt her, but maybe she can… fix it. Or maybe she has something I can fit into? Gods Evie, I can't show up in *this*."

Now, the panic was actually starting to set in. What if this was just an omen that I shouldn't go? I'm going to make a fool of myself while doing the display of flames, so I might as well look like a fool wearing a dress that's too tight and too short.

"Okay," Evie breathes. "Okay, just stay here. I'll go get her." She leaves swiftly through the door.

Two of the other girls are attempting to fix the back of the corset as if they'll fit me, while the other two are going through my wardrobe, looking for something remotely sensible.

Not even five minutes later, Celeste and Evie walk through the door. Celeste must have been in the middle of getting her cosmetics done because she's in her silk robe, her makeup unfinished, and hair in rolls.

She covers her mouth when she walks in.

"Shit," she mutters, and I hear her stifling a laugh.

"Celeste, this is so not funny right now," tears well in my eyes. I must be dramatic due to being overwhelmed or something because this is just plain foolishness.

"Oh, Ryenn, I know," she giggles. "You just remind me of your mom. The same exact thing happened to her when she became pregnant with you. Her dress was too small because her belly had grown. Then she started screeching because her pregnant hormones were making her emotional, which caused her eye makeup to run down her face."

I try to hide my smile.

"Gods, we were late and everything that Ball…" Her smile turns to a frown as I see her contemplating.

That had been my mother's last ball before she died.

I stripped my dress off, not being able to bear the sadness of seeing such a beautiful thing that didn't even fit me.

"Wait, I have an idea," she says and leaves quickly, leaving me dumbfounded.

Five minutes later, she returns, a wicked grin on her face.

"This was her dress. The one that didn't fit her. It's a sage green, so it goes with the pastels theme. It's also a corset-styled top, so if it's a bit too large, we can size it in or hem it a bit. She was a bit taller and bustier, but that should be an easy fix."

She takes a light green dress from the bag. Two handmaids assist me to get into it and have me stand looking away from the body-length mirror so they can get it to look just right. They steam it and pin it, tie it and fluff it. All five of them are swarming around me, and my heart is beating a bit too hard. Finally, they finish, and I turn to the mirror.

The dress I'm wearing is stunning. It's a soft sage green that is off the shoulders with balloon-styled sleeves. The cut of the top goes gently over the curves of my small breasts, leaving the entirety of my clavicle utterly exposed. The corset part of the top has silver detailing through it, outlining light details of ivy leaves. It cuts differently at my hip, causing it to flow out gently. The material is lightweight and soft. When I turn to observe the back, the lacing looks symmetrical and gorgeous with silver accents. The way the dress is shaped gives me a slight hourglass shape, making me feel mature and pretty. I look at Celeste, who has been sitting in the bed, watching the entire time.

Tears roll down her face, black and purple smudges of her

eye makeup follow.

"Celeste, your makeup!"

"Oh shoot," she dabs her eye with tissues that a handmaiden hands her. "Oh, I don't care. Gods, you look just like her. It's beautiful, Ryenn, honey. You're beautiful. I am so *so* proud."

I smile, feeling emotions knotting in the back of my throat.

"Stop, or I'll cry, and then Evie will get mad at all her hard work wasted."

"It's true," Evie grins, although I notice the handmaiden's eyes are glistening with tears, too.

Celeste stands and gives me a hug, inhaling deeply.

"Thank you," I say, my words muffled by her chest. I may have gotten taller, but Celeste still had a good head on me.

"It was meant for you. Your mother would be so proud. I must get back now before Marisa kills me for messing up my makeup."

"I'll see you later?" I ask her quietly.

"We can walk over together," she winks and leaves.

~

After another hour or two, my makeup is finally finished. It's light and pretty, highlighting my features. Silver sparkles spread across my eyelids, light pink gloss coats my lips, and a light pink blusher is spread across my freckled cheeks. My eyelashes are also curled with some blackener, which makes the silver of my irises pop out even more.

I decided to go with a pair of flat shoes instead of heels because I still haven't mastered the art of walking in them despite the lessons I have had with Celeste. You can't even see my shoes, though, because of the floor-length dress.

I stand and size myself up in the mirror. As stupid as it sounds, I feel pretty, which gives me some confidence for this evening. I am a princess. I am heir to the Emerald Throne. The next Queen of Sanctania. The first descendant in a millennium of the Drakōn Flame. And I am going to show the citizens that I belong here just as much as anyone else.

~

I sit on my bed, waiting for a knock on the door to retrieve me for the ball. Looking out the window, the gardens and courtyard are beginning to fill with pastel-colored Fae beginning to arrive. I decide to let off some steam and practice summoning and suffocating while I wait. All the handmaidens have left, besides Evie, who was still cleaning up the remnants of this morning's chaos. She picks up the purple dress and zips it into the dress bag. I suppose I will save it for when Pippa is able to fit into it in a few years.

The fire comes and goes easily. I hardly have to think about it anymore, honestly, and I don't know if that makes me feel good or nervous. I let the silvery flames dance. Evie stops and watches me.

"It's pretty," she says, her attention still on the flames.

"Thank you," I say and make them vanish. "Deadly, too, unfortunately."

"I do not think you'll use them that way unless necessary, princess." She smiles and leaves with some laundry.

Unless necessary?

What did she mean by that?

When would it ever be necessary for me to use it for deadly reasons?

Celeste and Emmet arrive at the door mere seconds later, shoving me out of those thoughts.

Celeste is wearing a pastel yellow dress. It scoops deep across her breasts and has thin straps. There are little white flowers stitched to the piping, and the same white flowers braided into her golden-blonde hair. Her crown sits atop her head, which she holds high. Emmet is wearing a matching colored shirt to that of Celeste.

It's more relaxed than his usual high-collared tunics, and the light yellow looks pretty against his sun-kissed skin. His tailored slacks are a cream-white color. His crown also sits upon his slicked-back caramel-brown hair. He almost looks out of his element with the light colors, considering the only thing I have ever really seen him wearing would be black or the emerald green of the kingdom.

"My Gods, that's the dress, isn't it?" Emmet's eyes go wide, and he smiles. "The one Ela had a meltdown over?" He was laughing so hard he nearly bent over.

Celeste and I laughed along with him.

"That's the one," she smiled.

"Well, now I can kind of understand why she was so distraught. It is quite stunning."

His compliment warms me in a good kind of way. Both hold out their hands, and I walk to them. Linking arms with them and walking in between them, we walk out of my bed chambers and into the central portion of the castle, which has turned into a swarm of Fae within the last day.

Chapter 34

The beginning of the ball is to start in the Throne room. The windows have been opened and curtains removed so that people outside in the courtyard will be able to see the commencement as well. The throne room looks quite different from the last time I had been in here, during the trial. There are hundreds and hundreds of Fae in beautiful attire, and floral arrangements are everywhere. It is beautiful, and I have a hard time finding words as I take it all in. The sun was also just now beginning to dull a bit, causing a golden hue to spread across the entire room and castle.

Celeste had explained along the way that the small Transitioning Ceremony would be the first thing to occur, and then the ball would commence. There would be music everywhere, live bands, and also different foods and other festivities scattered about the castle and its grounds.

The three of us made our way through the thick cowed, a path broken for us by scouts leading the way to the steps of the thrones. I was nervous, and my stomach swirled in distaste. I also had a clammy sweat coating my palms as fire pulsed in my veins, chomping at the bit for my performance. The heat of the early summer night was also warm in general, causing stuffiness in the air despite the open windows.

We made our way up the steps and sat on our thrones. I was

sat next to Celeste. Apparently, it is custom that we sit to the right of the King. There were many eyes on us, causing the flutter to make its way to my chest and hitching my breathing.

Turn it off.

You belong here. You can do this.

Celeste turned and looked at me and whispered, "Just block them out. Pretend they aren't really there. You can do this. You're gonna do great."

I nod and smile back at her. I couldn't speak. It would be impossible to pretend there wasn't a sea of Fae, most of whom probably did not like me or last saw me during the trial, looking at me with judging eyes. But I will do my best. I decided to try and pick out some faces that I do know instead.

I quickly spot Amalie, dressed in a beautiful pastel pink dress with pink flowers adorning it, standing close to the steps with who I assume to be her date that her parents forced her to go with. He's kind of hard to look at and looks utterly unimpressed by the whole thing.

Towards the south wall, I see the other three girls, Autumn, Hanna and Luna, giggling with each other. They are wearing purple, pink and blue. Grey stands close to the girls, and as I am watching, Autumn links her arm through his. Heat rises to my face as I watch this for some reason. I thought they broke up. Wait, why do I care what he does?

Tearing my eyes away, I see Braxton at the east wall. He is wearing a light orange pair of slacks and a white top. I actually catch his stare, and he smiles at me. I look away before the blush on my face becomes too noticeable. Butterflies flapped around my stomach. As I look away, my attention goes towards the main door of the throne room. Ser Arry is there, adorned in his sergeant outfit. I glance at Celeste and see that her stare is in the same direction that mine was, causing me to grin.

My thoughts cease as the King rises from his throne, and the room immediately goes silent.

It's go time.

"Citizens of Sanctania," he starts, his voice booming. "It is my pleasure as King to welcome you to our annual Summer Ball." The crowd claps in response.

"To begin our Ball, we first have an order of business to address. As many of you are aware, my niece, Princess Ryenn Embers, is the rightful Heir to the Emerald Throne." He looks at me, smiling, and I attempt to smile back. "It is a tradition that once the Heir completes their Transitioning, they receive a temporary crown of the kingdom as a means to a promise of the ruling, and that they also give a demonstration of the powers they have been blessed with."

He lets the crowd breathe for a second, and the wave of silence washes over me, making me slightly uneasy. I have to do this. I'll show them my flames, and then we will move on and enjoy the evening.

"Ryenn, please rise," I do as he says and walk to the front of the dais.

Off to the side, Ser Davis brings the tiara on a cushion. It is similar to the one Celeste wears but does not have the complete fullness of a crown. It is more meant to be pinned into the hair instead of just laying on the top of the head. Emmet takes the crown into his hands and holds it, beginning his speech.

I kneel in front of him as previously told to me by Celeste.

"Ryenn Embers, do you promise to have the kingdom's best interest at heart and to continue your studies so that, on your 21st birthday, you may take the throne and serve the Kingdom?"

"I do," I say surprisingly easily, in the voice Celeste had once taught me.

"Do you promise to use the powers you have been blessed with in only good fate and for the bettering of the kingdom?"

"I do," I say with the same confidence. The spice of the flames returns to my veins.

Emmet places the tiara gently on my head and pins it to my hair.

"You may rise."

I do as he says and turn towards the crowd of Fae. Their faces are blurry due to my nerves. Despite this, I remain steady and lift my hands to the front of me.

"Please show the kingdom your powers."

Without a second thought, the Drakōn Flames rise from the palms of my outstretched hands.

~

The silver blaze laps and dances through my fingertips. The heat from my veins cools, and I become more comfortable as they are controlled with ease. Smiling, I move my hands to my side, still outstretched and let the flames grow slightly larger, still dancing lightly. I look up and see the crowd's reaction.

Many people have slack jaws. Some are muttering to their neighbor, and some gasp.

The King, smiling as he watches me confidently control the flames before him, speaks again.

"Ryenn is the first descendant of the Drakōn Flame in over a millennium. She is an incredibly powerful Fae. She will use the flames for the Kingdom's best interest and already has great control over her abilities. We are blessed to be the presence of this sort of magic."

The crowd is still silent.

Worry settles in my chest, and I vanish the flames from my grasp.

They see right through me. Directly through the facade I've put up. They think I am going to be evil like my ancestor with the same flames before me-

Then I hear clapping.

I look down and see Amalie has started clapping and hollering like a crazy person.

Soon after, the other Fae begin to join, and then the entire throne room erupts in claps and cheers. Emotions threaten my ability to swallow.

They weren't scared?

I look to Emmet and then to Celeste.

Both are smiling and clapping along with the rest of the crowd.

I smile, bow and then take my seat on my throne, holding my head high, taking a shuddery relief of a breath.

Chapter 35

The King proceeded to thank the citizens again and then dismissed everyone to enjoy the evening.

The whole thing only took about fifteen minutes to complete, but it felt good to have it over with. Especially given the reactions, I was worried for a second, but it seemed as though the majority were accepting.

"Go enjoy yourself, Ryenn, honey. We aren't meant to stay on the thrones all night. Emmet and I will head down in a minute." Celeste turns in her throne and says to me.

"Okay. Have a good night," I say back.

"If you need anything, there are Scouts everywhere, or you can come find me, okay?"

"Okay," I grin and walk down the steps to the rest of the festivities.

Amalie is still waiting at the bottom of the steps for me, her date not paying attention and looking bored.

She grabs me before I even make it off the last step.

"Oh my Gods, you did so good, Ry! You look like a fucking Queen. I'm dead. You're so beautiful," she rambled while squeezing me.

"Says you! You look like a Goddess, Amy, truly." We pull apart from each other.

"I'm going to find a table," the date says and leaves us.

"Gods, he is the most boring Fae in this entire kingdom," she rolls her eyes. "My parents will kill me if I don't spend the entire godsdamn evening with him, though." She looks around, assuming to see if her parents are watching. "I can't hang out for long, but I just wanted to tell you that you're a badass, and Braxton is definitely reeling right now."

I laugh. "You're too funny. Have a good night, Amy. I wanna hear all about it tomorrow, okay?"

"Yes, you too, Ry. Love you," she says and squeezes my hands.

"Love you too."

With that, she turns to find her date.

Now, what do I do?

I decided to walk around the crowd a bit and look at all the flower arrangements up close. Peonies, poppies, lilies, snapdragons and so many more bouquets are scattered about it in carefully planned out systems. It's gorgeous. Celeste really outdid herself with the planning.

As I walk around, Fae, whom I have never met before,

congratulates me and some even bow. It's weird, and I just know my face is so red right now.

The live music plays beautiful light tunes, and some Fae are dancing in the centre of the room. I stand by and watch with awe. They move effortlessly. Some dance with partners, and some dance alone or with a group of friends. As I watch the enthralling dancing and listen to the calming tunes, I feel a tap on my shoulder. I turn quickly, a bit too quickly, as I almost topple over from my dress, getting caught around my legs.

"Careful there, Princess." Braxton catches me before I trip. "Didn't mean to startle you."

I smile, hoping it was going to be him. Gods, he looks so beautiful in the orange sunset that has deepened in the last hour to near dusk.

"You didn't startle me. I was just entranced with the dancers. They look so pretty," I said, glancing back out at the floor. More people have since joined them.

"Well, would you like to join them?" He asks, smiling and taking my hand in his hand.

"Oh, I don't know," I bit my lip. "I think I will look silly."

"Nonsense. You just have to follow my lead. You wouldn't look silly anyway. You look perfect."

My eyes widen, and the aching swirl returns to the warmth of my belly. Smiling, I decided to give it a chance.

"Alright then. Lead the way."

~

We made our way to the dance floor and waited for the next song to play. A slow, sultry-styled song and enticed many more Fae and their partners to join us. I hardly noticed anyone else, though. I didn't have a single clue where Celeste and Emmet went or where Amalie and her date were because my attention was solely focused on the gorgeous Fae currently leading me gently through the crowd by the hand.

Turning and taking both my hands in his, I look into his amber-hued eyes.

"I'll put my hands here," he proceeds to place them on my waist gently. "You put yours here," and then he places my hands on his shoulders. "Now we just feel the music and move to the beat. I'll lead. All you have to do is follow, okay? Simple."

"I feel like you're lying about the simple part, but I'll trust you," I decided to say.

The music starts up, and he begins to move.

As he said, I follow his lead.

Throughout the entire song, I am smiling. Gods, this just

feels so good right now. I didn't care about anyone else in the world. All I cared about was this perfect moment right here, right now.

We continue to dance through a few more songs, and our bodies end up drifting closer, and his hands lower slightly, resting right above the curve of my ass.

The butterflies swarm quickly in my belly, and the tight ache returns. It doesn't hurt; it just feels… different. Not in a bad way, though, I suppose.

After three songs, I began to get short of breath. Dancing is apparently a good cardio workout, and I am exhausted. Seeing my progressive struggle. Braxton stops moving so much, and we dance slowly, hardly moving, just swaying.

"I just want to tell you that your powers are really cool. I think you're going to be incredibly powerful. You already have the strength before you even transitioned, and I think the powers bestowed to you reflect that."

That statement hits me right in the chest. It was sweet. It made me feel… good. I know Amalie and Celeste, and everyone has said nothing but encouraging things, but hearing it come from Braxton's mouth just hits differently for some reason. I can't even respond to it as emotion knots in the back of my throat. He leans in closer. My Gods, is he going to kiss me?

"I need a break… or a drink," he whispers in my ear. "I'll see you later, okay? Here, let me lead you back to the sidelines."

Stunned a bit, I nod, and he eases his way through the dancing crowd.

"I think your friend wants to talk to you, by the way…" he states and motions his head to a table near the wall. Amalie is turned completely around in her chair and gaping at me with wide eyes. Oh my Gods.

"Thank you," I say to Braxton before he leaves. "I had fun."

"Me too, princess," he kisses my hand that he holds and leaves.

Heat crawls all the way from my toes to my face. It makes me feel a little sick to my stomach, actually. I stand there for a minute, forgetting that Amalie is nearly falling out of her seat, trying to get my attention.

I walk over to her with a silly grin.

"Holy fucking shit Ryenn Embers that was so hot," She yell-whispers as I get close.

"Oh my Gods, stop," I blush and laugh.

"Your night is going so much better than mine," she pouts.

"Where is your date, by the way?" I notice she is sitting alone.

"I keep sending him to get me drinks to keep him busy so I don't have to try and make small talk with him." She rolls her eyes and sips from a pink-fruity-smelling drink.

"Is that alcoholic, Amalie?" I narrow my eyes at her.

"I think so actually because I feel a little silly if I am being honest... oops," she giggles. "Well, I guess I didn't specify what *kind* of drink to get me..." She nearly tips off the chair.

"My Gods, how many have you had?!"

"This is my third... wait, no fourth? I don't know. Try it, though it tastes like summer," she smiles wildly.

"Your parents are going to kill you." I frown, causing her face to be pale.

"Fuck you are so right."

"Just don't drink anything else, okay? Eat some food and drink water. Only water."

"Okay, Ry Ry. I want you to stay." She pouts her bottom lip out.

"You know I can't interfere with your date, or your parents will hate me even more than they do already..." I look over my shoulder, feeling a stare on my back. Lord Seredi sips from a glass of wine. "Speaking of, I should actually get going. When he gets back, do not drink anything else, got it? I'll check on you in a couple of hours, but behave until then."

"Okayyyy," she grins.

I walk away hastily as her boring date gets back to the table. I hate to leave her there, but what I said was true: I didn't want Amalie's parents to dislike me as much as they clearly already do. Plus, they were serious when it came to finding Amalie the perfect Fae to be a lord, and that was something I did not want to interfere with.

Chapter 36

The night progresses and the sun has fully set. The candles and chandeliers light up the space beautifully. The castle is still stuffy with humid heat, but the vibes are calming in a way. I spent the last hour or so wandering around, looking at the different floral arrangements and listening to the different styles of bands playing. Fae still came up to me, congratulating me, which I was getting better at receiving without blushing. There were a scattered few who would stare with distaste or turn in the opposite direction when they saw me coming, though, and it stung a little.

I was now picking at the dessert table in the Main Dining Hall, which had been transformed into a floral masterpiece with dozens of tables of drinks and foods spread about. I pick up a cream puff and eat it, trying not to get messy.

"Hi," I hear from a voice behind me.

I turn and am met with a tall Fae woman, wearing a light purple, nearly white dress. Her wine-red hair is tied into a low sort-of knot with braids weaving through it. Her green, nearly lime-yellow eyes are piercing, and she wears heavy eyeliner, making her look feline-like.

It was Jess. Celeste's… companion from last night.

"Oh," I say, swallowing the rest of my cream puff, "Hello,"

I grin, blushing. Gods, why did my face always have to betray me?

She smiles. "I just wanted to introduce myself. I'm Jessibria, everyone calls me Jess though. We haven't been… formally introduced. I saw you last night though". Her voice is beautiful. In a raspy but feminine sort-of way.

"Yes, er, Celeste told me about you. It's nice to finally meet you." I attempt to smile but it comes out wobbly.

"It's nice to meet you too, Ryenn. Do you mind if I-" she doesn't finish before taking her thumb, which is adorned by long white nails, and runs it across my lip, a bit of cream puff filling wiping off. "Sorry. Wouldn't want you going around with whipped cream on your lip," she laughs, and I am sure I turn as red as her hair.

"Anyways, I just wanted to introduce myself and tell you that I think you're pretty cool. The Drakōn flame is gorgeous, and you did a really good job at controlling it tonight," she smiles.

"Thank you," I smile back. She doesn't turn away, though, and continues to look me over until she catches my eyes.

"Sorry. I knew your mom pretty well. I am sure you've heard you look much like her."

"I have. Were you two friends?"

"Yes, not as close as Celeste and her, but we all went to

schooling together. I was a good few years younger than them; my sister, Lady Juniper of Carlisle, was Ela's age and I was three years younger than her. Your mom was always very kind to me, though. I was a bit of a late bloomer and nerdy, but she always stood up for me when the boys would poke fun. I did some of her tattoos when we were older as well." I had noticed the female's arms had been inked with various images. She was a tattoo artist. *Interesting*. Tattoos weren't as common in Molisan, only fishermen had them, and they definitely weren't as pretty as the art covering her arms.

"That's cool," I say, smiling. I liked Jess, she seemed like she was an easy person to talk to. And she was quite pretty. Two reasons why Celeste probably liked her too. I blush again.

She smiles. "Celeste also told me you embarrassed as easily as Ela did too," she laughs. "Anyways, sweetheart, if you ever need anything, let me know, okay? I am in the capital occasionally for tattoos, but I am always travelling the kingdom for the same reason."

"Thanks, Jess. That's nice of you."

"Don't mention it, love. You look great, by the way. Super hot," she winks and leaves me standing by the cream puffs.

~

Walking down one of the corridors, I observed some of the paintings hung. I hadn't really paid much attention to any of them before, if I am being honest, but I guess I just haven't really had the chance to. At the end of the corridor, I walk upon a painting of who I immediately recognize as my mother. We do look alike. Eerily similar, actually. The main differences being that she obviously looks more mature than me, her hair is slightly darker brown, her eyes are emerald green, and her face looks… *kinder*. I'm not sure if that makes much sense, but it's true. She seems like the type of person you could tell anything to. A pang of sadness ripples through me. It hadn't really bothered me before, but I hadn't even gotten to meet her. Everyone always talks about how great she was, and that opportunity was ripped away from me mere seconds after I had been born. I wouldn't have had Rose and Mother and Father, though, if things had been different. But I didn't have them now anyways, so did it really matter?

I am drawn away from my sorrowful thoughts with the sounds of moans coming from around the corner. Confused, I walk around the corner of the corridor. What I see feels like a stab right through the heart.

There are two Fae, deeply enthralled with one another and kissing passionately against the wall. The female is on the outside, wearing an icy blue dress and has long blonde hair down her back, with her leg wrapped around the male, who is pinned against the wall with his hands grabbing her by the ass. The male is wearing light orange pants and a cream top. It's Braxton.

Braxton was the one making out with the pretty blonde and moaning deeply as he enjoyed every aspect of her touch. Bile started to rise in my throat, and I continued walking before any of them could open their eyes and see me there.

How could I be so godsdamned stupid?

He didn't like me. I had gotten my hopes up for no reason. Why would anyone like me anyways?

Gods, I am such an *idiot*.

I march outside the front castle doors to get some air. My skin was burning and aching. Tears stung my eyes. *No.* I am not going to cry over a boy. A boy that didn't even have feelings for me. One that I had a lot of feelings for, but it didn't fucking matter now, did it?

I flopped onto a stair, sitting next to the railing, and looking at my hands. In three, hold three, out three. Repeat. I needed to calm down. There's no need to get emotional. Had the dancing and riding lessons not meant more to him? He called me pretty, multiple times. Clearly, I wasn't as pretty as the female currently wrapped around his waist. You know what? Good for him. At least one of us is having fun. I don't even know why I bothered wasting my time thinking about the possibility between us. He was four years older than me, probably still thought of me as a child.

Stupid

Stupid

Stupid

I bury my face in my hands and drag them down. I need to blow off some steam before I burst into a ball of silver flames.

"Hey."

I nearly jump off the step as someone sits next to me. It's Greyson.

Sucking in a too-short breath and clasping my hand across my chest to still my frantic heart, I say, "You *scared* me."

His face pales a bit. "I'm sorry that wasn't my intent."

In for three, hold for three, out for three. Turn it off. *Better*.

"I saw you sitting out here, and I came out for a breath of air. If you would like me to leave, you can say so," he says in his deep, yet somewhat calming, voice.

"No, it's okay. I was also getting a breath of air, so you're welcome to join me," I grin, and he grins back.

We sat there in silence for a few moments. The quiet was deafening and awkward for some reason. My powers thrummed through my veins, itching for me to release them.

"I liked your display earlier, by the way. Fire powers are

sick," he says all of a sudden.

"Oh, thanks…" Why was he out here right now? Where is Autumn?

"Where's Autumn?" The question comes out boldly and before I can stop myself.

"Don't know and don't really care." He rolls his eyes.

"You don't sound impressed…" Why am I entertaining this conversation?

"I'm not sure why I agreed to be her date tonight. We have been a thing for a bit, sure, but the last little while she's been… anyways, it doesn't matter. My mother and her mother are in town, so I guess we just went along with the original plan for this evening, but I needed a break from the pretending."

A weird sensation washes over me, but I continue talking anyways, maybe to try and calm the burn I feel.

"Fair enough. What district are you from?" I decided to ask. I hardly know anything about Grey. I mean, he usually keeps to himself, and I just never really thought to ask.

"Carlisle," he states.

Oh my Gods, that meant Jess was his *aunt*. And Lady Juniper was his mother. The woman who stood up for me at the trial was Greyson's mom. I laugh, much louder than I intended.

"What?" He gives me a confused expression.

Now that I look at him, he does look a bit like Jess. The eyes are a very similar greenish-lime, and his skin is the same hue of golden tan. His hair is not red, though; it's a deep, rich brown, nearly black.

"Sorry, nothing," I say, a blush creeping to my face now that I realize I've been staring at this guy's eyes for Gods know how long.

The flames are agonizing. Why am I struggling so hard to keep them away right now? I grind my teeth.

"You okay?" He asks, looking genuinely concerned.

"Mhmm," I manage to mutter through a clenched jaw.

"Wanna go for a walk?" He asks next. The gesture is nice, but it also makes me a tad nervous. There *were* Scouts everywhere, though, so it's not like we'd be alone. Plus, I could burn off some energy.

"Sure," I decide.

He stands and holds out a hand to help me up. I take it, although I made it known that I didn't need it.

We make our way through the paths leading around the castle grounds. We walk past different musicians and some art and food. The entire time, we walk in silence, side by side. Mere inches from each other. We make it close to the north side of the castle, where the gardens are located. There are far fewer people in this area, hardly any, if I'm being honest. I guess no one needs to go to the gardens when the gardens are brought everywhere else.

Heat bounds in my body, and I groan.

"You can let it out if you need to," Greyson states as we come to a shortstop.

"What?" I say, looking up at him.

"Your powers. I know that's why you're in pain. You need to let off some steam. Go for it. There's no one around and I'm not gonna judge if that's what you're worried about."

"I don't think it's a good idea."

"Why not?"

"I just… I don't know. I'm afraid once I start, I won't be able to stop, and I've only been practicing for a week."

"You stopped tonight," he says. It's true I did, but I didn't feel the immense pressure behind them as I do right now.

"What if I hurt you?" I furrow my brows.

"You won't," he smiles, showing the peak of his canines, which makes the swirl of aching course through my belly again. He's quite handsome in the moonlit path.

Crackles of lavender-colored light spring to his fingertips. *Electricity*.

"You have electricity powers?!" I gawk at the lightning dancing up his hands and arms. It looks similar to my flames in a sort of sharper and sporadic way.

"Yep. Runs in the family. Lots of electricity Fae come from Carlisle actually." He makes the purple lights vanish, "You're turn."

"I'm not sure that's a good idea..."

"I never pegged you for the scared type," he teases.

"I'm not *scared* asshole," the flames burst into my hands in tall mounds. I immediately feel a sense of relief and cooling in my body.

"There ya go frisky." He still smiles and doesn't back away an inch, "Feel a bit better now?"

"Yes. And I am not *frisky*. I just don't like people telling me what to do," I glare.

"Sure."

The silver fire runs up my arms and circles calmingly through the bases of my fingers. I suffocate them with ease once I feel the pressure that has clamped on my chest ease a little.

"Thank you," I smile at Grey. He hasn't taken his eyes off of me.

"Don't mention it Frisky," I frown at the pet name. Before I can retort though water starts to shoot up from the ground.

"What the fuck!" I exclaim.

"Shit the sprinklers!" Greyson laughs, "Well I guess that's why no one else is out here."

Little sprays dart everywhere over the lawn, quickly making work of soaking the both of us.

We both start laughing hysterically and run from the sprinklers, making it back into the path.

"I'm so *wet* right now," I say, looking down at my dress.

"What?" Grey stops dead and stares at me and I blush.

"From the sprinklers idiot. Get your head out of the gutter."

I'm still smiling, and he is still staring at me, a curled grin on his chiseled face. We stand there looking at each other in silence.

"Thank you," I say.

"For what?" He asks, stunned.

"For what you did to Corbin. And standing up for me since. And for tonight. Just… thank you."

Grey takes a deep breath and brushes some of my wet curls behind my ear. An overwhelming tension comes over me, and before I know it, I'm on my toes, kissing Greyson right on the mouth.

Chapter 37

What the hell am I doing right now? The last shred of common sense tries to pry me back to reality, but I don't listen. I am kissing Greyson. And he kisses me back. It's like the entire planet stops spinning and it's just me and him; soaking wet in the castle gardens from sprinklers during the Summer Ball. I don't know what came over me, but it felt *right*, like something I needed to do. And it still does. His tongue breaks through my lips and circles my fangs. I return the favor and a deep growl comes from his throat. His hands are tangled in my hair behind my head, and I have my hands on his chest. Warmth courses through me as it has been all night but this time it feels… *thicker*. The tension swirls in my belly. I open my eyes. As I pull back for a breath, there are flames on my fingertips, nearly burning through Grey's jacket.

Shit.

What the *fuck* was I doing right now?

Oh my Gods Ryenn get ahold of yourself.

I take a step back, forcing my hands to my sides and smoothing my dress. Grey's hand drops from my head, and he smooths his thumb over my lip. The same lips he just gingerly sucked on. *Fuck.*

"You okay?" he asks, those lime eyes searching mine.

"Yes, I'm okay I, uh, just remembered I have to find Amalie. I told her I'd meet up with her and she's probably wondering where I am. I, uh, thanks again? I'll see you at class, okay? Goodnight."

I take off before he can say a word, running back through the paths and up the stairs to the front entrance of the castle.

I really had lost my mind hadn't I?

"Princess."

I whip toward the sound of a man's voice.

Ser Arry is walking towards me through the entrance of the castle.

Shit I probably look so guilty right now.

"Good evening, Ser Arry…"

"Can you come with me please?"

My stomach drops, "Why?"

He looks me over and grins a bit. "You're not in trouble. I fear that your friend Miss Seredi may be though."

"Oh Gods what happened?" Worry churns in my stomach.

"I found the young girl sick as a dog in a flowerpot outside the throne room. I brought her to the ladies washroom and was going to find her mother but she 'forbade' me from doing so and requested your… *assistance* instead. I think she may have had a few too many drinks."

"Oh Gods. Thank you for finding me, Ser Arry, can you lead me to her?"

"Yes, your Highness, follow me." I followed Ser Arry through the crowd, getting multiple confused stares, most likely due to my soaked gown. We reach one of the private Ladies Washrooms, reserved for Ladies or Royalty. Amalie would probably get in trouble if found here, actually.

"Thank you… You're not going to tell her parents about this, are you?" I ask the tall man. He is quite large and could most likely squish me like a bug if he wanted to. And he was handsome in a rough way, not at all like Emmet.

"If that's an order, then I will not," he grins, and I can tell he is joking. "Think of this as an… apology for what you saw last night?"

I flush deeply. "Yeah, okay, thank you." I open the door to the private washroom and hear him chuckle to himself on the other side.

Then I immediately hear Amalie puking her guts up.

"Amalie? It's Ryenn. What stall are you in?"

Luckily, the rest of the washroom was entirely empty.

"Here," she groans from the last one and opens the door.

The sight I see next is not a pretty one.

Amalie is sitting on the ground, the bodice of her pink dress soiled with some sort of liquid, her hair down out of her bun and her eye makeup in streams down her rosy cheeks.

"Oh, *Amalie*," I sat next to her. "What happened?"

The girl starts to cry. "Well, after you left and told me not to drink anything else, Rykard, my *horrible* date, had brought me another drink, claiming it wasn't alcoholic. But it *was* and he apparently spiked it with something, causing me to feel the effects even *worse*. I can't remember much from it, but Autumn and her bitch friends were in on it, and I only found out when the four of them were laughing at me from puking in a fucking flowerpot. Ser Arry found me and brought me here…. Oh Gods, it's coming again."

I hold her sticky blonde hair back as she vomits in the toilet. Nothing but pink fruity liquid comes up. I should've been here. Was Greyson in on it? Is that why he took me for a walk, so I'd be distracted? Gods, how could I be so stupid and naive?

"I'm so sorry, Amy," I say and rub her back as she heaves again.

"I'm going to get in so much trouble." She lifts her head up and her lip quivers.

"No, you aren't. Ser Arry owes me a favor and he promised not to tell your parents. You can come back to my chambers for the night, okay? Celeste can come up with a good lie to tell your mom." I smooth her hair.

"Okay," she sniffles. "This really really sucks so bad."

"Yeah, I know."

"I love you, Ry. You are my bestest friend ever," she pats my cheek with her sticky hands.

"And you are so drunk right now. I love you too though… Let me go get Celeste, she'll be able to room-jump us up to my chambers, so we don't have to walk through the castle, okay?"

"Mhmm," she groans, and I go to the door.

Ser Arry is standing guard on the outside and has put up a sign that says, "Out of Order." I smile at the gesture.

"Is she okay?" he asks.

"She will be… Can you do me another favor?" I grin sheepishly.

"Depends," he raises a brow. "I am meant to at least look like I'm on duty right now."

"I need you to go get my aunt… please. I'd go, but I kind of don't want a million stares as to why I am currently soaking wet and smell of alcoholic vomit."

He laughs deeply. "Okay. That I can do."

~

A long vomit filled five minutes later, Celeste walks through the doors of the washroom. A very confused look accompanies her face.

"What happened? Are you girls alright?" she asks as she rushes over to the stall.

I still hold back Amalie's hair.

"We're okay… We just need you to room-jump us back to my chambers… Please?"

I was relieved to see her, I realized. Tonight had been really freaking weird and I needed some normalcy back before I lost it altogether.

"I can, but I expect an explanation when we get there, okay? Arry left out details and scared me half to death, Ryenn."

I stand and hug the woman. Breathing in that familiar perfume. "Are you sure you are alright, dear?" She whispers, grasping my face in those cool delicate hands.

"Yeah, it's been a long night. I'll tell you upstairs."

"Okay… This is going to be tricky with both of you…" She walks over to the sink and grabs a small trash bin, handing it to Amalie. "Here, honey. In case you get sick from the Locus, okay?"

"Thank you, Aunt Celeste… I love you. More than *anything* right now. Well, not more than Ryenn because she's my bestest friend ever, right Ry?"

Celeste looks at me with wide eyes.

"Again, I'll explain. Just get us out of this bathroom."

Celeste sighs. "Alright. Hold on."

Chapter 38

We make it back to my chambers easily. The whole room-jump thing is still incredibly disorienting, but I don't vomit from it this time. Can't say the same thing for Amalie, though, but she had the trash bin to save herself from getting it all over my floors. Celeste stayed back and helped me clean Amalie up and then myself. The entire time, Amalie was babbling about many different things and when she wasn't, she was crying. I felt like a bad friend the entire time. I could've prevented this from happening. I should've stayed with her after I realized she was already tipsy. I finally helped her get comfortable in my bed, and she was out in a matter of minutes.

"Alright, spill," Celeste says to me as I fashion my robe around me, and I join her over by the windows on my chairs.

"Shouldn't you get back?"

"I should, and I will, but I need to know what happened first."

I take a deep breath.

"I'm not mad, honey. Just worried."

"Where do you want me to start?" I rubbed my temples.

"First, tell me what happened to Amalie. She's clearly *very* drunk and her mother is not going to be impressed. She's not of legal drinking age yet, and neither are you."

"I know… Amalie's parents set her up with a date, as they usually do, and to keep him busy, Amalie sent him to get her some drinks so she wouldn't have to maintain small talk with him. Anyways, she didn't specify what kind of drink to get her, and he must have assumed to get alcoholic ones, which she didn't realize until she had three or four drinks in and already very tipsy. I told her not to drink more, and like the horrible friend I am, I left her with her date, thinking that if I stuck around too long, her father would get mad. I came back to find her, and Ser Arry found me and told me she was in the bathroom. She was so sick and told me that her date was in on a prank with the other girls in our class, where he spiked the rest of her drinks, making her even more sick. It's all my fault, really I should've been there, and now I feel horrible. Ser Arry promised not to tell her mom. Please don't tell her, Celeste, okay? They're so hard on her and it was an honest mistake. Just come up with something as to why she has to stay the night? Please? I never had anything to drink. I was too busy doing… other things."

"Okay, Ryenn, *breathe*. I believe you just calm down."

Flames had started to creep to my fingertips like they had out in the garden. *Turn it off.*

"Okay." I take a shuddery, deep breath.

"I won't tell Vada. I can see it was a complete accident. Well, not necessarily, considering her date clearly drugged her, but still, it wasn't Amalie's fault. She's a good kid, and I agree her parents are… Strict. It's also not *your* fault, why do you think it is?"

Tears sting my eyes. "Because I am naive and *stupid.*"

I bury my face in my hands and cry.

"Why do you say that honey?" Celeste moves closer and rubs my back.

"For a multitude of reasons. Boys are idiots."

"Well, yes, but did things not work out with Braxton? I saw you two dancing earlier."

"Oh, they were going fine until I found him and another female, a gorgeous blonde who is clearly older than me, making out in the corridor."

"Oh *honey,*" her brows lowered with empathy.

"Yeah. I am not even that surprised. I mean, he was just probably being nice to the new child of the kingdom. I don't even know why I thought he actually liked me. Then to make matters even worse, I went outside to get a breath of air to calm the flames coursing through me, and Greyson met me out there." I take a deep breath to steady myself.

"Then he took me for a stupid walk to the stupid garden, and I was comfortable enough to release some of said stupid flames and found out he was an electricity Fae from Carlisle. Oh yeah, I met

Jess earlier too, *his fucking aunt*. She's really hot and I can see why you like her. Anyways, the stupid sprinklers turned on and then we ran away laughing, and like the stupid naive little girl I am, I kissed him. On the lips. Not just a little friendly kiss either, Celeste. No this was…intense. Then I ran away to go find Amalie. But now that I think about it, he was probably in on the prank to hurt Amalie, so it really was my fault, wasn't it-"

"Ryenn, stop."

I realized I was pacing back and forth and that I had summoned a ball of silver flames in my palms.

Shit.

"Sit and breathe with me."

I suffocate the flames and sit.

In for three.

Hold for three.

Out for three.

Repeat.

"None of that was your fault. Yes, boys can be idiots. What Braxton did was not nice, leading you on only to not feel the same as you. And are you certain Greyson was in on the 'prank'? He may be innocent. As for kissing him, that is something you unfortunately can't take back. Maybe talking to him, once you are calm and maybe not tonight, would be helpful. Everything will be alright, okay? Just try to relax a little, tonight was overwhelming, it is to the best of us. I am glad Ser Arry came to get me when he did because he got me out of a particularly heated conversation. Anyways, I'll just tell Vada that Amalie had brought you back to your room because you were tired and that you both ended up falling asleep, okay? Scouts are on guard outside. I have to go back, unfortunately, but just try and get some sleep, okay? All these problems won't seem as big as they are feeling right now tomorrow, okay?"

"How can I be sure I won't burn this room down?"

"Do you feel like burning this room down?"

"No, but that hasn't stopped me before-"

"Then it won't happen. You know you control it. You are *strong.*"

I sigh and climb into the bed next to an already snoring Amalie.

"I'll see you in the morning. There's a garbage bin next to the bed in case she gets sick again, okay?"

"Thank you."

Celeste walks over and kisses the top of my head before leaving.

Chapter 39

I woke to the sound of a knock on the door early the next morning. Amalie was still sound asleep next to me but woke when I went to answer it. It was only Evie, bringing breakfast up for both of us. I laid the tray on the bed and climbed back in. I was exhausted. Last night was a lot. Amalie looked even more exhausted than I was.

"What the fuck happened last night?" She groaned and rubbed her eyes.

"I don't even know where to start, Amy." I bit into a sausage. "Here, eat something."

She bit into a piece of toasted bread. "It's like it's all coming back to me in flashes. Fuck, my head hurts." She flips back on the pillow, and I grab some of the pine-needle-tasting pain medication from my bedside table.

"Take some. It'll help."

She does so without even looking at the bottle.

Then she sits up straight. "Oh fuck."

"What?" I say with my mouth full.

"Oh, I am going to be in so much trouble."

"No, you won't because Ser Arry promised not to say anything, and Celeste won't either."

"No, but Rykard's parents might. Or he might. Oh Gods, I made such a fool of myself." She pulls the pillow over her face.

"Amy, it's okay. No one will remember. They were too involved in their own affairs to care about you. Rykard and Autumn and her friends should be ashamed of themselves, and this is technically considered harassment."

"Just leave me here to die," she says, muffled by the pillow over her face.

"I can't do that," I laugh. She starts to actually cry, and I feel a pang of sadness blossom in my chest.

"I'm sorry, Amy. I should've been there. I'm a horrible friend."

She sniffles and takes the pillow out of the way. "No, you're not," she pouts. "I distantly remember telling you that you were my 'bestest friend ever' multiple times last night."

"I still shouldn't have left you alone. And I don't even have a good excuse like I could blame it on the fact that Greyson and I went for a walk through the garden together and that he was attempting to distract me, but I was still outside anyways and not where I should've been."

"Wait, hold on. Back up," she sits up straight again. "What do you mean you and Grey went for a walk together?"

I pinch my brows together with my fingers.

"Okay, so I saw Braxton making out with an older female in the hallway, which upset me and then I went outside to get air, and Grey joined me and asked if I'd like to walk with him, and I agreed and we ended by the garden where I felt comfortable enough to use my powers to burn off emotion and steam and then the sprinklers turned on which is why I got soaked and then we laughed and then we kissed and then I ran away."

"Ryenn Embers!" She squeals, "You did *not* kiss Greyson Bryce."

"I did. But I regret it because I think he was trying to distract me from finding you."

"Oh my Gods."

"I'm sorry."

"Ry, do not be sorry. You know that if you would've stuck around, my parents would've gotten mad anyways. Plus, how were you supposed to know he'd spike my drink or that he was in cahoots with Autumn and bitch one and bitch two? I'm sorry that Braxton did what he did, though. That's messed up. He led you to believe he had feelings and made you develop feelings only to go and make out with a chick in the hall? Who's most definitely not as gorgeous or strong as you? That's fucked up. But it doesn't matter because you still got action, you son of a bitch. Oh man, Autumn is gonna be *pissed*. I'm not mad at you. In fact, I'm kind of proud of you."

Both of us laugh.

"Autumn cannot find out. That was a one-time thing, and I must have been confused or something because I do not know what came over me. I do *not* like Greyson." The last part felt almost like a lie. Maybe I respected him, and I could see us as potential friends if he was, in fact, innocent of the whole drink-spiking thing, but that does not mean I liked him.

Amalie and I sat there, talking and eating in my bed for a little longer. It was nice to just sit there, and everything felt normal. Like I was a normal teenager with my normal teenage friend eating brunch in bed after a sleepover. It was something I read in books and never thought I'd get to experience myself.

That sense of normalcy didn't last very long, though, as an urgent knock sounded on my door. Amalie and I gave each other a confused glare, but I told whoever it was to come in. It was Ser Davis.

"Ser Davis?"

"Princess, Miss Seredi, I have been told to come get the both of you immediately and bring you to the meeting room."

"Is everything alright?" I felt all the color drain from my face and my heart went to my feet. Amalie looked like she felt the same.

"I can't say for certain. You both need to come with me."

Amalie and I scrambled to our feet, quickly putting on a robe each and slipping on our shoes. We followed Ser Davis down the hall, flanked by four more guards.

~

Celeste, Emmet, Juno, Hunter, Normani, Bradley, Lord and Lady Seredi, Ser Arry and the other five lords and ladies of the other districts were in the meeting room when myself and Amalie arrived. Other Scouts lined the perimeter of the room. The tension in the air was palpable and did not help the ball of nerves forming in my stomach.

I walked over to Celeste and Emmet, standing between them to seek some sort of comfort in this scenario. Vada took Amalie by the shoulders and brought her over next her father. I noticed now that the other Fae from our class were actually with their parents as well, besides Corbin's parents, who were alone. A weird sensation washed over me and threatened to weaken my knees.

"What's going on?" I ask Celeste quietly and shakily.

"There's been an attack. We need everyone here before we discuss the details," she whispers and smooths my tangly hair down.

"Everyone, take a seat, please," Emmet states and everyone obeys.

My heart is beating out of my chest. What kind of attack? Did they think I was behind it somehow? Why was everyone here?

"As most of you are aware, there has been an attack last night." He takes a deep breath and clears his throat. "During the Summer Ball, an attack was made by rebels in two areas. Now, since the majority of us were in the capital, as we are now, it is clear these attacks were thought out and motivated."

Hunter clears his throat and speaks up, "Scout troops were higher in number in the capital last night to ensure safety, because of this, we had fewer troops at the borders and also fewer on patrol outside the walls."

"Yes," Emmet continues, "the attacks last night took place to the east side of the wall, the section bordering Carlisle and also up from the wall on our southern front…from the mortal side."

Chapter 40

Attacked from the mortal side? I swallowed deep to try and rid the knot building in my throat.

"Were… were the mortals attacked?" I ask sheepishly and all eyes fall upon me.

Emmet bites his lip. "The rest of what was left of Baytown, according to our sources…," he glances at Ser Arry, who looks slightly distressed, "was attacked and seized by Dark Rebels. There is nothing but ashes left in that town. There were no survivors this time."

Something cracks within me. Something that has been building for a long, long time. But I don't feel anything. I feel numb and like this is all *fake.* I sit there and stare at Emmet.

"That's how they attacked the Molisan side of the wall then. They went from Baytown up through the Forbidden Forest and attacked the same side of the wall that I once entered through. Makes sense considering they were most likely able to use the bay to enter Baytown and the humans left there had no means to fight back," I concluded.

Everyone is still looking at me with what seems to be a mixture of both confusion and slight fear.

I didn't care though. I felt nothing. I didn't even feel the agonizing burn in my veins. I welcomed that pain, but it didn't come.

"Yes, that's what we assumed as well… The attack on the east side, on the wall bordering Carlisle to Aclos, was one of the first we've seen, and we can't understand the reasoning for *two* attacks."

I remembered that Aclos was the name of the kingdom that the Dark King rules and where his rebels and hundreds of fire Fae lived.

"Seems like they thought one attack, if we were not already distracted enough by the ball, would distract the remaining troops further so they would attack another weaker point. Sounds like we almost expected them to attack Molisan, so it would've made sense that they would attack there first and then try to get in through Carlisle, considering it borders their kingdom and it's a shorter distance to act upon… Am I correct in saying that Ser Arry?" I looked up at the tall man resting against the wall, his arm was in a sling, which was new since last night. He looked tired. He must have gone out and responded to the attacks after Amalie and I went to my chambers.

"Yes… that *does* seem likely, princess. The attack on Molisan was the first. The attack on the east occurred nearly an hour later. There were fewer troops left on that side of the wall because most had been summoned to respond to the threat to the south." The look on his face looked something like he was impressed by what I said. Again, I didn't care. It was simple to understand the motives and I am not sure why everyone was so shocked.

"Did we lose many Scouts?" I ask next and turn my attention to Hunter, who is staring at me with an open mouth.

He clears his throat. "Yes, we lost nearly 200 men. We defeated the rebels, but it is true we took a large hit… if Ser Arry and his men looking after the capital did not respond, we would have lost more."

"Princess, I believe you should let the adults talk. You have no experience with war and shouldn't be making assumptions about matters that do not pertain to you." Lord Seredi cuts in and heat rises to my face.

"Do you have experience Lord Seredi? Because if you have, then why haven't you made the basic assumption of the rebel attack that I have just now? Seems like common sense to me and if you were that experienced in war, you could've put together those puzzle pieces, correct? Also, these matters *do*, in fact, pertain to me. Not only am I Heir to the Throne, thus *all* matters of the kingdom shall pertain to me and my future, our men were hurt and so were innocent mortals. I care about our kingdom, whether you want to believe that or not."

I was unbothered by the confrontation I was dishing out. I looked at the rest of the group then; Greyson had a smirk on his face that matched his mother's, both Lord and Lady Seredi had their mouths slammed shut and a distasteful look, and pretty much everyone else either looked a mix of impressed or slightly scared.

"What Ryenn says is entirely true and seems entirely likely. Based on the patterns of the rebels last night we can see they were attempting to weaken the east wall so they would have a better ease of bringing their own forces through. What exactly their motives are is still up in the air. Scout troops are to be increased on the perimeters as soon as this meeting is over. I will come to Carlisle myself over the next few weeks to focus some much-needed attention on said troops. Does anyone have further questions?"

The adults went back and forth, asking questions regarding the safety of their own districts and then the safety of their children in the capital. It made the most sense for it to be the safest in the capital anyway, so I am unsure as to what their concerns were there. I kept my mouth shut for the rest of it though. That doesn't mean I wasn't listening, I was, and taking mental notes of how to go about protecting the people better.

I still felt numb. Like a shell. I didn't hyperventilate or feel crushing panic. I felt kind of broken and like I only had one purpose or motive left in me; protect the kingdom and protect mortals. It makes no sense as to why innocent people had to lose their lives when so many of us had been dealing with privileged problems last night. It made me sick to think about it. I needed to figure out the rebels' motives and put an immediate stop to the actions; it can't be as simple as not liking mortals or just wanting more power. There has to be more to it.

~

The meeting went on for another hour or so before Emmet dismissed everyone; leaving me, Celeste, a few scouts and himself in the meeting room.

We sat there in silence for a few moments. Celeste stood, walking behind me and began braiding my hair. I knew she was burning off nervous energy and that her perfectionism was probably screaming at the state I was in, so I let her continue without saying anything. Emmet massaged his temples. The air was still tense despite all the others leaving.

"I apologize if I said something to upset you," I say, looking at my uncle.

He looks up from the table. "You said nothing to upset me Ryenn. I am actually quite impressed by your critical thinking... How did you come to the conclusions you did? I had already been talking to the sergeants of each troop and neither could understand the reasoning behind the purpose of the two attacks."

"I don't know... just common sense, I thought."

"Nadine mentioned she had good critical thinking skills and sense when doing history lessons with her," Celeste chirped in. There was still a weariness to her voice and her hands shook slightly. She hadn't really spoken at all during the meeting either. I wondered if it was this whole thing that had frightened her or if she was upset that Ser Arry had been hurt.

"Anyway, you sounded much like your mother… a Queen. And although I should technically reprimand you for speaking to Lord Seredi the way you did, I won't, though because he was being an ass," he grinned, fangs peeking through his lips and I choked on a laugh.

"When will you leave for Carlisle?" I ask. He was gone so often and I was hoping our deal would stand regarding my combat training.

"I will leave with Lady Juniper and Lord Azariah when they head back today."

"Oh"

"Why?"

"Well, I was hoping our deal was still standing… regarding my training? I feel like it could be useful now, more so than ever to be able to defend myself against potential threats. I am not saying I'd be anywhere without Scouts, but still."

"Right… Ser Arry is going to be out of commission due to his injury for the next couple of weeks so he should be able to train you. He trains new recruits all the time anyway, so I cannot see it being an issue. Celeste, you can talk to him about it right?" he raised a brow at her and Celeste stilled as she finished my braid.

"Mhmm," she said. That was weird.

"I have to go get ready. I trust both of you will be fine in the capital. I will return in a week, but if I need to stay longer, I will send word. Be on your best behavior Ryenn and be careful while training. Don't overdo it."

He patted the top of my freshly braided head before leaving, not saying another word to Celeste.

I didn't like this side of him… he seemed stressed but also withdrawn. He had reason to be both of those things, but still, it made me a tad uneasy.

Chapter 41

Back in my chambers, I change into a comfortable gown. It was already late afternoon, but it was warm and nice outside; the opposite of how the vibes were. Fae were making their way back to their districts which meant a lot of the castle had already cleared out. Celeste had walked me back to my chambers and stayed while I got dressed, cleaning up a little and picking up random things around the room. She was quiet and hardly said anything. I didn't ask her to stay, but I got the sense that she didn't really want to be alone either. Her unease made me slightly uneasy as well.

"Celeste?" I say, coming out of the washroom. She was standing by the window, a fair hand placed on the glass.

"Mhmm?"

"Can we go for a walk?"

"Sure dear. Where would you like to go?" She turns and smoothes her dress down.

"The gardens maybe? Or to that clearing, you took me to before. I just don't want to be cooped up in the castle. I feel like I have too much energy or something."

"I know what you mean…," she sighs. "Let's go."

~

We walked the same way we went before, three Scouts following from ten feet behind. The gardens were a bit too busy from the gardeners cleaning up from the ball, so we decided to head towards the clearing in the woods. There was a breeze in the air, but it was warm. It wasn't as humid as last night, which was definitely nice. We took the fifteen-minute trail to the clearing, Celeste ordering the Scouts to stay down the trail for some privacy. We didn't really speak the entire time we walked, but I could sense something was wrong. When we got to the clearing, the burned ring remained, sticking out like a sore thumb in the lush green meadow. I looked away from it and followed Celeste over to the river to sit on the bank.

"Celeste, are you okay?" I ask sitting down next to her.

"Not really," she sighs and tips her head back, a tear escapes her eye and she swipes it with her thumb, "Sorry."

My eyebrows pinch together and worry springs through my chest.

"What's wrong?"

"Just the whole attack and everything… It's very stressful." she lies back on the fluffy green grass.

"Is that the only thing? Not that it's not a big thing, of course, but still." I look down at her and she looks at me with watery blue eyes. "Did something else happen last night after I went to bed?"

"Well, about an hour or so after I left you and Amalie in your chambers, we received notice of the attacks. I was… *talking* to Ser Arry and Jess when the messages came in, and he had to leave. It was terrifying. We had heard there had already been dozens of deaths and I… I wasn't sure I was going to see him again," more tears spilled from her eyes, and I reached for her hand.

"As you could tell, this morning he was injured. It may not look bad now, but that was *after* being healed by Juno herself. He came back in pretty rough shape and will take weeks to recover. Emmet saw my reaction to seeing him like that and immediately knew there was something…more between us. I've told you before that he's fine with me not loving him and having relations with others, but the way I reacted to seeing Arry half-dead was like how someone would react to seeing someone they loved hurt. Or that's what he accused me of anyway. Anyway, I hurt his feelings, hurt Arry's feelings because I wasn't there when he woke up and haven't spoken to him really since and then last night was just a lot to deal with for a multitude of reasons. Plus, I haven't slept yet, so forgive me for being dramatic. Gods, I don't know why I am telling you all of this, but I have no other friends to really tell, do I? Sorry, I am rambling." She rubbed her hands down over her face.

"I'm sorry about all of it, Celeste. It isn't fair to you. You never got a choice with any of this. And you're the Queen, which is a shit position to be in when the kingdom is under attack. Plus, I am a good listener, so you can tell me anything, I am much more mature than my age." She reaches up and clasps my cheek with her palm.

"Thank you honey. You are very mature. You've had to grow up far before you should have. I am so proud of you for this morning, by the way, you handled that meeting with grace."

"Thank you." I lay down next to her and looked up at the sky.

"How are you feeling about it all? I am so sorry about Baytown."

"Honestly… I feel nothing. I feel utterly numb Celeste, and I don't know if that's a good thing or something I should be terrified of."

"Sometimes, as a means of survival, our body buries bad things or trauma to keep us from feeling them too harshly. Sometimes, it only takes something small to tick that off, though and then you may feel an overwhelming amount of emotion all at once. Right now, your body is in survival mode. Just remember it is okay to feel vulnerable and feel all the emotions, okay? No one will judge you for being upset. You have the right to your own pain." She turns her head and looks at me and I do the same and look at her.

"Thank you."

"Your mom was actually the one who told me that for the first time. It's something I'll never forget."

I wanted to ask her what circumstances had led to my mom telling her that, but I figured it was best not to bring it up, considering she was already upset.

"Can we just stay out here a little longer?" I ask.

"As long as you want," she grins.

~

We stayed on the grassy bank for a good two hours. I think Celeste actually fell asleep for a bit; her head rested near mine and I heard her breathing slow and steady, along with her frantic heart that had been beating out of her chest earlier. I still haven't gotten used to the heightened hearing and the fact that I could hear those things so easily now when I couldn't before. I did it now without realizing it. It reminded me of a predator and prey in a way; a skill only a predator would really need.

While she rested peacefully, I lied there and looked at the clouds, attempting to make my fire into different shapes in front of me. I had been successful in making a sphere, the easiest, and a wonky heart shape. Summoning, holding and suffocating were easy, but manipulating it differently, was definitely going to take some practice. Luckily, lessons with Juno would be starting again tomorrow after class and maybe she would let me do something else now that I mastered my previous lessons.

I am startled slightly by the sound of footsteps approaching down the path; ones I recognise to be a Scout. I sit up and Celeste's eyes blink open as she supports herself up on one arm.

One of the three scouts near.

"Your Highness, someone has come down the path and would like to speak to you," he states.

"Did they say their name?" She asks with sleepiness undertones.

"Yes, they said they are named Jess, and that she has been looking for you."

"Okay, she may come down. Return to your post afterward please," she fully sits up and smoothes her dress again.

The Scout does as she says and Jess comes up the path not even minutes later.

"I've been looking for you all afternoon Cece," Jess says as she rounds around the corner, not realizing I am sitting next to her. "Oh… hello Ryenn. I didn't realize you were out here too," she goes to bow, but I hold up a hand to stop her and she smiles.

"I have been out here for the last… how long have we been

out here?" She looks at me.

"About two hours. You've been snoring for the past hour."

She looked at me with wide eyes, her cheeks reddening, "I don't snore."

Jess laughs and sits next to Celeste.

"Sure you don't," Jess says and winks at me.

Celeste puts her face in her hands and Jess and I laugh.

"Why have you been looking for me?" Celeste asks.

"Oh, um, I heard about the attacks. I just wanted to make sure you were okay. I was talking to Arry, er, Ser Arry…"

"Ryenn knows everything, so don't hold back for her sake," Celeste mutters and I grin.

"It's true" I shrug my shoulders.

"Okay…" Jess exhales. "Have you talked to him since? I know you were upset last night and Emmet said something to you and then I didn't hear anything from you afterward."

"It doesn't matter. I can't have feelings for him. Or you. You know this. While I was too busy being evoked in two Fae, that I shouldn't have been because I am a married female, our kingdom was being attacked. I am the fucking Queen and I couldn't stop being selfish for three seconds to be able to see this attack coming and then when Arry got hurt-" the last word sounded strangled and tugged at my heart.

"Celeste you cannot possibly blame yourself for this." Jess stopped her and tears began to run down Celeste's porcelain face again. "Honey, you can only do so much. You wouldn't have known these attacks were going to happen. Even if you had been out on the wall yourself, you couldn't have stopped it. Arry is a Scout, he knows his job means he could get hurt or killed at any second."

I sat back, unsure of what to say. I felt bad for Celeste, truly, I loved my uncle don't get me wrong, but I cannot imagine having to marry someone you've been betrothed to since basically being born. She could never truly love someone else because of it. It wasn't fair. I wasn't sure what Emmet had said to her, and I am sure he most likely didn't mean all of it and was probably stressed from the attack, but still, I had never seen her like this and it worried me.

"I know…fuck I'm sorry," she sobbed quietly and Jess took her face in her hands and wiped her tears with her long white nails.

"Don't apologize. You are allowed to be upset and have feelings despite what you give yourself credit for. You are a very good Queen and the citizens are lucky to have you, right Ryenn?" The stunning female glanced up at me with her lime-green eyes.

"Yes. That's what I have been *trying* to tell her." I smile and lay my head on Celeste's shoulder.

"Thanks guys." Celeste smiles and wipes the rest of her tears. "Okay, I'm okay. Enough of this sob-fest, we need to get back to the castle. I have duties to attend to," The last statement seemed directed to Jess and I immediately got the hint and blushed. Both females looked at me and laughed.

The three of us met the Scouts back on the path and headed back towards the castle. I still felt somewhat numb by everything and like I was floating as I walked. Almost like I was dreaming. I pinched myself to make sure that I wasn't; which turned out to be true, this was all real. Still seemed like living in a nightmare occasionally.

Chapter 42

The rest of the day went by in a bit of a blur. When we got back to the castle it was already dinner time, so I opted to eat in my chambers. Emmet and the others had already left and the halls were near vacant besides the usual buzz of servants and handmaidens. It was now evening and the sun was starting to set. I attempted to take my mind off things and read a book, but I couldn't focus. Why were the rebels and Dark King attacking now? That was something that plagued me all evening. They've never made to attack Sanctania before, it had only really been petty attacks on the mortals. What were their motives?

Taking a deep breath and ceasing my pacing, I decided I wanted a cold bath. The caress of the frigid waters may put my mind at ease. The heat had also somehow gotten worse even as the sun set and the humidity suffocated the castle once again.

I drew the bath, stripping off my gown that now clung to me from the sticky sweat that covered my skin and submerged myself in the welcoming coolness. A gasp left me before going completely under the water and holding my breath. I got to 102 seconds before having to come up for air; a new personal best. As I sat there in the cold water, my mind wandered to the events of last night. They seemed so miniscule compared to it all now. I don't know what truly came over me when it came to Greyson and honestly, I didn't care, it's not like I will let that happen again. As for Braxton, I don't need riding lessons anymore, so maybe I will be able to avoid him. He'll probably be trained to be an early recruit now anyway, considering the losses of troops last night, so I hopefully won't be seeing him at all. Thinking about that female wrapped around him caused my blood to run hot, the first bit of anger that I had felt all day, actually. Before I realized, or could stop it, my bath water heated to nearly scalding temperatures.

Well, that's new.

I got out, no longer feeling at ease from a cool caress and put on a thin nightgown.

I knew I wasn't going to get any sleep tonight, but there was no way in the seven depths of hell that I would be taking that sleeping medicine again. So instead, I lay there, staring at the candlelight burn like I had those first few weeks since arriving at the castle.

~

The next morning, I got up before the sun rose and donned some training leathers and a lightweight sleeveless shirt. I was starting my training with Ser Arry this morning, which had to be at the asscrack of dawn apparently. I hadn't slept a wink anyway, so I was eager to get out of the stifling bed. When I had gotten back to my chambers yesterday there was a note left by him to meet him in the training gardens near the west side of the castle at 4:30 am. Training would be an hour and a half each day which gave me time to come back, bathe, meet Celeste for breakfast and then head to school.

Leaving my chambers, two Scouts flanking me, I headed through the quiet castle and out to the training ring. I hadn't actually been over here before, I mean, I had observed the Scout training from the windows, but I hadn't been outside to see it in person. The ground was slightly raised and the covering was lightly cushioned. There were racks of different styles of weapons near the castle and a couple of other training equipment like weights and bands to the other side. Ser Arry was off to the side preparing something when I neared and nodded for the scouts to leave or stand guard somewhere.

I walked up to Arry with a smile on my face, it wasn't until I got close to the large Fae that I realized there was someone else with him. Greyson.

"What are you doing here?" I raised my brows.

"Good morning to you too princess," Grey grinned back, causing me to scoff.

"Good morning Ryenn. Grey will be your combat partner."

"I thought *you* would be training me?" I ask.

"I will, but clearly, I cannot be hands-on for combat

training." He motioned to his arm currently resting in the sling. "Plus, you need someone who is your age and closer in height. Although he is still 8 inches taller than you, I suppose, but he was the best I could find considering I don't train females usually," he says matter of fact, causing me to frown.

"Ser Arry trains me this time every morning anyway, so maybe I should be wondering why *you* are here," Grey smirks.

"None of your business," I roll my eyes.

"Alright then…" Ser Arry glances between us. "Let's get started."

For the first 45 minutes of our session, we do warm-up exercise, which includes running laps around the large arena, jumping jacks, sit-ups and push-ups. By the time I am finished, I am drenched in sweat and nearly gasping for air. Grey looks as though he hardly has a hair out of place and he was using weights during the whole thing. Ser Arry doesn't take it easy on me, though which I appreciate, that's the last thing I'd want.

"Take five minutes to have a drink, then we will get to some basics," he states, smoothing his stubbly face with his good hand.

I follow Grey over to the table with the water bottles and he tosses me a small towel; presumably for the sweat glistening on my face. I roll my eyes again but use the towel anyway. He grins while taking sips of his water, but I do my best to ignore his stare. He doesn't say anything though.

We walk back to the arena and Arry has us run over some different hand-to-hand positioning and even gets to the first trick, which is flipping someone over your shoulder. Grey lets me try it without fighting back, and I feel pretty proud of myself when I manage to do it with ease.

"Good. You're a quick learner Ryenn. For the last 10 minutes before cool-down, I want you both to attempt flipping each other for real. Fight back. Pretend this is real. Whoever flips who the most wins." He takes a step back, folding his arms and grinning.

I narrow my eyes at Greyson and take the prep stance I just learned.

"I'm not going to go easy on you," Grey smiles, taking a similar stance to mine.

"Good, I wouldn't expect you to," I bark back.

We go back and forth at each other for the first minute or so and then he catches me, flipping me over with ease. Fire burns in my veins, but I get back up and keep trying. It only takes another three minutes before he's flipped me again twice.

"Come on Ryenn, plant your feet down and get him! Don't give up," I hear Ser Arry say off to the sidelines. The roar of flames in my ears deafens everything around me and then he grabs me and flips me again, nearly knocking all the wind from me.

"Come on Frisky. Get up, we still have four minutes, I'm sure I can flip you another three or four times-"

My eyes pierce through him and my lip curls up over my fangs. Standing, flames burst into my palms and I march towards him, snarling like a godsdamn predator.

He doesn't move though. "Ah ah ah, no powers," he tilts his head and smiles.

"Put those flames out Ryenn, this is hand-to-hand combat; powers cannot always be relied on," Arry says with a grunt.

"Fine," I growl, flicking the flames from my grasp. The momentary relief that summoning them brought me cleared my senses enough that when Grey took a lunge for me, I stepped out of the way, ducked a bit, catching him off guard and flipped him over my shoulder. Then I pinned him there with my foot.

"Ha! I did it!" I shouted and smiled wide, looking at Ser Arry, who was also smiling.

"You did. Ten minutes are up now. Grey wins 4-1. Take the last five minutes to cool down, you two," he walks over to the sideline to put some weights back on the rack.

I go to move my foot from Grey's chest and he grabs it at the last second, sweeping my legs out from under me, causing me to fall right on my ass next to him with a yelp.

"Rule number one; never let your guard down, Frisky," he said, mere inches from my face and I blushed.

"Asshole," I muttered under my breath as he stood and offered a hand to me. I stood on my own, not taking his stupid hand, and started doing some stretches to cool down. The entire five minutes, he never took those feverish green eyes off of me, but I pretended not to notice or care.

~

Back in my chambers, thirty or so minutes later, I look in the mirror after getting out of my cold bath. I already had a few bruises from being flipped so much, but I was somewhat proud of them. This morning was exhausting and I already wanted to crawl back into the bed and sleep the rest of the day, but I had too much to do. I donned my usual schooling uniform and Evie showed up briefly after fixing my hair into a pretty braided bun.

A different handmaiden, one I recognize to be one of Celeste's arrived just as Evie finished up.

"Hello Princess, Her Highness is not feeling well this morning. She will not be going to the dining hall for breakfast and just wanted to know if you could meet her in her chambers prior to school and eat there instead of alone."

"Oh, okay thank you. Have my tray sent there please? Let her know I'll be there in a few minutes." Confusion and concern panged me a bit. Is she okay?

The handmaiden nodded and left swiftly, Evie close behind.

I grabbed a couple of books to bring with me to training with Juno after class, I had some questions that I had read regarding fire powers and the Dark King and I figured she was most likely the best one to ask. I left my cloak though, knowing it was going to be another hot day just by the way the sun blared through the blue sky already.

A twist of nerves swirled low in my belly as I neared Celeste's room. I didn't think Fae got sick very often, I mean they are nearly immortal, really. I twisted the brass knob and let myself into the large chambers. Celeste lay in her massive bed, hair down, making her look so young. There was a deep flush across her face and her eyebrows were pinched.

"Hi," I whispered as I got near, laying the books and my satchel on a stool near the door and padding across the soft carpet to her bed. "Are you okay? Your handmaiden told me you aren't feeling good."

She smiled sleepily. "Yes honey, I'm okay, no worries. I just started my cycle this morning and have been in quite some pain. That explains why I was so emotional yesterday, though." She chuckles.

"Oh," I blush lightly. That makes sense. At least she wasn't truly sick then.

"Yeah, I may not be able to have children, but Goddess of Nature has a cruel side and still makes me go through this about three times a year," she exhaled deeply, and a few handmaidens and servants brought in some breakfast trays, laying them on the bed. I sip from my orange juice and then Jess, wearing a thin lace nightgown, leaving nothing to the imagination, comes out from the washroom carrying some towels and a basin of water. I just about choke on my juice and look away.

"Oh hello, Ryenn!" She says cheerily and takes a seat on the bed next to Celeste, not seeming to care in the slightest that what she's wearing is nearly invisible.

Celeste's cheeks deepen in color as the red-haired Fae rings out a towel with cool water and places it on her forehead.

"Jess, you don't have to do this," Celeste says but then groans as a wave of pain must grips her.

"Stop it. Just because you're used to suffering doesn't mean you have to." Jess clicks her tongue, "how was training this morning

Ryenn?" She asks me.

"Right." Celeste sits up a bit, towel still draped across her head as she speaks, causing me to grin a bit. "How did it go?"

"It was good," I said. I decided to leave out Greyson-details considering his aunt was right there. "I am definitely tired now though," I laugh.

"Did you sleep last night?" Celeste asks.

"Mhmm," I try to lie while eating a piece of sausage.

"Ryenn, don't lie to me," she scowls.

"Okay fine. No, I didn't, but it's okay."

"Why? Did you have any nightmares?" She takes the towel off her face and places it in the basin, causing Jess to shake her head lightly.

"No, I just couldn't sleep. I was too warm and everything." I blush, feeling slightly embarrassed we were talking in front of Jess. I like her, don't get me wrong, but she just reminded me so much of Greyson and that was not a face I wanted to picture right now.

"Do you want me to ask Sara for something to help you sleep? It doesn't have to be the nightshade stuff you took before, I am sure there are many things-"

"I'm alright, Celeste. Really. It was just a one-night thing.

I'm sure I will be okay tonight. I should get going though, because I am sure Amalie and Pippa will be at the dining hall any minute now." I leap up from the bed and start to make my way to the door.

"Ryenn," Celeste says in a cool tone that sends shivers down my spine. I turn and look at her. "You promise you're okay?" Her blue eyes swallow me whole.

"I promise… I'll see you after lessons with Juno. You'll take care of her, right Jess?" I glance at the female who is flaked out on the bed, chewing a piece of bacon. I keep my gaze on her face as I ask her this.

"Of course," she smiles, her tone thick like honey.

"I do not need anyone to look after me," Celeste argues. "I am a grown woman and have had a cycle before- *fuck.*" She grabs her abdomen and flops her head back on the pillow.

"Uh huh," I laugh and Jess shakes her head, reaching for the basin again and smoothing the cool water over the queen's face.

"Have a good day Ryenn. Tell Grey I said hello," Jess gives me a wink and I leave immediately, my face on fire. Did she know something?

Chapter 43

I met Amalie and Pippa in the hallway after leaving Celeste's room, and we headed to the schoolhouse. Amalie still looked exhausted from the other night's events and was on edge going to class. I assured her it was going to be fine, and she smiled. We talked a bit about the meeting we were summoned to yesterday morning and that she thought I looked queenly while talking to the group. She also apologized for her father's remarks, which I told her was unnecessary because it was not her fault.

Class went by as it usually did but there was an energy that I can't quite describe in the air, almost as if *everyone* was on edge. I mean, they had the right to be. Their parents went back to their respective districts yesterday, and there had been an attack, so I can see why some were nervous.

At one point, though I had left the schoolhouse to go to the washroom, it was in a separate building for which you needed to cross the yard. When I got there, I heard someone crying, one of the younger children in the class. She was sitting on the floor in one of the stalls, and I heard her silent sobs as I entered.

"Hello?" I asked quietly, "Are you alright?"

I heard her gasp and what sounded like a hand slap over her mouth.

"It's alright… Open the door and talk to me. I can help," I said, pressing my hand on the stall door. The poor thing sounded so distressed, and I could sense her desperation. The cries reminded me of Rose, which tugged at my heart a little.

"I- I'm okay…" the little voice said back with chattering teeth.

"Open the door, sweetheart," I whispered.

The stall creaked open and two blue eyes looked up at me, wide as saucers. It was Corbin's little sister. I believe her name was Lilly.

"What's wrong?" I ask, sitting down next to the shivering child. She was a couple of years older than Pippa, maybe seven? The title of Lady of Vermuse would be passed to her now that Corbin was gone, so I can imagine that has to be a lot of pressure on a young child.

"I'm scared," she says, tears streaming down her face. She looks a lot like her brother, but not at the same time. She has the same eyes and colored hair, but her features are soft and innocent.

"Scared of what?" I ask and rub her back, attempting to soothe her like I once did Rose.

"The attacks. I miss my mom and dad. I wanted to go back with them, but they-they said I have to stay and learn, but I-I can't focus, and I couldn't sleep, and then I was so worried in class, and I couldn't breathe or listen to Mrs. Langerfeld anymore and I- I got sick," she takes shuddery breaths and closes her pale blue eyes.

I noticed then that she must have thrown up over herself while trying to get to the washroom because there was a stain down over the front of her green dress.

"It's okay… shh," I attempt to soothe her and pull her closer to me to stop her from shivering. "It's alright. I'll help you get cleaned up, okay? Don't worry about it; it happens to the best of us. Even me. You don't have to worry about the rebels here; you are safe. Your mom and dad wouldn't leave you here if they didn't think you were safe. Scouts will keep the bad guys away, okay?"

Her blue eyes blinked open, and she looked up at me "Why- why are you being so nice to me? My brother hurt you…"

"You aren't your brother." And it was true. She wasn't. She was a little girl who, at the moment, was terrified.

"I'm not like him, I promise. I-I am a good kid. I would never hurt anyone, especially not a princess. I'm sorry he did that. He never did like me either-" she started to ramble and shake again.

"It's alright, Lilly. Calm down. Okay, let's take some deep breaths together?" she nodded and followed my usual breathing sequence. Once she stopped quivering, I stood and helped her from the washroom floor. "Let's go get you cleaned up, alright?"

I led her out by the hand, and we walked over to the boarding houses where the children of the Lords and Ladies of the other kingdoms stayed. It was only a two-minute walk from where we were and still on castle grounds so I knew it wouldn't take us long. The girls stayed on one side of the house and the boys on the other. The older Fae stayed on the upper level. There were a few handmaidens around, and the Lady at the main desk recognized who I was, I guess, and let us go to Lily's room. The child grabbed one of her clean uniforms and went and changed in the bathroom. I waited outside the stall and looked in the mirror at myself. I still felt that numbness that had taken root when I found out about Baytown the other day.

Lilly came out and threw her dirty dress into a laundry basket and washed her hands. She still had tear stains on her pink cheeks, so I grabbed a towel and wetted it. "Come here," I said gently, and she turned to me.

I cleaned her small face as she looked at me over the face, her gaze falling to the scar on my lip. "It's okay to be scared. Everyone gets scared and anyone who tells you any different are liars. Being able to admit you are scared takes serious strength and bravery."

"Really?" She blinked her thick lashes.

"*Really*. Being able to ask for help also takes a pile of courage. I'm here if you ever need someone to talk to or someone to listen to, okay?" I fixed her black hair into a low braid and patted her on the back, looking into her eyes in the reflection.

She grinned at me. "Thank you."

"Don't mention it. Let's get back to school before Mrs. Lagerfeld wonders where we went. Remember, you are safe, and you are incredibly brave Lilly. If you ever feel that fear again, try the breathing technique I did with you, okay? Works for me."

We began walking back out to the yard, and the handmaiden smiled at me.

"You get scared?" Lilly asks as she takes my hand.

"All the time."

~

We had only been gone maybe 15 minutes and no one noticed when we returned to class. I gave Lilly a reassuring nod, and she went to her table near the front of the group, taking a big breath.

The rest of the day passed, and I soon found myself with Juno. This time, she was getting me to attempt to light things on fire just by looking at them, like a candle wick or a crumpled piece of paper. By the end, I managed to light the paper on fire once. The candle wick I did not. I felt defeated by the end, but she reassured me that I could just be tired and that it would all take practice. I think my overall numbness had something to do with it before. While training with Grey this morning, I hadn't felt that heat in my veins. I also asked her my questions regarding the Dark King, which she didn't give much detail on.

"Who *is* the Dark King?" I asked, wiping my brow.

"He is the King of Aclos. He is not a good king and thus has earned the title 'the Dark King," she answered without glancing up from her literature.

"But did he come from Sanctania? I haven't been able to find much information on him or his motives besides that he and his rebels are not welcome in Sanctania and that they think mortals serve no purpose unless it is to serve Fae."

"And that's all there is to know." She glances up with a bored expression

"But why? Why don't they like mortals? Why are they banned from Sanctania? How old is he? Why-"

"Child, if you have not found your answers in books, why would you think I have the answers you look for?"

My cheeks heated. "I don't know. I just thought you knew everything."

"One cannot know everything. Especially if it has not been

documented or been erased from documentation."

"What do you mean?" I narrow my eyes at her.

She closes her book, and a puff of dust flies up in her face. "I mean what I said. There's no documentation on the Dark King, his origins, his motives, nothing. No one has spoken to this Fae in centuries, and if they have, they either haven't lived to tell about it or have it documented. Any history does not mention him and unfortunately, being one of the oldest Fae in this kingdom, you won't find anyone before me that may know his origins. All we do know is that he is dangerous."

A mix of emotions swirled through me: confusion, anger, distaste, uncertainty, and sadness, but numbness still seemed to trump all of them.

"Anyways, try not to dwell on it. I am sure we will know his motives soon enough. That's it for our lesson. Ser Davis, escort her back through the castle, please."

I am sure we will know his motives soon enough

What the hell did she mean by that?

Chapter 44

I met Celeste back in her chambers afterward. Apparently, Jess had left a few minutes before I arrived, and Celeste had dressed and done her hair since this morning. I had stopped by my chambers to change out of my sweaty school uniform and don a summer dress that was light and cooling compared to the thick summer air surrounding the entire kingdom.

"How are you doing?" I ask.

"Oh, I've been better. Nothing I can't handle, though, dear." Celeste smiles lightly.

"Have…have you heard anything from Emmet? Any more information on the attacks?"

"No, unfortunately, I have not. I know he has made it to Carlisle, though, because Jess received a message from her sister that they made it back safely." I could sense a wave of sadness wash over Celeste.

"Everyone seems to be on edge… The energy at school were a bit *off* today; I could almost palpate the anxiety in the air. It was weird."

"Remember how I told you that Fae could essentially smell different emotions or have a heightened sense of awareness? That's pretty much what that is, but if you can feel it more strongly and pinpoint the exact emotion, especially that of a group, the exact term for it is *Katiase*. Only strong Fae can do it, and I wouldn't be surprised if you're manifesting it. I can only pinpoint an exact emotion if it's strong and if I am focused on one person, like how I can tell when you are embarrassed or lying."

"Lying isn't an emotion," I scowl.

"No, but guilt and tangy shame accompany it," she retorts, and I close my mouth.

Am I able to *Katiase*? I feel like it could both come in handy and also be a huge annoyance at the same time.

"Anyways, where did Jess go?" I decided to change the subject.

"She has a job, Ryenn. One that she will be doing all evening."

"Oh, right! She's a tattoo artist. That's something that isn't common in Molisan. Mainly, only fishermen had tattoos, and they were not as pretty as the ones covering Jess's arms and legs… Do you have any tattoos?"

"I do. I can hide it, though. Some Fae still have an odd outlook on tattoos and think they are distasteful."

"Really? I think they are beautiful… Where is your tattoo?"

Celeste grins a little. "On my back."

"Oh…cool."

"You want to see it, don't you?"

"Well, duh, but I don't want to be rude."

She takes a deep breath and laughs. "Here, help me with the lacing."

I do as she says, unlacing her corset that starts at the nape of her neck all the way down to her hips. As I pull it down, I see the ink etched along her spine.

It's a beautiful line work of sun and other stars, like a linear constellation with nothing but stars; no planets, no moon, just the sun and stars. It's beautiful, and I can't believe I didn't realize she had it before; I suppose she always wears dresses that cover her back so it's not like I would see it.

"Wow," I breathe.

"Celeste, or *Celestiana*, is the name of the Sun Goddess in the old language. I got the sun to match what I was named after, I guess. Jess did it for me a few years ago. I love it, and I wish I could show it off more, but that's something I cannot do. Not many have seen it, actually, just Jess, Ser Arry and my handmaidens. Now you."

"Emmet hasn't?" I say before thinking. I can truly be stupid, can't I?

"No, he hasn't." Her face blushes a little, and I lace her back up. I can taste remorse on my tongue; it's thick and heavy.

"Sorry," I whisper.

"Don't apologize, honey," she looks at me. "You look tired. Are you sure you're doing okay?"

"I'm okay. I *am* tired, though if I am being honest, today drained me," I yawn.

"Go lie on my bed while I do some paperwork if you'd like to rest. What I am doing isn't interesting anyway."

"No, I need to learn…Even the boring paperwork stuff. I'll just watch you, and then we can go to dinner after."

"Okay, if you say so." She smiles and reaches for the stack of papers on her desk.

~

I wake up in Celeste's bed, covered by a light fur blanket. How did I get here? The last thing I remember is Celeste showing me the wax seal of one of the districts…I must have dozed off. And she must have carried me to the bed. A tinge of embarrassment seeps in, but also the warmth of comfort. I turn over to Celeste's desk and see her still sitting there.

"How long have I been asleep?" I ask groggily.

"Only an hour. Dinner is in thirty minutes." She looks at me, smiling.

"Sorry…Gods, I must have been *really* tired. I really was trying to pay attention."

"It's alright, Ryenn," she laughs. "Although your snoring has been making it difficult to focus on my work."

I gasp, "I do not snore! *You* are the one who snores," and I flick a pillow at her.

"You did not just throw a pillow at me," she glares, her fangs peeking out through her lips as a smile creeps across her face.

"I apologize, Your Highness and the pillow simply jumped from my arms," I giggle.

"Oh, you're going to regret that." She picks up the pillow and throws it back at me, nearly knocking me over.

We both erupt in laughter and keep throwing pillows at each other. Celeste must be cheating because there is the force of the wind behind each of her throws. One of the pillows bursts from the impact, and feathers fly everywhere. Right on time, Ser Davis enters the room.

Both me and Celeste look at him like guilty children.

He looks at the both of us and shakes his head. "Dinner is ready, your Highness…"

Celeste clears her throat. "Mhmm. Thank you, Ser Davis. We will be right behind you."

He looks around the room again and then between us before

sighing and turning to leave. I see a slight grin on his face before he turns.

Celeste and I looked at each other and burst into laughter again.

~

Dinner went by smoothly, and it was delicious, too. Just me and Celeste. I liked the simplicity of it. I went to my chambers shortly after, taking one of my baths to wash off today's events and heat before climbing into my bed. I slept almost immediately but woke from an odd dream shortly after. It wasn't a nightmare, but it still left me feeling uneasy.

It was just fire. That's all the dream was. Silver flames clouded my vision. I don't know why it left me uneasy. I mean, I have come to somewhat accept my flames, but still. I was half expecting to wake up to another scorched quilt, which Evie would have killed me over, but no unexpected destruction was caused. I also didn't get upset, cry, or hyperventilate; I just *was*. The numbness worried me a little bit, but I also welcomed it. Maybe I had finally succeeded in truly turning off my emotions; not silly ones that came to the surface occasionally, like laughing with Celeste or spite from being called 'frisky' by Greyson, but the deep emotions that hindered me and kept me in that everlasting state of panic. I could no longer feel that.

Chapter 45

The week went by in a blur. Every day was as hot as the day before it; hardly any clouds covered the sky, and rain was nowhere to be found. I trained every morning and started noticing a difference in my strength. By the end of the week, I had added three-pound ankle weights to my cardio. According to Ser Arry, who still wasn't cleared to remove the sling, Fae built muscle rather swiftly. What takes a mortal three months to gain is easily gained in one week by a Fae. I also learned a few more hand-to-hand combat techniques. Greyson was a good partner, as much as I didn't want to admit it. He'd always let me try something but wouldn't hold back when we were allowed to attempt to fight. He still won, but I was just happy I had been able to at least catch him off guard at least once through each session. That tight spite in my chest was welcoming every time we fought, and his stupid smirk would usually send me over the edge, especially if he dared to mutter that stupid pet name he enjoyed so much.

We don't speak outside of training, though, especially not at school. I am unsure why, but it feels… *weird* to do that. I think Autumn still has feelings for him, too, if that serpent can even feel things, and not that I care if she does, but I am not one to be a second choice for anything or anyone. Amalie had finally started being herself by the end of the week, though, which was a relief. I was starting to get concerned about her, and she didn't want to talk about that night, even though I had tried. I think her parents got really mad at her, what they said or did though she wouldn't tell me. Pippa wouldn't even speak of it when she heard us talking one day, and I knew she knew something by the way I could sense the fear off of her.

I had a new friend, though. Corbin's little sister, Lilly, had seemed to grow quite fond of me over the last week, and I often saw her watching me when out in the schoolyard or class. Occasionally, when Amalie had to leave to go to her dance lessons, I would walk with her to the boarding house. She told me all about the other kids in the class, something I never thought to ask about before. Greyson was the only one in the class who was an only child. Autumn had two younger brothers, Luca and Kai; one was 7, and the other was 6. Luna had three siblings, Bennett, Jolie and Percy; they were triplets, actually, and all of them were the same age as Pippa. And Hanna had a younger sister, Thea, who was the same age as Lilly. All together there were eight of them in the younger group, then six of us in the older group. Lilly was the only one who didn't have an older sibling anymore, something she didn't seem remotely bothered by, which concerned me. She never got into detail but had mentioned that Corbin was never nice to her and thought she was a nuisance, which made me hate the bastard even more. She was a sweet kid and incredibly smart. I think she latched onto me because of that kindness that I had shown her because now, every time she saw me, I got an overwhelming sensation of safety and comfort coming from her, which made me happy, of course, but also made me miss Rose a bit.

Lessons with Juno had been the same, and I haven't bothered to ask her any more of my questions, considering she would most likely shoot me down anyway. It doesn't mean I don't have questions, though; I have loads. I have been able to light the paper and candle on fire by the end of the week, though, with ease. I got a reassuring nod from the old female and felt pretty proud of myself every time I got that sign of approval. She was a woman of little words and even little kindness but still helpful.

Braxton was also nowhere to be seen in the stables, which was lovely. I heard from a few of the other hands that he was summoned to Carlisle to complete his Scout training, which meant I could see Blaze without worrying about walking into him. Some days, I would ride the freckled horse through the many trails in the forest near the castle and other days, I would spend with Celeste, reading different materials and practicing different Queenly duties. My least favorite was still walking in heels. I preferred the brown laced boots I wore daily or a pair of thin flats, but she insisted it was more lady-like. I'm not sure what about rubbed heals or tripping every few minutes was ladylike, but whatever. I hadn't seen Jess since the beginning of the week, though. Celeste said she was busy with tattoos and that she was a traveler, so whenever she came to the city, she had a long list of clients. I could sense a pang of almost regret or sadness from her, though I knew she also hadn't spoken to Ser Arry yet either because he asked every morning before training how she was doing. Celeste was a proud woman who also liked to be perfect and in control, and I think the feelings she had were unnatural to her in a sense. I knew she was also worried about Emmet as he hadn't sent a message about his endeavor yet, and we didn't know if he would be coming back this evening or if he planned to stay another week.

Despite his absence, along with Hunter's, small council meetings were held twice weekly. And that's where we both were as the sun set over the castle.

"Tensions are rising in the city, Celeste. I was out to lunch today with my handmaidens, and there were many concerns regarding the attack. What do you plan to tell the citizens? I know Emmet has given a statement, but we have not heard from the King since," Lady Seredi asked her sister, drinking from a glass of red wine. The smell of the wine turned my stomach, and I had all I could do to keep from vomiting.

"I know tensions are high, and I imagine everyone sitting here is still anxious... Vada, you know as soon as I hear anything from Emmet, I will relay that information to-"

The doors to the meeting room open before Celeste is able to finish her sentence. Hunter and Emmet walk into the room together. I smiled at my uncle, it was good to see him. He looked well, too, like he always did: well-kept and groomed, not a hair out of place.

I glanced at my aunt; her face paled slightly, and her mouth hung open.

"Good evening, small council members," Emmet said before walking to his usual seat and patting me and Celeste on the shoulders. Celeste nearly flinched at the touch. I could sense the shock rippling off of her. The rest of the room had a mixture of the same shock and relief.

"Well, how nice of you to join us, your Highness," Lord Seredi says, an evil shrew smile across his face.

"Yes, myself and Hunter just got back from Carlisle mere minutes ago. There is nowhere else I'd rather spend my time right now, Garrett," he sighs.

"Do you have any updates for us, your Highness?" Juno asks from the other side of the table.

"None that are all that… *reassuring*, unfortunately. Hunter will be able to tell you all about the efforts to replenish our Scout troops, which have been going quite well. No citizens lost their lives in Carlisle the night of the attack either. The rebels were unsuccessful at fully breaching the border. They have, however, made a significant… dent in the force fields surrounding Sanctania."

Worried glances are exchanged among the members.

"What do you mean by… force fields?" I ask, not being able to remember that from my lessons with Nadine.

"The kingdom has been kept safe and unscathed due to the nature of the magic that has been able to protect us. It is near ancient, spells derived from Emerald stones and the gravitational pull of the Gerios Mountain scape. Usually, it means you would not be allowed to pass the borders without being granted access or being a citizen of Sanctania." Juno responds to me.

"Yes, and somehow the rebel attack has weakened that. The force field still stands, just not as it did before. We are working to repair it, luckily Fae from Carlisle had strong electricity roots, which may be able to charge the spell to be whole once again, but right now, there is the threat that if there is another attack, it could wipe out the force field entirely," Emmet answers.

I swallow deeply. This could be bad. They would be able to fix it, though, right?

"How did the rebels even know about the force field? I don't even remember learning about them…"

"The force fields are something only the lords and ladies and small council members are aware of. It was meant to be kept a secret so that no one could use it against us, if that makes sense. We are still uncertain how the rebels or the Dark King came to figure it out," Emmet answers again, staring at me almost apologetically with his green eyes.

I search for that feeling of panic or sense of fear that once would have sent me into a panic attack or spiral. I found nothing but the hollow emptiness as I took in what I was learning.

~

The meeting ended far past the sunset. I was exhausted, and my temples pounded from feeling everyone's anxiety throughout the whole thing. Hunter had explained all the good things that had happened over the week, but none of it seemed to ease anyone's mind. My mind was swimming with thoughts. The rest of the council members had just finished piling out of the room as I stood and straightened my dress. The large emerald doors closed behind the last person, leaving me and my aunt and uncle in the meeting room.

"You could've sent word," I heard Celeste say as she took her eyes from the table and looked at Emmet, who had just stood.

"I told you I would if I needed to stay another week. I didn't need to stay another week, obviously, because I am here now," he states bluntly.

"But you could have warned me, warned *us*, about the news

you just sprung on everyone instead of keeping me in the dark." Celeste pushes back her chair and stands. She may be tall, nearly still a head over myself, but Emmet still towered her.

My heart rate picked up as I heard Celeste's do the same.

"Sucks to be kept in the dark, doesn't it, Celeste?" He answered in a tone I haven't heard from him before.

"No, we are *not* doing that. What happened between me and another Fae does *not* equate to not telling me about the state of our kingdom Emmet. I have been worried sick all *fucking* week."

The wind started to pick up in the room a bit, causing the hairs on my arms to stand.

Emmet glanced at me. "Go to your room, Ryenn." But I stayed frozen in place. I didn't want to leave. I *couldn't*.

"Well?" Celeste narrowed her eyes at him. "Do you have anything to say?"

"I don't want to have this conversation right now."

"Well, that's too godsdamn bad because we *are*. Maybe if you had given me a heads up about the whole force field weakening shit, I wouldn't be lashing out right now."

"Celeste, if I had thought it was that big of a deal, then I would have let you know. I had it handled by myself."

"This is supposed to be a two-person job! That's what you once told me when I said I didn't want to be the Queen. You can't just leave me out of things because you get mad that I was fucking someone."

"I wasn't mad that you were fucking him!" Emmet shouted, which caused me to take a step back. "I was mad that you seemed so concerned over him when he came back near dead. I knew he meant more to you than your usual whores. I should've known that you weren't incapable of love. You're just incapable of loving *me*. That's something I have come to terms with, Celeste but don't you dare try and bring the kingdom's trust down with you because of some stupid girl crush on the Sergeant of the first Scout Battalion. If I could see that, I guarantee the citizens will, and then where will their trust lie during this time? Not on the people who are faking a happy marriage and having affairs left, right and centered."

Celeste's eyes filled with tears, and I tried, at that moment, to be invisible. "You're not innocent in that, Emmet! You have your fair share of fun just as much as I do."

"My fun stops in my chambers; it doesn't follow me to public parties. So forgive me for not wanting to speak to you, but I couldn't stand to look at you, let alone let you know of my whereabouts," he snarled, sounding like a predator.

"*She died that way.*" Tears were now running down over Celeste's face as she took a deep breath. "Me and Ela got into an argument over something petty the night she left to go help Baytown. That was the last I heard of her before the announcement came that she had *died.*" She was now sobbing through the words,

"I don't have to love you in a married sense to fucking *care* about you. I couldn't sleep all godsdamn week because I thought the next message I was going to get would be from Lady Juniper saying that you had been hurt or worse-" She buried her face in her hands and was shaking as she sat back down on the chair, her blonde hair coming undone from the wind that had been circling the room like a cyclone. My chest cracked open for Celeste, and I felt all her sorrow and grief rush to me. It was so powerful that she nearly knocked me off my feet. Emmet's hateful expression had faded, and he now felt... bad. He felt guilty, tangy and overwhelmed.

"I'm sorry," he whispers, going to Celeste, taking her in and embracing her as she cries harder. "I'm sorry. I shouldn't have done that. I forgot that had happened, Celeste. I'm *so sorry.*"

My eyes were wide, and emotion clogged my throat. That layer of emotion temporarily drowned out the hollowness I felt by the numbness, but not in a good way, in a heavy, exhausting way, one that made it tricky to swallow.

"Ser Davis, please escort Ryenn to her chambers," Emmet looks up at me. "It's okay. I'm sorry, okay? I will talk to you tomorrow."

I nod hesitantly as Ser Davis approaches me and leads me out of the room. Celeste's sobs follow me the whole way out.

Chapter 46

I felt heavy as I sat in my room. I only wore a thin night dress and couldn't let the blankets even touch me as I felt the scorching heat. It was the middle of the night, maybe an hour since I had left the meeting room. I tried to take a cool bath, but not even that calmed me. Celeste's cries haunted me. She had mentioned before that she blamed herself for my mother's death, but I didn't know the reasoning behind that. And the fact that Emmet knew this had happened knew what happened to Celeste after my mother's death, yet did the same thing and didn't send her message due to petty reasoning angered me a bit. I suppose all men were idiots, whether you were a king or not. I lay there tossing and turning before I decided I had enough.

I needed to wake in three hours anyway, so maybe going to see if she was alright would calm my nerves. Leaving my robe behind because I was too fucking hot, I shuffled down the hall, not saying a word to the Scouts on duty. It wasn't their business what I was doing anyway.

There was no scarf tied to the brass handle, and it was unlocked.

I let myself in quietly, my footsteps nearly non-existent against the lush carpets. Celeste lay in her massive canopy bed and appeared to be sleeping. Good. She *was* okay. My Katiase reached out to her, and despite the calm, sleeping look on her face, I felt the depression and exhaustion seep from her.

Her room was much cooler than mine, though, and maybe it had to be due to the fact that she could control the temperature with her wind, even while she slept. At that moment I want to crawl into her bed and curl up next to her. Childish, I know, but despite the numbness, I just had this deep-rooted feeling that I didn't want to be alone, and I could sense she didn't want that either. So carefully, I crossed the massive bed, trying not to disturb her, and lie next to her. The blankets are cool to touch and welcoming.

I lie there and shut my eyes, and I am sure she won't mind if I just relax for the next few hours before training. I could slip out before she woke anyway.

Suddenly, I feel the bed shift slightly, and she wraps her arms around me, her skin cool to the touch. "You okay?" she says, merely a whisper.

"Yeah… Are you?" I say back in the same volume.

"Mhmm," she hums back.

She stays there, holding me in and embracing me, fearing to let me go, as we both fall asleep.

~

I woke up a few hours later, or what I thought was only a few hours later, but the sun had already begun to rise, even though the orange hue barely crested the trees. Shit, I was late for training. You know what? I don't care. I needed a break. I'm sure Ser Arry wouldn't mind.

I laid there groggily, Celeste still snoring lightly to my left. She was tired. I felt it in my bones. I looked at the clock on the wall; I had a few hours before I had to get up for class, but I figured it would be polite of me to alert Arry that I won't be there this morning. I roll off the bed, being extra careful not to disturb Celeste and go out to the hall, where Ser Davis awaits.

"Ser Davis, would you mind telling Ser Arry I won't be attending training this morning? Just tell him I have a headache and am not feeling 100%. I am already 30 minutes late, so he's probably wondering where I am…" I looked at the ground, feeling a little guilty about skipping out.

"I already told him," he said. "I figured you needed the rest. As does the Queen."

"Oh," I look at him with a blush across my face. That was kind of him. "Thank you."

"It's alright. Go back to bed, princess. The handmaidens will wake you for breakfast."

I do as he said, letting myself into Celeste's room again and carefully crawling back into her cool bed. She didn't disturb once.

~

I woke again after two hours as the handmaidens entered the chambers and opened up the curtains, letting the full strength of the sun inside the room. It was blinding at first, and I groaned against it. They then went to Celeste's bathing chamber and started drawing a bath.

I flipped over to my side and looked at Celeste, who was now sitting and rubbing her eyes. They were slightly red and puffy from crying yesterday.

"Hi," she whispers, looking down at me.

"Hi," I smile.

"Thank you," she whispers and pets my hair. Her touch is gentle and soothing. One I now welcome without a fight.

"I need to get ready for school… I'll meet you in the dining hall?" I ask, sitting up.

She nods and begins to work her fingers through the tangles in her hair.

I still sit there, looking at her.

She catches me staring and stills. "Everything alright?" She asks, her tone calm and cool.

I leap over and hug her, burying my face in her hair and inhaling deeply.

"I'm so sorry, Celeste. About all of it. I know I don't have to apologize, but I want to. You don't deserve any of it."

"Oh honey," she breathes deeply, hugging me back. "*Thank you.*"

I pull back and look into her watery blue eyes. "I love you."

"Love you too, Ryenn. Now go get ready, or you'll be late." She gives me a playful shove, and I smile, leaving the chambers and heading down the hall to my own.

~

Not even thirty minutes later, I am dressed, my hair is done and I am going down to the dining hall. That was the quickest time I have ever gotten ready for school, actually. When I get there, it is only Emmet sitting at the head of the table.

"Good morning," he says in a cheery tone after taking a long sip from his coffee.

"Where is Celeste?" I ask, my tone flat as I take my usual seat.

"On her way down, I imagine," he says, offering a pitiful grin. "You're mad at me."

I scoff and look at my plate, stabbing a sausage with a fork.

"You have the right to be mad. What I did was not nice, and believe it or not, I do regret said actions."

"Good," I mutter.

"Ryenn," I look up at him as he addresses me with his tone when addressing a crowd as the King, "I am sorry not only for hurting Celeste the way that I did and for keeping you in the dark as well all week but also for all of it. I haven't gotten to speak to you since all of the news about the attack unfurled. I am also sorry about Baytown."

"Thank you for your apology," I say. I can't stay mad at him. He knows what he did was childish, but I also knew Celeste wasn't without her faults, but he had hurt her badly.

"How are you holding up with all of it? I have been talking around, and the handmaidens and Scouts say that you've been quite busy but are doing well. Juno says your powers are being harnessed nicely."

"I'm holding up fine," I say, swallowing the rest of my sausage. "Training is going well, too. I'll have to show you what I know later," I grin, knowing it would probably be near impossible to flip a man his side over my shoulder but I was still going to try it.

"I'd like that," he says, grinning. Celeste enters the room, donning a pale blue summer dress with white markings. It's pretty and one I have not yet seen. She looks better than she did waking up this morning. I suppose cosmetics hid the red bags under her eyes.

"Good morning," she breathes, taking a seat next to me and Emmet.

"Good morning, Celeste," he says in a calm tone. "How are you doing this morning?" He looks at her with all-knowing eyes.

"I'm alright," she says, and I don't sense lies off of her, just a cool, minty feeling, one that I can't quite pinpoint. Maybe peace? I'm not sure, though.

"You slept?" He asks next.

"Mhmm," she sips her tea and both their gazes fall to the doors as Amalie and Pippa walk in.

"Have a good day, Ryenn," they both say at the same time.

~

A little while later that day, all the students are eating their lunches outside; the heat in the school house is sweltering, although it isn't much cooler outside either.

I bite my sandwich as I notice Grey nearing from the log he was just sitting on. I swallow my bite like a lump, and Amalie glares between both of us with a smile tugging at the corner of her lips.

"Where were you this morning?" he asks, tilting his head.

"None of your business."

"You're not going to be the first female warrior by sleeping in on practice," he smirks.

"I wasn't '*sleeping in*', Greyson. Quiet down. I'd rather people didn't know about my training sessions."

"Why not? I thought you wanted to be a badass. Or is it because you don't want people to know you're training with me?" He quiets his tone.

"Neither I just- I don't know. I don't care what people think." I roll my eyes at him, taking another bite of my sandwich

"Then where were you this morning?"

"Again, none of your business. Why do you even care?"

"Kinda hard to do hand-to-hand combat with no partner."

"So you missed me then?" I joke.

"I guess I kinda did Frisky. Anyways, I'll see you tomorrow morning?" He smiles again, and heat rushes to my face.

"Yes. But do *not* call me that." He walks away, chuckling, without answering me, and I turn to Amalie, who has her jaw nearly in her lap.

"Amalie, close your mouth. You'll catch a bug." I roll my eyes

"Okay, the *tension*. Ry, I knew you were training with him, but *that*. That was some serious spice," she giggled, and I gave her a shove.

"Shut up."

A siren began to sound overhead. One I hadn't heard before, almost like an incredibly loud horn. Before I got to ask Amalie what was happening, Mrs. Langerfeld came rushing out of the schoolhouse, and Scouts flanked the schoolyard.

"Everyone gets to the castle now!" She yells.

Amalie and I exchange worried looks and stand to run. Pippa comes running over for her sister. All the Fae children take off in a sprint, and Scout races by us, heading to the castle's main doors past the gardens. I spot Lilly frozen in spot, eyes wide like a deer in headlights.

"Lilly, come on, we have to go!" I ran over to the young girl, the group still running ahead. I noticed the child had wet herself from fear and was shivering, hardly breathing.

"It's okay, we have to go to the castle. The Scouts are here, see? We are safe." I touch her back, and she looks up at me, tears streaming down her face

"I-I can't m-move," she shudders.

I take a deep breath, seeing the group running ahead up in the distance.

"Okay, hold on tight, alright?" I scoop the girl up in my arms, and she clings her small hands around the back of my neck. She hardly weighs anything, and running with her in my arms is easy.

I picture the *need* to get inside. The Scouts were starting to lower the main gate, and I didn't think we could get in time. I had become faster with training for the past week, but still. I closed my eyes then, *willing* us to be inside. *Desperate* to get there. When I opened my eyes again, we had jumped over 100 yards of the garden and were on the bridge with the rest of the group. Greyson came up next to me, putting his hands on my shoulders.

"I couldn't find you," he breathed heavily. "How the fuck did you get up here so fast?"

"*Locus,*" I panted. I must have room-jumped. Gods, that was so fucking cool. Now is not the time to be proud of that accomplishment, though. I grasped Lilly tighter and rubbed her back.

"Lilly, are you okay? We are inside now. It's okay, honey, we are safe."

She was still shivering against me and clung to me as if fearing that if she let go, something bad would happen.

"I feel sick," I hear her small voice whisper.

"Oh yeah, the room-jumping can do that... Are you going to throw up?"

"N-no, I don't think so," her teeth chattered.

I walked up next to Amalie and Pippa. Pippa was clinging to her sister's legs, and tears rolled down her rosy cheeks.

"What is going on?" Amalie looks at me, eyes wide with fear

"I have no idea-"

Emmet came to the main entrance, then Celeste in tow. I could sense their stress and anxiety but also the relief that washed over their features when they saw me.

"All children are to be escorted to the Throne Room, please. Further instructions will come shortly."

Chapter 47

The Scouts escorted all 14 of us into the Throne Room. A few other citizens were also in there: some handmaidens and servants, Mrs. Langerfeld, and a bunch of Scouts, including Ser Arry. Once we entered the room, Lilly finally settled enough to get down. The poor thing was terrified, I could tell from just looking at her, but *sensing* her made my heart ache for the young girl. The fear and a tang of embarrassment felt all too real. Evie, who had luckily been in the Throne Room, came up to us, saying she was relieved to see me and that she would find something for Lilly to change into so she could get out of her wet dress. The rest of the Fae sat with their siblings, soothing the younger ones' nerves. It was the only time I actually saw Autumn, Luna and Hanna being remotely kind. Grey sat close to Lilly and me, not having said anything since finding us on the bridge outside.

Evie returned shortly after with a new uniform dress for Lilly to change into. I assisted her behind one of the curtains near the back of the room where no one could see us. We weren't permitted to leave the Throne Room, so we had to make do. The heat of embarrassment from Lilly was overwhelming, and even though I tried to comfort her, she still cried.

Now we were sitting on the floor, Lilly in my lap, fiddling with the end of my braid between her small hands as I waited for

Celeste and Emmet to return. Besides the emotions and feelings I was picking up from the group, I still felt numb. Hollow. I should probably have been worried. Instead, I welcomed it instead of that dreaded feeling of panic I knew was deep down in there, festering.

~

It's been a good thirty minutes since the horn blared since we've been sitting here without anyone talking to us. The nerves and tension in the throne room were smothering me.

"Lilly, I need to go speak with Ser Arry. Would you mind sitting with Greyson? I promise I'll be right back, okay?"

The child took a shuddery breath, and I looked over to Grey and met his stare. He could almost sense my need to get up and do something.

"Come over, Lilly, we can play I-Spy," he says, then reaches a hand towards the girl.

She looks up at me, blinking her thick lashes. Her eyes are still puffy and red, but the tears have stopped.

"It's alright," I whisper calmly, and she crawls from my lap and sits next to Grey.

I mouth the words "thank you" to him, and he winks back, starting the game of I-Spy.

I brushed my dress off, one that I couldn't wait to change out of for many reasons, and walked over to where Ser Arry stood by the wall.

"I need to speak with my aunt and uncle," I said as I approached the tall man. He scowled at me.

"I have orders not to let anyone leave this room," he says flatly.

"Well, I am ordering you to let me see the King and Queen," I retort, crossing my arms, and he raises a brow.

"Your orders don't trump theirs," he says.

"Please, Arry," I whisper, letting my guard down a bit. "I need to speak to them, or I will lose it in this room. You've seen me lose it before on my first-day training with Greyson. Fire and fear do not seem like it mixes well does it?"

"Fine," he sighs, "follow me."

I follow behind him, aware of the attention that I may have drawn from the rest of the group, and am led into an adjacent meeting room, the same one where the council discussed Corbin's punishment during the trial, I believe.

Celeste, Emmet, Juno, Hunter and Normani were there.

"What the hell is going on?" I ask as I step into the room, and their attention flies to me.

"Ser Arry, you were given orders-" Hunter starts, but I cut him off, raising a hand.

"I gave him orders to bring me here. I want to know what's going on. There's a group of 13 children in that room who are scared shitless, and I'm on the verge of being one of them. What happened to not being kept in the dark, Emmet?" I direct my attention to my uncle.

Celeste stands and walks over to me, guiding me to an open seat next to her.

"There was another attack," Emmet starts, and I suck in a breath. "It was on the mortal lands, the next town over from Baytown; St.Marie's."

"And what of our safety? The force fields? Has there been an assault on Sanctania?"

"There has not. Yet. That's why all the children were summoned to the safety of the castle. If the rebels are planning an attack similar to their last, then we wanted to make sure you were all safe and in one place. There has not yet been an attempt on us, but we wanted to have proper precautions in place just in case."

I let out a little breath of relief. "Why couldn't you just tell them that? Do their parents know? What about the rest of the small council…"

"The rest of the small council members were outside the castle grounds when we went on lockdown, so they are not allowed back in until lockdown is lifted," Celeste states calmly. "All the children's parents are aware of the attack and agree it is safer for them to stay in their respective districts while the children are kept in the castle for now."

"Okay… okay, good."

"I was just about to go tell the group that before you burst in here," Emmet says, smiling.

"You left us waiting for hours!" I throw my hands up.

"It hasn't even been 30 minutes," Celeste says.

"When have you both ever known me to be the patient type?"

All the members laugh at that, and a bit of weight lifts from my chest. We're still safe. The force fields stand. It's just safety precautions; a good idea, honestly. Hopefully it stays that way.

~

I walked out with Emmet and Celeste and sat on my throne as he gave the same speech to the children and other citizens that he had just given me; that there was no immediate danger and that this was all a safety precaution. He also followed up by saying that everyone was to remain in the room until tomorrow morning so food, sleeping cots and other necessities would be brought here. There were quite a few groans at that, including Amalie, who had then argued that she technically wouldn't be leaving the castle if she went home, but since an outdoor bridge attaches the west side,

Celeste said they couldn't risk it.

I returned to Grey and Lilly after the speech, the girl rushing to her feet and hugging my legs when I got near.

"I told you we were safe. You feel a bit better now?" I asked her.

She nodded, still grasping my legs

"Listen, I gotta go talk to the Queen and maybe change my clothes, but I'll be back, okay? It's going to be like a big sleepover."

"You promise you'll be back?" She looks up with worry on her face.

"I promise, chicky". *Chicky*. That's what I used to call Rose. I take a sharp inhale and look away. Lilly wasn't Rose. That doesn't mean I didn't like her, but I do not need to dwell on Rose. She's gone whether I like it or not.

Fuck what is wrong with me? Am I really that numb?

I shake off those thoughts and walk over to Celeste, who is chatting with Mrs. Langerfeld. She finishes her conversation and then turns to me.

"Am I permitted to leave? To at least get changed? I'll come back afterward, and I promised Lilly I would anyway."

She sighs but then raises a brow. "I was going to say no, but I'm looking at you now, wondering what that stain is on your dress and why you look so disheveled."

"Two things: Lilly had an accident, and I had to carry her. Hence the stain and I look disheveled because I room-jumped," I grin.

"Aww, poor thing. *Wait*- You room-jumped!?" She smiles.

"Yep, right from the archway of the gardens to the bridge of the castle. It was cool and not as disorienting as when I did it with you. Well, Lilly said it made her sick, but luckily, she didn't vomit, or I'd have another bodily fluid stain on my dress."

"That's far too focused on your first try. *And* with another person, even if she is small, that's crazy. Congrats, honey," she pets my head.

"Thanks. Anyways, can I please go get cleaned up?"

"Fine. But you will have two Scouts plus Ser Arry escort you and enter your room to ensure no threats. I have to go meet with the council for the foreseeable future," she rolls her eyes, "but I promise I'll let you know if we hear anything else, alright?"

"Okay, thank you," I exhale.

"Just be careful, please." She looks at me, and I taste the concern.

I nod and head for Ser Arry to give him the wonderful news that he's my newly appointed babysitter.

Chapter 48

It didn't take me long to get changed into something lighter and cleaner. The three scouts stayed in my chambers as I did, which was weird. Arry didn't seem too impressed by his involvement, honestly. He must be kind of upset that he isn't able to respond to the attack due to his injury; I got a sense of frustration from him.

Back in the Throne Room, servants were bringing rolls of cots to set up for the 14 children. The younger kids were on one side of the room, playing some sort of game, except for Lilly. As soon as she saw me come back, she hadn't left my side since. Autumn, Luna and Hanna were talking about something stupid, I assumed. Grey sat against a wall, picking at a piece of wood with his pocket knife, and Amalie was reading a book that I snuck in for her. I sat beside Amalie, braiding and combing Lilly's dark brown hair. When I used the Katiase, I could feel that there wasn't a heavy tension in the room like before, people were starting to calm down. Now and then, though, I'd feel a tumble of panic rise from Lilly.

"You sure you don't want to go play with the other kids? Looks like they are having fun," I ask her.

She shakes her head and looks down at her lap.

Finishing her braid, I turn her around so that she's looking at me. "Do you wanna talk about it?" I whisper.

"No," she shakes her little head, not looking me in the eyes.

"Hey, look at me." I tilt her chin up with my finger.

Her big blue eyes flick to mine.

"It's okay. We're safe."

"It's true. Ryenn wouldn't lie. She's going to be the Queen, remember?" Amalie looks up from her book and winks at the little girl.

"You'll be a good Queen," Lilly says then, grinning.

"Why thank you, Lady Sapphic," I smile.

"I'll be a part of your council then," she smiles wide, exposing her lost front tooth. Fae children lost their teeth like mortal children until the fangs came in during their Transition.

"You will. And so will Amalie. She's going to be the Lady of the Capital." I look at my friend but she looks back at her book, face red. I get a sense of despair from her then, and I'm not exactly sure why.

"I didn't want to be the Lady. I knew Corbin was going to be the Lord, especially if he never won the heir champion title. I never thought he would, and he was unkind. He wouldn't have made a good king. He fooled lots of people to like him though. But now I'm happy to be Lady because you'll be the best, nicest Queen."

I blush a little. "Thank you. Lilly, did Corbin ever… hurt you?" I decided to ask. Not that it would make a difference, but I wanted to know. There was something about her that I couldn't quite grasp. She was mature for her years but also absolutely terrified of being hurt or in harm's way.

"Sometimes…" She whispered, twirling her hair around her finger. Amalie looks up from her book, her face flushed, and I can feel anger coming from her. I feel the same.

"Does your mom and dad know that?" I ask again, straightening my back and easing the tension in my muscles.

"Yeah. They loved him, though and never said anything. They just told me it is what it is and to not be a nuisance or bug him, but I *never* did. Or at least I didn't try to. I don't know; sometimes he'd get angry and just come to my room and…" She took a deep breath. "It doesn't matter now anyways. He's gone. Mother is still upset, and Father is just quiet anyway, so it's weird, but I don't know. I still love them, and I miss them. Not Corbin; I never loved him."

Hearing her admit what she did sent shivers down my spine. Amalie had a hand clasped over her mouth as she looked at me with wide eyes. How could anyone possibly hurt Lilly? She was so small and innocent. How could anyone hurt a fucking child in general? Gods, sometimes I wish I had killed him on the spot instead of him being exiled. That thought disturbs me a bit.

Fuck.

I pull the girl closer and give her a tight hug. She inhaled deeply and stayed there for a few minutes, relaxing. The sweet smell of lavender accompanies the sense of relaxation.

"What the fuck?" Amalie whispers.

"I know," I whisper back, rubbing Lilly's small back. Even though she was seven, she was probably smaller than Pippa, who was 2 years younger than her.

Lilly ends up falling asleep in my arms, and I stay there, rocking back and forth. It's bittersweet, really, reminding me so much of Rose. We stayed like that for nearly an hour, myself and Amalie talking back and forth about what the attacks could mean, about my training and other things. I still have yet to see my aunt and uncle again, and I worry that I should be attending the meetings. I hate being left out, and I feel like I have a right to know what is going on. Servants begin wheeling meal trays of soups and other foods for the kids. I wake Lilly, and we go over together to get our dinner. We go back to the cots and eat our stuff as Greyson walks over with something in his hand.

"This is for you," he hands the thing to Lilly. It's a small wooden Drakōn, carved from the chunk he was working on earlier.

"Wow!" She exclaims, looking up at Grey, smiling. "It's a Drakōn, right?"

"Yes," he smiles. "A creature that's strong and brave, just like you." he winks, and she clutches the little wooden creature to her chest.

"Thanks, Grey," she grins.

"You're welcome, kid. Now, eat your soup before it gets cold." He looks at me then, and warmth spreads across my face.

A tight curl of emotion squeezed my abdomen, a similar feeling of recklessness that caused me to kiss him at the ball. I suck in a breath. Gods, now is not the time to be thinking like this. But that was so nice of him. Then I feel a fruity emotion come from Grey as he looks at me, something that is unfamiliar to me. It's like grapefruit, acidic and sweet, and it makes my heart speed up. *Lust*.

Chapter 49

Celeste comes to the throne room to retrieve me later. Lilly has fallen asleep on her cot by now, clutching the wooden Drakōn to her chest. I follow Celeste outside the doors, where Emmet is also waiting.

"Any more news?" I ask, half worried they will say yes.

"No, thank goodness," Celeste grins, "but we do have to tell you something."

"Okay, what?"

"Celeste and I need to go to Carlisle for a few days. They are working hard in attempts to fix the force fields, and they think our help would be of value. Juno will be joining us, along with Hunter and Bradley," Emmet says.

"Oh," I say, feeling like my heart deflates a bit.

"Ryenn honey, if there weren't a danger, we would have allowed you to join us, but you know yourself that you'll be safer in the castle. You'll stay with Vada and Garrett, okay? We should only be gone three days," Celeste says, touching my shoulder.

"No, it's okay. I understand." And I did. Still, it hurt a little when I knew I could maybe help. Plus, I didn't love the idea of having to stay with Lord and Lady Seredi, but at least Amalie would be there. A little pang of panic bubbles up from the pit of hollowness; what if I had a nightmare or something? Celeste wouldn't be there to assist.

Calm the fuck down, Ryenn, you're being childish. She's only going to be gone for three days.

"Good, well I have to go pack… Celeste, I'll retrieve you from your chambers in the early morning. Be on your best behavior Ryenn," Emmet winks at me and walks off down towards the familial quarters of the castle.

"Ryenn," I look to Celeste, feeling worried pour from her. "Are you going to be alright?"

"Mhmm. I will. It's only three days…"

"Jess is still in the city. I was able to speak to her briefly today, and she said she'll check on you daily, okay? You'll be fine. Vada and Garrett weren't necessarily pleased, but they'll do anything for the kingdom."

"I'll be *fine,* Celeste." I gave her a smile that I knew wasn't from happiness. It was to make her feel better.

"Alright," she hugs me tight. "By the way, I think what you're doing for that young girl is very, very kind. She clearly feels comfortable with you. You're a good girl." She kisses the top of my head, and I breathe in her familiar perfume.

I allow that blanket of numbness to suffocate me once more, welcoming it.

~

The night passed uneventfully. I didn't sleep, and I couldn't actually. I just lay on my cot with the rest of the children. Lilly snuggled against me for the whole night. We were all dismissed from the Throne Room early that morning and permitted to return to our actual chambers to bathe and rest. Schooling was canceled for the day.

Evie assisted me in packing a small bag to bring to the west side of the castle, to the Seredi's tower. I had a quick bath, a nice cool one, and donned a cream-coloured dress.

The day wasn't that bad; I mean, I hadn't seen the Lord or Lady yet, most likely because they were far too busy, but we were meant to meet them for dinner in a few hours. Right now, the two girls decided to go for a short walk to the gardens, followed by three Scouts, of course, Ser Arry being one of them.

"Is Greyson your boyfriend, Ryenn?" Pippa asks, skipping along and humming a tune.

"What?" I choke on my surprise, and Amalie starts laughing like a crazy person.

"He looks at you with goo-goo eyes," she giggles, and my face heats. "Ha! You do like him because you are blushing."

"I do *not*," I counter back.

"Do too," she giggles, and I grab her and tickle her ribs. She runs off ahead, laughing and skipping like a little puppy.

"Do you like him, Ry? Be honest. I won't tell anyone, and I think it's kinda sweet if you do," Amalie asks as her sister picks flowers up ahead.

I sigh. "I don't know. I feel weird. I knew I liked Braxton, and he was kind and sweet…until he wasn't. But with Greyson, I don't know, and I know I kissed him randomly, but like I don't know what I feel. He's nice but also so fucking annoying with his stupid smirk and stupid pet names… I don't know."

She grins, "Okay," and I roll my eyes.

Did I like Greyson? I think I probably already knew the answer to that, but now is not the time to care about boys.

We circle the gardens and slowly make our way back towards the castle. A red-haired Fae is leaning against the rails of the bridge as we are near, and immediately, I know it's Jess, keeping her word and seeing that I was doing okay.

"You guys go ahead. I'll meet you inside in a minute."

Amalie holds her sister's hand and walks in with the other Scouts, and Ser Arry stays behind to watch me.

"Good afternoon," Jess says in her raspy voice, smiling with her fangs glistening in the afternoon sun.

"Hi Jess," I smile back.

"Just checking up to see how you're making out. Your aunt is a bit of a control freak, as you know."

"Yeah, slightly," I laugh. "I'm okay. Really. How's tattooing going?"

"Same shit, different day," she smiles, and her gaze flicks to Ser Arry. "Ser Arrington," she lifts her chin at the male as he towers behind me.

"Jessibria," he says back, his voice merely a rumble.

I'm standing in between their weird emotional cyclone. Sultry spiciness and that fruity lust ripple between them.

"You guys are gross," I say, causing both of them to laugh.

"I didn't do anything," Jess argues but winks.

"You didn't have to. Anyways, Ser Arry is clearly on babysitting duty, so we must get back before Vada and Garrett chop off my head for being late to their dinner," I roll my eyes.

"Yeah, good luck with that." Jess flicks her thick hair over her shoulder. "I'm staying at the Geltic Inn in case you need me," her gaze flicking from my face to above my head where Arry stands. *Gross*.

"See you tomorrow."

"Bye, Ry. Have a fun night," she says in a joking tone before walking down the bridge towards the city, her tall high heels clacking on the cobblestone.

Chapter 50

I don't think I've ever been to a more awkward dinner than the one I'm attending right now. Picking at the chicken with my fork, Garrett and Vada silently watch me. The entire time, we've all been silent and haven't said a word. I clear my throat and set down my fork.

"Something wrong with your dinner?" Garret asks, breaking the 10-minute silence.

"No, it's fine. I'm not very hungry," I replied. It was the truth. I wasn't hungry and hadn't had much of an appetite since yesterday.

Vada scoffs.

"Is there an issue?" I ask her before really noticing I'm speaking.

"Besides the fact that you have no manners, child. Celeste is doing a pretty shit job at raising you if you think talking to an adult that way is acceptable," Garrett says then. Heat rushes to my face.

"Father, stop," Amalie mutters then from my right.

"Amalie, do not speak to your father that way. Or would you like twice as many lashings as the last time you spoke back?" Vada glares at her. Amalie turns red and looks at her plate. I feel both fear and embarrassment through the Katiase. It's potent and clogs my throat. I also felt anger. Maybe the anger was mostly from me, though. *Lashings*. They had been whipping Amalie?

Bile rises in my throat.

"Celeste is doing quite a good job last time I checked. And I will not sit here and listen to you talk bad about the Queen of the kingdom," I say back, spite filling my mouth. I feel that familiar stinging burn in my veins.

"Temper, temper, temper." Garrett mockingly shakes his head, one meant to belittle me. I won't stand down, though. "That temper won't get you very far in this kingdom, child. Unlike your mortal shack, you won't be able to burn down the castle when you get angry."

I clamp my mouth shut. What did he mean by burning down my home? I didn't have my powers then…

"What the fuck are you talking about?" I seethe.

"*Language*. And don't act so stupid, Ryenn. The entire small council viewed your memories when you first got here, we saw what happened to your cottage, how it burnt down around you. The flames were *silver*. Gods, I figured you would have put two and two together by now." Garrett looks down at me, an evil grin across his face.

Breathing became difficult.

What was he talking about?

Why hadn't I known they had seen my memories?

The flames weren't silver... *were they?*

"My house burning down was a rebel attack..." I say, my voice quiet. It was... right?

"The only rebel attack on Molisan since the day you were born was the recent one on Baytown. You caused the fires that initially wiped out a good portion of the stupid little town." Vada rolled her eyes. "Gods, I'd say everyone on the small council has figured that out by now. Did you really not know?"

My chest began to tighten as I felt a crack ripple through me.

Had I caused my house to burn down?

Had I killed my little sister and father?

Had I been the one to burn down half my hometown?

All of it flashes back to me.

The nightmares; *silver flames* crept up those walls, blocking every entrance.

I must have been in such a fit of anger that my powers manifested and caught the house on fire.

I did it.

I hurt them.

I killed them.

Emotion rushes to me then, knocking me back against the chair. The Katiase picks up confusion, anger, pity… satisfaction. Lord and Lady Seredi were satisfied. This must have been their plan all along.

My own emotions drown out the ones I feel through the Katiase, that long-asleep panic shooting to my core, sorrow and guilt accompanying it side by side.

I can't breathe.

Heat burned my veins.

Everyone was looking at me.

Smoke.

Smoke left my hands, those silver flames following suit.

"Don't you dare even try," Garrett said then, that satisfied emotion leaving him. "You're dangerous and not fit to be heir to the Emerald Throne. That fire will be the end of us all. The same way, it was the end of your family."

"Don't fucking talk about my family!" I yell then, standing.

"Ry," I hear Amalie say distantly. Pippa was crying, but I could barely hear it over the crash of flames in my ears

Flames encircled my wrists, leading up my arms, circling my

head. I'm sure I could breathe fire if I tried, taste it and relish in its comfort.

I had killed my baby sister.

Agony took hold then, a crashing and debilitating feeling

"I only speak the truth. Not my fault you cannot control yourself."

Flames light the tablecloth on fire, spreading towards him as he takes a step back.

A grin creeps across Garrett's face.

"Scouts, *seize* her."

Scouts, who were standing by came near me with manacles made of a dark, rich metal, advanced towards me.

"You can't do that," I spit back at him.

"Oh yes, I can. If I had it my way, I'd whip you senseless until you started obeying, but that would, unfortunately, be an act of treason. However, you are a danger to yourself and others. Therefore, the clasps are to nullify your powers, and you are to be put in the dungeon cell until I am no longer in charge of the safety of this city. I pull rank on you right now, child. Celeste and Emmet aren't here. *I* am in charge."

The Scouts came closer. I realized then there were two that I hadn't met before, and that I was not sure where Ser Arry was.

They attempt to put the large clasps on my hands, and the metal stings to the touch.

I yank my hands back. "Don't you fucking touch me!" Flames erupt from me, Amalie, Pippa, and their mother step back from the table.

"Father, stop this! She's upset, and you're only going to make it worse," Amalie yells.

"Don't you talk back, young lady!" He yells back at her.

"Do not speak to her that way, and I will have your head on a fucking stick when I am-"

The manacles are slammed onto my hands, and I scream against the pain, nearly making me fall to my knees. The clasp is another set around my ankles.

"Get the gag," Vada says, venom coating her tone.

A ball gag is placed around my mouth, and they hold me up by the chains linked to me.

They can't do this.

This was a trap.

I could feel that stupid satisfaction coming from them again, along with the fear from the two girls, both of whom were sobbing.

I'm a monster.

Oh, my Gods.

I can't breathe, choking against the gag in my mouth.

"Lead her down to the dungeons. No one is to see her, and no one is to let her out. Celeste and Emmet won't be returning for two more days at the very least. Maybe now she'll learn that actions have consequences." He stalks towards me and holds my chin. "Not so powerful now, are you, Princess?" I yank back from him. If looks could kill, he'd be so fucking dead.

~

The two manhandling Scouts grab and push me down the winding hallways until I get to the cells, just down the corridor from the wine cellar. The memories flash to me, and I'm haunted.

They latch the chains that encircle the manacled cuffs and my ankles to the anchor on the floor in the middle of the room. It's cold, dark and damp. There is no way out.

One of them yanks the ball gag out of my mouth as I'm hyperventilating against it.

"We're ordered to leave this off so you can breathe. If you start doing anything wrong, we have orders to put it back on."

They both leave then, shutting the large metal door with a tiny barred window at the top behind them.

I'm alone.

Chapter 51

I burned down my house.

I killed my sister and father in the flames.

I ran away from the destruction.

I blamed it on a rebel attack.

I usurped a throne I'm not fit for.

I was attacked.

I was raped.

I was cheated.

I exiled my attacker.

I'm a monster.

~

I'm not sure how many hours have passed in the cell. I can't move against the chains; they dig in and burn my skin.

I can't use my flames no matter how hard I try. The pain of the fire coursing through me that I can't relieve myself from is unbearable.

I hate myself.

Panic, agony, guilt, grief, fear, rage; all the emotions swirl in my stomach. I throw up for the fifth time since sitting here. Hardly anything is left in my stomach at this point.

I'm trapped.

I'm going to die here.

I can't fucking breathe.

I can't do this.

"Let me out!" I scream. I scream, and I scream, and I scream.

My throat is raw, and no one is listening.

This is definitely the end.

I hope it's soon.

~

I hear footsteps and look up at the door. Someone is coming.

I see a female with red hair pop up behind the small window.

Jess.

"Ryenn, oh my Gods," she gasped.

"J-Jess?" I manage to whisper against my scratchy throat.

"Oh, honey. I can't talk long. Arry and I tricked the stupid Scouts who won't let anyone down here. Amalie escaped yesterday morning and went to get help and found Greyson. Both came and got me. I have just sent a message to Celeste and Emmet, and they should be on their way back. I'm so sorry. You don't deserve this.

Fuck I'm going to kill then," she was nearly out of breath.

"Please let me out," I whimper.

"I- I can't. I'm so *so* sorry."

"Jess, please don't leave me here," I cry. How I have tears left is beyond me.

Jess is crying now, too. "I don't want to. Shit, they're coming. Hang in there, Ryenn you can do it. You're so strong. They're on their way home."

"Hey!" I hear a man's voice from down the hall. "Get away from there!"

Jess disappears.

"Jess!?" I yelled.

I'm screaming again, hauling in the chains. Blood trickles down my arms and my legs.

"Let me out!" I scream.

Let me out!

Let me out!

Let me out!

Let me out!

Let me out!

Let me out!

*Let me ou*t!

A Scout enters and shoves the gag in my mouth.

~

My tongue is stuck to the roof of my mouth against the metal ball that cuts into the corners of my mouth. I lie there on the cool cobblestone flooring, my hands and ankles still anchored to the floor. I can't move much against them without the torturous metal digging back into my skin, making it bleed.

I lay on the floor, shivering. My head pounds, and although I feel cold on the outside, there is still a steady burn in my veins.

The dress I am wearing is no longer an off-white. It is stained red from the blood I have lost and black from the dirty floors.

I dry heaved against the gag again, and luckily, I had nothing left in me to throw up; I nearly aspirated the last time I did because of the ball gag. It has been hours since it was placed, maybe even days since I have been here.

Then I heard something.

I sit up as much as I can, my breathing picking up, and my heart beats loudly.

There's a crash up the hall.

Someone is coming.

No, multiple people are coming.

Please, please, please, please.

Then I see them.

Ser Davis and Ser Arry beat open the metal door and came into the room.

Juno and Sara are right behind them, and I catch a glimpse of Amalie, Jess and Greyson. And then Celeste makes her way to the front of the group, Emmet by her side. Everyone takes a moment to stop to take in what they see.

I close my eyes; maybe this isn't real. Maybe I am hallucinating.

Then I smell her perfume and feel her arms around me.

"We're here. We're going to get you out." She is shaking, trying to get the clasps from the gag out of my mouth.

I am sobbing.

The gag finally releases, and I shut my mouth, tasting metallic blood.

"We need the keys," Celeste says, and I open my eyes.

She's on her knees, attempting to unlatch the manacles.

They are locked, and they don't have the keys with them.

Sara and Juno are near me, and I flinch.

"Get them off," I rasp, sounding like something out of a nightmare.

"Emmet, we need the keys," Celeste's eyes well, and she looked at Emmet, who was still standing in the doorway, dumbfounded.

"Seize the lord and lady of the capital; get those fucking keys," Emmet addresses Arry and Davis, and they take off down the corridor.

"Get them off," I say again, shaking.

"They're going to get the key, honey. It's okay. You're okay."

"No, I need them off Celeste. *Please*," I cry, pulling against the chains. My panic drowns out the agony, and blood pours down my arms and legs again.

"Ryenn, stay still. You're hurting yourself."

"*Please*," I repeat over and over. I can't take it anymore. Panic is taking over, and my vision is clouding. I fight the chains. I need them off now. *Right now.*

Celeste is trying to calm me, holding my face in her hands,

trying to use her cool wind to calm me, but it doesn't work.

I need them off.

Jess, Amalie and Greyson stand to the side and say something. Amalie is crying.

I need them off.

Celeste is talking to Juno and Sara, but I can't hear them. I can't hear anything. All I hear is the crashing flames, the panic and my pleading screams.

I need them off.

Sara is searching through her bag, grabs a syringe of something, and gets close. I am still thrashing against the chains, and blood is going everywhere. My blood. I am going to die.

I need them off.

Something sharp pricks my arm. I look over at Sara; she has injected something into my arm. My vision gets even cloudier, and my body feels heavy. The crashing stops all at once and I collapse to the cold cobblestone floor.

Chapter 52

Waking from a dreamless sleep, I bring my hands up and rub my face. Bright lights hurt my eyes as I tried to pry them open. Memories of what happened to me hit me all at once, and I surge upright, grabbing at my wrists. There are no manacles, no chains; just gauzy white bandages.

My vision finally comes back fully, and I realize where I am: the infirmary. Familiar beeping comes from the monitor above my head as I scan the room. I am alone.

My body starts shaking. I observe my arms, bandages covering my wrists, and tubing with medications and fluids attached to my hands. I don't feel my fire, though; that aching burn, that unbearable pressure, it's not there.

Panic takes root like a weight in my gut. Oh my Gods, did I hurt anyone? Is that why I am alone?

You're dangerous.

You're a monster.

You killed your sister and father, and you probably burned everyone else to smithereens.

You'll be a Queen of nothing but scorched ashes.

Air escapes me, and the monitor beeps louder, red blaring

across the screen.

Sara comes running from that same door as before.

"Ryenn, breathe. You are safe." She sits on my bed, trying to lay me back. "In and out; do it with me."

I try to listen, and I need to speak and to do that, I need to fucking breathe.

"Where-where is everyone?" I squeak out, my throat still raw.

"I'm going to alert them you are awake. Celeste literally just left to get something to eat. Honey they're okay, you're okay too. You just need to rest and heal up," she says in her hushed, calming voice.

"How-how long?" I manage to get out through breaths.

"You've been in the infirmary for two days." She rubs my arms and then grabs another blanket to lay across me.

"No, how-how long was I *there*-" I try again.

"Four days," she says hastily, and I suck in a breath. "Lie back, love. Your heart is beating far too fast. You need to relax a little bit."

I do as she says, mainly because I feel as though I may faint if I don't.

"I am going to go get them, okay?" She says.

"No- no, don't leave." My eyes blur with tears.

"Okay. Okay, I won't." She calls in a Scout then, one that I recognize used to stand guard outside my chambers to go retrieve my family. She holds my shaking hands and uses her healer powers to attempt to take the edge off the nerves I have.

Not even five minutes later, Celeste comes rushing back into the infirmary. She mustn't have been far down the corridor as she was the first to show up. She stops briefly, looking at me in the bed, and I sit up. Emotion clogs my throat again, and tears blur my vision. The Katiase makes me feel both relief and sorrow coming from Celeste, and she walks over and wraps me in her arms.

I sat there, sobbing into her hair and clinging onto her like how Lilly had clung to me when we ran from the schoolyard. She rubs my back, lavender-smelling cool breezes caress me, and she whispers soothing things to me, trying to calm me so that the monitor will shut up, beeping in the background.

"I'm so *so* sorry," she chokes. I feel the guilt then, potent and prickly.

I pull back to see her face, and I wipe my wet cheeks with my hands.

"It isn't your fault. It's my own," I rasp out, sucking in a too-short breath.

"*No*. No, that is *not* true, Ryenn. Garrett used his 'authority' to imprison you after causing you to snap. What he did was incredibly horrible. None of this was your fault. Vada, Garrett and the two Scouts involved are currently being held at trial."

"It is my fault," I whisper. "I *killed* them, Celeste. I killed my father and my baby sister. I wiped out half the population of Baytown. *I'm a monster,*" I break again, deep, rasping sobs escaping me.

"Oh, honey." She holds me and rocks me back and forth. I am somewhat aware that more people have begun to show up, but Sara keeps them outside my room for the time being while I am a complete mess.

I sniffled. "Did you know? Did you know it was me?"

"No. I didn't put two and two together, and it was *not* your fault. You didn't even know you were a Fae at that point; you didn't even know about fire powers or any of it. You had an emotional breakdown, and your powers were summoned before you even woke up to realize. It was all an accident. I know that doesn't bring them back, honey, but you did not purposely hurt anyone. You are *not* a monster." She spoke calmly but seriously, holding me against her.

I suppose it was true; I hadn't meant any of it, but it still didn't change the fact that they had all died at my hands. I don't think I'll ever be the same after that. Knowing that I was capable of doing that while being completely and utterly unaware before I had even Transitioned it haunted me knowing what I could be capable of.

I take a deep breath and lie back against my pillow, and Celeste hands me a tissue to wipe my nose. The monitor finally stops beeping as I start to un-clench and relax.

"You have a few visitors waiting outside." Celeste brushes a piece of my hair behind my ear. "Would you like me to send them away for now, or would you like to see them? They have been very, very worried."

"I want to see them," I rasp back.

~

My room in the infirmary had quickly become packed with people. I was still uneasy but have calmed down a bit seeing everyone. There was also no intense pressure of flames, which kept me a bit more comfortable; plus, whatever medication was running through the line in my arm must have been something to cease the panic.

Celeste sat on a chair next to the head of my bed, Ser Arry and Ser Davis stood by the entrance, Jess stood near Celeste, Amalie was sitting at the foot of my bed, and Grey was on a chair in the corner of my room. Emmet was apparently holding a council meeting with everyone to discuss what was to become of Vada and Garrett. Pippa and their younger baby brother were being watched by Evie and some other handmaidens in the familial quarters. I shut out the Katiase for now. The feelings of everyone started to get overwhelming and I could barely handle my feelings, let alone everyone else's. Sara was in the process of braiding my unruly, thick hair as everyone chatted. I hadn't said much due to my throat hurting.

There was a moment of silence, though, and I decided to be bold.

"I want you to tell me what happened," I said to the room, hoping someone would answer.

"Ryenn, maybe you need to rest first-" Celeste starts.

"No. No more being kept in the dark. I want to know it all. Jess?" I turned to the red-haired female, and she sighed uneasily but sat on my bed near my hip.

"I'll tell you what I know. I owe that to you," she says and then clears her throat. "After I left you that evening, as you were heading to dinner, I headed back to the tattoo shop and had a few more clients. Not long after finishing for the night, Ser Arry came and said he was off duty and was hoping to be fit in for a tattoo, which I obliged even though I was tired."

"Anyway, we ended up back in the room at the inn, and… anyway, that part is not important. The next day, I was swamped with clients, so I didn't make my way to the castle until late that evening to go check up on you like I promised Cece I would. When I got there, the vibes were just weird. I made it to the west side of the castle and hadn't seen Arry since. I ran into Vada, though and asked where you were. She got mad that I was supposed to be checking up on you, saying she was quite capable of watching you for Celeste anyway. We got into an argument, and her Scouts escorted me out."

She took a deep breath but continued, "I went back to the Inn, feeling uneasy about everything because I had promised to keep an eye out for you, and the whole situation was just…*weird*. I couldn't sleep the whole night. Early the next morning, Greyson showed up at my door, carrying Amalie in his arms." She looked over at the two; Amalie was abnormally quiet, and Grey shook his head at his aunt.

"Anyways, as I told you when I showed up to your cell, Amalie had told Grey what happened to you and then found me. I went straight to the castle, finally finding Arry, who had been put on main bridge duty."

"Garret and Vada told me their Scouts sufficed to keep you safe and that I would be better on my usual post. I argued, but his orders trumped me…" Arry said then from the door.

"We were able to distract the guards in the dungeon, or Arry did by telling them they were needed elsewhere, and I found you…" tears sprung to her eyes, and Celeste grabbed her hand.

"Ryenn, you looked like a *ghost*. You were pale, probably from puking and losing so much blood, too much blood. I was terrified for you, I needed to get you out, but then the fucking guards came and got me, despite Arry attempting to help… Let's just say I was slightly reprimanded for my actions, and I was able to escape them though. Before I had set out for the castle, I had sent messages to Celeste and Emmet, as well as my sister." I noticed then the purplish shadow under Jess's left lime-green eye. She had been hit. I took a shuddery breath and took Jess's hand, and she looked up at me, tears still streaming slowly down her face.

"Thank you," I croak.

"I wish I could've done more, Ryenn. Gods, I really tried, but they had you guarded so heavily and-" She takes a sharp inhale.

"Stop. You did what you could. Thank you," I say again, and she nods, wiping her eyes.

"What happened after?" I look to Celeste, and everyone exchanges worried looks.

"We never received Jess's message until early the next

morning. We had been busy attempting to fix the forcefield the entire evening and then fell asleep. As soon as we received it, we took off to head back home, Emmet even sent a message to the guards to stand down, but they never listened, thinking they had to obey Garrett's orders or they'd be reprimanded. Gods, Ryenn, I freaked out the entire way. It took us way too long to get back and I am so sorry.

We got back, there was a big fight, but we ended up making our way to the dungeons. Jess, Amalie, Grey and Ser Arry met us at the gate; they had been waiting for our return and had already been attempting to bargain. Anyways, we finally got down to you and-my Gods, I really thought you were gone." Celeste's worry makes me feel sick to my stomach. It was uncomfortable; had I really been that bad off?

"Ryenn, the cuffs they put on you not only nullify powers but also torture the person it is used on; it has been known to kill people in *days*. It is ancient magic, like the Septor, and I am not sure how on earth they got ahold of them. They also dig in when you move, as I am sure you are aware, and you have already lost so much blood. Juno had obviously accompanied us back to the kingdom and had made sure to grab Sara, who was unaware that any of this had happened."

"The entire kingdom was unaware. They met us down there in case you were badly hurt, which you were. They also had you gagged and chained down; I really don't know how you survived. Just about four whole days went by with you like *that*. And then you started to panic when you saw us because we didn't have the keys to remove the manacles, and we had to sedate you so you didn't hurt yourself more than you were."

Gods.

I don't even know what to feel. The air was thick and heavy, and my heart started racing again.

But everyone looked like there was more to the story.

"What else?" I asked nervously.

Exchanging worried glances with the group, Celeste continued, "Honey, when we removed the manacles, all your pent-up powers *exploded* out of you. Now, you never hurt anyone, so don't worry about that; it wasn't fire; it was more like an earth-rattling explosion of pure power. It was felt all over the entire kingdom. We all thought it had killed you, but Juno was able to keep you stable enough to get you down to the infirmary, and you've been here ever since."

Oh my Gods

That's why I didn't feel the fire in my veins.

"Ryenn…" Celeste continued, biting her lip. "It shattered the forcefields."

Chapter 53

I broke the forcefields, the main thing keeping Rebels and the Dark King out of Sanctania. Celeste had attempted to explain that just because the force fields no longer stood didn't necessarily mean we were doomed. That old Fae who were well versed in magic were already attempting to come up with a solution to rebuild them, but still. That sense of security was *gone*. And it was me who ended it.

I was exhausted at this point, emotionally and physically, hardly able to talk any longer, and I think Celeste got the hint and asked people to start to leave to give me some time to rest. To take in everything that had happened. I stopped Amalie before she made it all the way out of the room and asked Celeste if I could have a moment along with her.

Amalie slowly made her way up next to me, and I sat up.

"Are you okay?" I squeeze out.

She shakes her head and brings her hand up to her mouth, squeezing her eyes shut.

"Amalie…" I whisper and lean forward, embracing her in a hug. She sobs.

"I'm sorry, Ry. I'm really, *really* sorry."

"*I'm* sorry," I say to her and touch her back. She flinches at the touch and straightens.

"Amy, what did they do to you?" I looked into her golden hazel eyes that were soaking wet.

She takes a deep breath "I never told you what would be my punishment before. I was always embarrassed that they hurt me. It happened too often, and… I don't know why, but I was ashamed."

"*What did they do?*" I clench my jaw.

"They whipped me. Father has a horsewhip that he kept in his office in case I needed a… lesson. Like the night after the ball, he whipped me three times. That was the most he had ever done before, and it didn't draw blood, but it was still shameful. He'd make me strip off, and then he would make me bend over his desk and apologize…" she sniffed, and I wiped her tears with my thumb.

"I tried so hard to get to you, to make them stop. He locked me in his office, stripped my clothing and made Pippa watch as he whipped me over and over. I stopped counting because I was sure I had gone unconscious. He drew blood this time. I am still… sore. Anyway, after waking up, Pippa snuck back to the office with some clothes for me, and I was able to gather enough strength to leave. I ran all the way across the castle to Greyson, who was outside of the boarding house. I didn't know who else to get, and I didn't know where his aunt was staying. I was able to mutter out what had happened, and we started running to get Jess; I collapsed along the way from blood loss, I guess. Grey carried me. I have been staying at the Inn since. Pippa and Samuel were left in the tower, and I couldn't get them out. I couldn't go back. Gods, Ry, I am so sorry. I tried so so hard-"

We stayed together, hugging each other and apologizing back and forth. I had never wished someone was dead before, but at that moment, I really, *really* wished her parents were dead. If Emmet didn't end them, I vowed I would. Screw this whole being afraid of hurting people shit. Those fuckers deserved the worst kind of torture.

~

I woke up later, realizing Amalie had fallen asleep next to me in my infirmary bed. Celeste was sitting in the chair reading a book, and she looked up at me as I sat up.

"Hi," she whispers.

"Hey," I whisper, my throat still scratchy.

"How are you feeling?"

"Kind of shitty if I am being honest. Sore," I sigh and rub my eyes, taking a deep breath. The panic that had been plaguing me since taking over that hollow cavern was still there, but the effects were hampered by whatever medication was still being injected into me and probably since I had slept.

"Would you like to try and eat something?"

My stomach growled at that. I definitely was hungry, but I felt similar to how I had before when I was attacked. I didn't want to be weak and frail like that again, so I nodded.

She left to get something. Amalie was still sound asleep, and I didn't want to disturb her. I am sure she needed just as much rest as I did, so when Celeste came back with some soup, she helped me into a chair to eat it.

"She told me everything," I whisper to Celeste then.

"She told me too…" Celeste emits worry and sadness from her. "I can't believe my sister had a part in that. I knew she was strict, but I had no idea they were hurting Amalie. Pippa denies them ever laying a finger on her or Samuel, but Pippa still had to sit by and watch her big sister be tortured," she sharply inhales.

My face flushes with anger.

"What is going to happen to them? Is the meeting completed?"

"Emmet will come to tell us when they finish up. Amalie and her siblings will never be subject to them again, though; I am taking custody of them."

I smiled, and my heart felt like it lit up.

"Really?"

"Yes, dear. I am never ever going to let them be in harm's way again. Amalie is still going to be Lady of the Capital, but we will find someone to take her place until her 21st birthday. Evie and the other handmaidens are already preparing some of the spare rooms in the familial quarters for them," she smiles.

"Does Amalie know?" I look over at my sleeping friend; she looks so young and innocent right now.

"Not yet… she's been quite emotional and everything, so we decided to wait until she gets some rest. This is the first time she has slept since waking up in the office."

My heart swells.

Fuck I want to kill them.

"Ryenn, I think it's sweet that you care for them so much, but I want you to care for yourself too. What happened to them was not your fault. We are going to fix it and make it better, and that's all we can do, unfortunately. We won't be able to take back what has already been done. Simply go forward and make things right, okay?"

I knew that, still deep down I made my whole body tremble to think about the past. I nod, though, stupid tears welling in my eyes. I am not sure why I start to cry, but I do.

"That goes for what happened to your cottage and your

family, too. You didn't mean to do it. You are not a monster; far from it. We can't take it back now. Just move on from it. What Garrett did was cruel but also calculated. Just so you know, he was trying to get a rise out of you to implement the plans he had already been planning with Vada to put you in that fucking dungeon with those gods-forsaken manacles and then hopefully let it kill you before we came back-" she takes a deep breath, her whole chest rising,

"- Anyways; You survived. You will continue to survive, and you want to know how I know that? Because you are *strong*. Not only as a means of being a powerful Fae but also brave and strong as a whole. And you are *good*. The force fields were weak, and yes, they broke, but it will be fixed. We will move forward and implement new plans, okay? None of this was your fault."

She strokes my cheek as the stinging tears fall.

I believed her. I really did. I just needed to heal, and then I would be able to help make up for the mistakes I had made... There's no reason to dwell on it, even though my mind will unfortunately try and trick me into going back to those places, but I *can* move forward. I have to. I will be a Queen, a good one.

Chapter 54

Emmet came by later and explained all the plans that were in place as we advanced. Vada and Garrett were currently being held in the dungeons until their punishment was entirely decided and a true trial could be held. It was also decided that, given their bravery and willingness to save me, Jess and Ser Arry would be the new Lord and Lady of the capital until Amalie came of age to take her rightful place. I was over the moon to hear this; they deserved it. Plus, I am sure Celeste was quite happy that her friends would be in the castle.

He also explained that while the force fields were shattered, there had been no rebel attempts, and he isn't sure that they even knew the force fields were shattered. Nonetheless, there were increased numbers of Scouts on the perimeters and the walls to ensure there were no attempts. Juno also went back to Carlisle to assist with the rebuild; apparently, they were able to find the initial spell, but there needs to be work on figuring out how to actually complete it, considering it is ancient.

Amalie slept in my bed the entire time; she was utterly exhausted, and I wanted her to rest as long as she needed. Pippa and Samuel were also doing good, according to Evie who had popped by to say hello and to bring a card that they had made. It was very sweet.

Sara was now in the process of changing the bandages on my wrists and ankles. I winced through my teeth, and she applied a cool but stinging cleanser on the open wounds.

"I know it hurts. I am almost done. You'll most likely scar, and it is going to take a while for them to heal because it was caused by magic and that metal, which prevents the fast healing ability of Fae and that of healers," Sara says, looking above her glasses to look me in the eye.

"It's okay," I say. I already had plans for what I was going to do about the scarring. I just needed them to heal enough so I could get tattoos over them.

Amalie rolled over then and yawned, sitting up groaning.

"How long have I been asleep here?" She squinted at the lights.

"About a day. I didn't want to disturb you." I wince again as Sara dabs my wrists with some cotton.

"Shit, Ry, that looks like it hurts," she winces as she looks at my wrists.

"Yeah, it does… My ankles aren't as bad, though. She just finished up."

"Amalie, I need to change the bandages on your back as well, dear." Sara looks at her, and she blushes. I get embarrassment, thick and uncomfortable spider walk like a shiver up my spine.

Sara finishes wrapping clean gauze around my arms and then goes to get supplies for Amalie.

"Would you like me to leave?" I ask Amalie.

"No… Can you actually stay? Maybe hold my hand?" she asks, face red.

"Absolutely," I smile.

Sara comes back and has Amalie undress and lay on her stomach in case she passes out. I sit on the bed next to her and hold one of her hands. Her back is covered with a large white bandage; there is some blood visible on the outside already, and I take a deep breath.

"Now, dear, I am going to use my powers, as you know, to try and ease some of the pain, but I am giving you a warning that this will hurt."

"I know," she whispers. "Just do it."

Sara carefully removes the tape and then the bandage in one sheet. My eyes widen and tears start to gather.

"Amy…" I whisper and tighten my grip on her hand. There were at least a good dozen open lashes spread across her small back. Six were raw and still had blood pooling at the surface. This didn't include the marks that hadn't broken skin, which accompanied bruises at different stages of healing.

"I know," she sobs then, embarrassment seeping through her every pore as she shivers.

"It's okay. It'll heal. You don't need to be embarrassed or ashamed; this was not your fault," I say, and she sobs harder, but her emotions feel lighter.

"Thanks, Ry," she sniffs.

"Alright, honey, I need to put the cleansing salts on now, okay? They stay on for a minute, and then it's over."

"Fuck I hate this part," she winces, and Sara spreads the minty-smelling salts over her back. Her whole body tenses against the contact.

"You can do. it, Amy. You can do it. You're so strong." I say and pet her head

Sara removes the salts a minute later and dresses Amalie's back again. Amalie passed out halfway through the minute from the pain, which was probably better than suffering through it. According to Sara, she believes the whip used may have been covered in some sort of venom to make the lashes sting more and have more effect. It was tortuous and cruel. I laid the blanket up so that she could rest from the pain and decided to go for a little walk just out to the desk and back, trying to regain some of my strength.

As soon as I left the room, Grey walked into the infirmary. I was suddenly hyper-aware that the only thing I had on was one of those papery white gowns, and my undergarments were completely visible through the open back of the gown. Sara, being the saint she is, must have realized and brought a second gown to tie around the backside of me so that I was less exposed. Grey smiled as he neared me by the desk.

"You're up," he states.

"I couldn't sit still any longer. I can't wait to get back to training, and I feel like I have lost all of my progress."

"Yeah, well, maybe you should take it easy for a few more days. Wouldn't be a fair fight, frisky" he smirks.

"Good excuse." I roll my eyes and then meet his gaze. He doesn't feel pity or sadness. He feels relieved and happy. Also, that fruity lust undertone; how can he look at me with lust when I look like this? I clear my throat. "Thank you, by the way. For everything."

"I wish I could have done more," he says then, his smile dropping slightly.

"You did more than enough. I wouldn't be here right now if Amalie hadn't found you, so thanks. And thank you for protecting her."

"Don't mention it. She was in pretty rough shape. You were

too…. Scared me shitless." His features paled a bit, and mine turned bright red. He was there and saw me in the cell yet he still feels *things* towards me. That reckless flapping of butterflies decided now was a good time to make a comeback.

"Sorry for scaring you," I whisper, and he inches closer and brushes a strand of my hair out of my face. His fingers linger, and I hold my hand on his

"Don't go all soft on me, frisky," he says.

"Why not?"

"Makes me want to do things you might not like."

"Like what?" His face is mere inches away from mine

"Kiss you." He smiles slightly so that his fangs are visible.

"What makes you think I won't like that?" I grin, matching his sultry one. He growls low in his throat.

"Just an assumption."

"Maybe we should test that assumption."

Then we collide. He kisses me deeply, passionately. Similar to how we kissed in the garden the night of the ball, but also with a sense of relief and urgency, like he's been waiting to do it since. I let the kiss devour me, let it wash away all of my negative thoughts and fill me with other interesting feelings.

At that moment, I didn't care if the entire godsdamn kingdom saw us, me in my paper-thin infirmary gown and everything. My stomach tensed, that curling desire going deep, my breasts swelling. *Lust.* The acidic grapefruit filled my senses, my own and Greyson's twirling together between us. It was overpowering and made me sway slightly, and I reached out to grab the desk.

Greyson stopped then, pulling away from my lips and catching me against him.

"You okay?" he looked at me worried.

"Yeah," I squeak and clear my throat. "I think I am still adjusting to standing for this long," I laugh nervously.

"Let's get you back to bed then." He holds me under my arm and guides me back to my room. Amalie is sitting up on the bed now, smiling widely as we enter. I realize she just had a front-row seat to whatever just happened. Grey helps me back into the bed next to Amalie.

"Thanks," I say, a little embarrassed. Not by what happened. I had no regrets about that. I was just embarrassed over nearly fainting in his arms.

"No problem. Listen, there's a little girl who keeps nagging me to bring her to see you. She doesn't know exactly what happened, only that your infirmary. I keep telling her that you need to rest, but

I feel if I come back to the boarding house and she finds out I came here without her, she'll have my head," he chuckles.

"I assume you're talking about Lilly," I laugh back.

"That would be her," he sighs.

"Of course she can come," I smile. I missed the kid; I am sure she missed me too.

"Okay, I will bring her to visit this evening. See you later, frisky." he winks and leaves the room, leaving me blushing and leaving Amalie giggling.

Chapter 55

The rest of the day, I just relaxed in bed, Amalie at my side, and people were coming in and out visiting. Celeste was there the majority of the day; she also told Amalie the news about her taking custody of her, and Amalie was thankful. I also got some hesitance from her, but she was nervous overall so I completely understood why she would feel that way. Jess came by, saying how busy it was now that she had to sit in on the council and everything.

The usual calm and confident woman did seem frazzled, but she was ecstatic when I asked her to tattoo my scars once they healed. Emmet also came by to check in occasionally as well; he wasn't very talkative, and I could tell he was nervous and felt bad about the whole ordeal. Greyson also brought Lilly in to see me, and she drew me a picture. She nearly lept all the way from the door onto the bed. I missed her more than I think I realized, some of that also brought up the sorrow of Rose once again.

I feel like I was taking it all in stride, though. I didn't let the fear overwhelm me, but I wasn't numb like I had been after the attacks on Molisan and Carlisle. I had feelings; they were big and threatened to make me snap, but I breathed through them and kept myself busy while talking to people.

Sara had also said I was medically cleared to go to my chambers the next morning so that's where I currently was. Celeste had washed my hair for me. I couldn't get in the bath due to my injuries, but she was able to wash it under the running faucet. It felt good, freeing, actually. Amalie had been escorted to her new chambers just down the hall; she still had to share with Pippa, but she requested it stay that way.

I looked in the mirror above my sink in my bathroom, the first time I had since… well, you know. I didn't look that bad; pale, sure, but besides the injuries to my wrists and ankles, I had already healed elsewhere due to being a Fae now. My lip scar was still there, and there were two scabbed scars on either side of my mouth from the gag. Thinking about that ball in my mouth made me take a deep breath, feeling too closed in.

I had to keep the sliding door to my bathroom open when I was in there because it felt too *small*. I actually panicked a bit when I first came in to pee, feeling like I was back there. Celeste had to come in and keep the door open so I knew I wasn't alone, and I knew I wasn't trapped. Stupid, I know, but it was going to take some time to get over.

Leaving my washroom and taking a seat on my bed, I started to do some schoolwork that I was once again behind on. It only took me a few hours to catch up, though. Celeste sat by the window at my desk doing some paperwork. The real trial for Vada and Garrett was going to be held tomorrow, and their fate would be decided. I hoped it ended in their death. Emmet was now busy assisting with all the lords and ladies from the other districts arriving in the capital. I am sure they are sick of traveling at this point.

"Celeste, will Amalie and Pippa have to attend the trial tomorrow?" I ask. I was hoping they'd never have to see those monsters again.

"Sadly, yes, both girls will be asked to make statements, and the council may want to use the Septor on Amalie. Ryenn, you should be prepared that they may have to use it on you as well."

Fuck I hadn't even thought about that.

I am not sure I can handle doing that again.

My breathing picks up.

My vision starts to narrow.

The walls are closing in.

No windows.

No escape.

Chains.

A gag.

I felt hands around my face, cool and gentle. My vision came back, and I focused on blue eyes in front of mine.

"In and out," the gentle voice says.

In for three,

Hold for three,

Out for three.

I am in my chambers. I am no longer trapped. *This is real.*

"It's okay," Celeste says, smoothing my back. "You can refuse the Septor if you need to. We don't have to do it. No one will blame you if you can't."

"I will do what needs to be done," I whisper.

~

I don't sleep well all night. Celeste stayed as per my request. I was still too nervous to be alone, and although I should have been more ashamed, I wasn't. I went through something traumatizing, and it's okay to be vulnerable. That's what I keep telling myself to make myself feel better anyway. There is a mean, evil voice in the back of my brain that I am attempting to drown out by doing such, but it occasionally makes it through.

Monster.

Pathetic.

Weak.

No. I am not. It would hitch my breathing for a second, but I won't let it affect me any further.

Sara comes to my room in the early morning to change my bandages before the trial. I am wearing a long-sleeved red dress to cover my arms. I also go to Amalie's chambers and hold her hand while her bandages are changed. Celeste took Pippa for a walk to get some juice while we were doing that. She didn't pass out this time, though, and I could notice some difference from the last time the bandages were changed two days ago. I was assisting her get dressed now, she was still quite sore and could hardly get her dress on herself.

"Pippa had a nightmare last night," she says quietly. "She wet her bed and everything. She was so distraught. She slept with me for the rest of the night. Not that I slept, but still. I feel horrible for her, Ry. She's too young for this like Samuel is a baby, so he doesn't know any different, and I am older anyways, and it hurts me, but I can't imagine how it must be affecting her."

"Poor thing," I say.

"I don't know what to do to help her. I can't even help *myself*." I realize tears are starting to fall down her fair face.

"Amy, you are still a child too. Indeed, it isn't fair for Pippa, and it isn't fair for you either. We will do what we can to help, and she'll be okay. You are both strong. You guys aren't on your own; you have a whole slew of people to help, and I am at the top of that list."

"Thanks," she whispers. "I really wish we didn't have to do this today."

"I wish that too."

~

The air was sticky and humid as we all walked together through the corridors of the castle. I walked with Amalie, holding her hand while her little sister held the other. Celeste and Emmet walked directly in front of us, and Jess and Arry walked directly behind us. Ser Davis led the group, and seven scouts surrounded all of us. My hair clung to the nape of my neck, and a shimmer of sweat glistened on my forehead.

The Throne Room looked far too familiar this way. All the Fae gathered, waiting for the trial to commence. I was to sit on my throne with Emmet and Celeste, while Pippa and Amalie would sit near the front with Arry and Jess. Not only was the air heavy with humidity, but it was also heavy with so many emotions. It made it tricky to swallow.

Sitting on my throne at the top of the stairs I spot Greyson sitting next to his mother and father. He gives me a curt nod, almost as if saying, "You can do this," and I give him a sheepish grin back. Could I do this, though? Guess we are going to find out.

Garret and Vada are led in by Scouts minutes later. They are placed on stools, similar to how myself and Corbin were during his trial. I immediately feel a pang of fear coming from the two girls who look at their parents with similar distaste. It makes my heart ache for them, and the burn returns to my veins. It kind of surprised me that I felt those flames. I hadn't even felt them at all since the apparent earth-rattling explosion when the manacles were removed from me. I swallow, trying to snuff out some of that persistent heat.

Emmet begins the trial in a similar fashion to the previous one, but I barely listen. My main focus is on my best friend, who almost looks as though she may faint, and on keeping my burn to a minimum.

"Before using the Septor, I would like to offer the opportunity to confess to what you two conspired against and to the assaults you have committed," Emmet says then.

"Your Majesty, you use the terms conspire and assaults as if you have already determined me and my wife to be guilty. We are guilty of nothing besides attempting to raise good children, ones with respect for authority, and for also offering the same to your niece while she was under our care. We did nothing to hurt Ryenn, and she was a danger to herself and others and in that moment, I saw it fit to put her somewhere she could not lash out. You know yourself just what those fire powers could do. You saw with your own eyes what she did to her own family-"

"That's quite enough, Garrett," Emmet stands, voice booming.

All blood feels like it leaves my body, leaving nothing behind but an agony of fire in my body.

"Let me rephrase for you what you seem to believe is good parenting: whipping your child with a horsewhip coated in Yeres Venom on more than one occasion, forcing your child to watch as you assault their sibling, shove the heir of the kingdom into enchanted manacles, ones that have been known to kill Fae in less than a week, keep in her in a dungeon without food or water, leaving her in her filth and ball gagging her so she could not scream for help. Tell me how you believe those actions to be not guilty."

There were hushed voices throughout the crowd, and feelings of mainly disgust and distrust rose from the crowd. My anger and disgust mixed along well.

"If you think that is what is considered to be guilty, then I guess you have already made your decision," Garrett says. "Just know that she-" he points a finger to me "-will be the end to this kingdom."

I look down at the man and smile wide as his eyes look horrified. Let him think that. I don't give a damn anymore.

"Vada, do you have anything to say?" Celeste says.

"The only thing I have to say is that you are a coward and should never have been nominated to take the Throne when Elanore was murdered. She may have been a shit queen, but you somehow have done an even worse job than her if you think letting this atrocity of a Fae be the heir is a good idea," Vada sneers.

Celeste sits back upright against her chair, and I catch a tang of hurt coming from her. My veins ache against the pressure. Fuck I want them dead.

"As king, I have made my decision; they are guilty of treason, assault and battery, child abuse, neglect and conspiring against the crown. Any objections from the council?" He scans the crowd, and I do the same. Not a single person raises their hand or stands. That act, or lack thereof, makes Garrett furious.

"You pieces of *shit*," he spits to the council. "I have been Lord of the Capital longer than most of you have even been on this fucking council, and you sit there and betray me. You are all idiots and will get what's coming to you when she burns the fucking kingdom to *ashes.*"

Pippa starts to cry at her father yelling, drawing his attention.

"You are both disgraced if you are to stand by and let them do this to your parents," he says to the girls. The fire curls in my throat.

They say nothing. Amalie looks pale, and Ser Arry lifts Pippa as she cries into his shoulder.

"Just as I thought. Amalie, you are a disappointment. I knew you would never have what it takes to be Lady, let alone the fucking Heir Champion, if that title hadn't been eradicated. You disgust me, and I hope those lashes *sting*," he snarls.

Amalie turns away from her father as she cringes at the last sentence. Jess holds her into her. I feel the cracking agony ripple through her.

That's *enough*.

I stand, flicking my wrists as the flames rise from my hands. The audience that was just talking and arguing over Garrett goes completely silent as I walk toward the edge of the dais.

Emmet and Celeste don't stop me; they know what I have to do.

"Don't you *ever* speak to her again," I say, my voice booming similarly to that of Emmet's.

His attention flicks to mine then, and he goes as pale as a ghost as he sees me making my way down the steps.

"What are you doing?" he asks, his voice not so full of the spite and confidence he just had talking down to his daughter.

"It's Your Highness," I say, and he stills. "Say it." My flames grow.

"Y-Your Highness," he mutters.

"Get on your knees," I sneer. He does so without hesitation. "You too," I say to Vada, and she grapples to the floor.

I turn my head to Arry then, Pippa still curled in his large arms, face pressed against him. "Take her out of here" he does so with a nod and leaves with the small child. I looked at my friend then, her face flushed and tears streaked. She gives me a nod of approval. *Good.*

Garrett lifts his face to look at me, then to look at the king and queen sitting idly by.

"You're going to let her do this? She is a *child-*"

"Did I say you could look at them?" I take my foot and guide his face so that it looks at mine.

He says nothing and looks down at the ground.

"Bowing looks good on your Garrett. You should do it more often," I scoff. Vada shivers next to him. "You too."

"You are a *bit-*" he doesn't get to finish.

Flames erupt from me then, effortlessly, and engulf him and his wife.

"Go to Hell," I straighten, flicking the fire from my palms.

Nothing but ashes remained in front of me.

Chapter 56

The entire Throne Room is quiet. I don't use my Katiase; I don't want to feel what they are feeling. I don't want to feel anything. I look up at the emerald doors and walk out of the Throne Room. Gazes follow my every step.

~

I end up walking out to the bridge at the main entrance. Why I came here, I don't know. I needed a breath of air, not that I felt bad about what I did. I felt nothing, or maybe I felt a bit glad, but still. I didn't last long alone before my family started to come through the doors to join me. Celeste, Emmet, Jess, Arry, Ser Davis, Amalie, Greyson, Juno, and a few others came out. I think they thought I was going to jump from the bridge. But I was fine. Everything was fine.

Until it wasn't.

The sky began to cloud over for the first time in the entire season, making it eerily dark. Before anyone could say anything to me, there was a crash above, and then the gates to the Castle property blew off their hinges.

Thick smoke leaked through, and figures started to walk forward.

Emmet came and stood in front of me, the rest of the group hanging back slightly except for Celeste, who stood close behind me.

A tall, dark figure came out of the shadows then.

A Fae.

A Fire Fae. He had been the one to blow the gate off its hinges

The Fae removed his hooded cloak then, revealing a hard jawline, well-kept appearance and stark white hair. A black crown, one with embedded rubies, sat above the white-as-snow hair.

I knew immediately he was the Dark King.

A smile crept over his face as he looked down at me. He was the same height as Emmet, maybe slightly taller. He was flanked by hundreds of cloaked figures, the rebels. One small one stood next to him, cloaked and masked.

"Well, well, well," The Dark King says in a mockery voice, one that is gruff but not what I was expecting. "Been a while since being allowed in the kingdom. Looks the same, though; boring."

"Who are you, and what do you want?" Emmet announces.

"Seriously? You don't know who I am?" He motions to the crown. "I am who you people like to refer to as 'the Dark King'. Has a nice ring to it, actually. I am King Deveron of Aclos. What I want, I believe I have already found." He looks back at me and my heart thunders. Why does he want me?

Emmet says nothing.

"Do you know how long we have been attempting to get in here? Never worked, though, and we couldn't figure out exactly why. That was until someone by the name of...Corbin was it? Showed up on our doorstep seeking refuge. Seems as though he was exiled from this lovely little kingdom. Anyways, Corbin said quite a few interesting things, one being the new heir to the throne randomly showing up, which didn't make sense to me for many reasons, but also that he knew there was a force field protecting this whole kingdom." He laughed then, evil and loud. "It's funny, you know, clever actually in most senses-

"You and your kind are not welcome here," Emmet states, standing up straighter.

"Gods, you are annoying."

Before I can blink, the Dark King grabs Emmet and presses a knife to his throat. Celeste screams, and I immediately push all of them back, using a wall of fire to prevent them from coming forward and risking the rest of them being hurt.

"Interesting." He smiles and sizes me up, and then the fire.

"Let him go," I say, looking up at the man.

"Nah, I think I'll keep him here for a minute so I can actually finish my story... As I was saying, we had no idea about said force fields. Our attack weakened them, and we were planning on how to take the rest of them down before they were reinforced, but then a beautiful, strong power shook the entire planet and broke it for us. I assume that was *you*."

"Why would you assume that?"

"Because you have the Drakōn Flame, clearly. You are strong. And you are also the heir Corbin spoke of, making you of my interest." He steps closer.

"Don't you touch her," Emmet mutters against the blade.

"Yeah, I am done with you," he slits Emmet's throat, ending up in a pool of blood on the ground.

I scream something and hear screams coming from behind me, ones I recognize as Celeste's as she watches through the silver flame barrier.

"Oh, stop it." The King rolls his eyes. "Don't act like you didn't just incinerate a lord and lady inside that castle."

"How do you know about that?"

"I didn't, but now I do. You are so easy to read. A flaw like your mother had." He wipes his dagger in a cloth from his pocket.

"What do you *want?*" I seethe through my teeth, staring at the blood pooling on my shoes. Emmet's blood.

"We have already established this. I want *you*. Anyways, try to keep up," he laughs. "Oh wait, forgive me and my manners."

He motions to the Rebel standing next to them, and they step forward right into the pool of blood.

"Take down your hood and mask, child, don't be rude."

The rebel did as ordered, revealing a young female. She had the same color hair as the king but everything else… She looked *identical* to me.

The freckles, the eyes, her stature, literally everything besides the stark white hair, which I had two strips of.

My mouth falls open as the girl stares at me with a clenched jaw. I feel the confusion and shock rippling from those behind me, feel it myself as I take in a near reflection of myself.

"Say hello to my daughter; Fallon," The Dark King says then, clasping the girl on the shoulders. "Your twin sister."

THE END

Acknowledgments

There are many people who made this book possible and I fear simply an acknowledgments page does not entirely do them justice, but I will try. To begin, I want to thank my biggest supporters; my parents. Without you I would have never taken my dream and turned it into a book. Without you I would have never made that first step to look into publishing my book. Without you I would have never dreamt this to be possible at all. You both fuel my confidence and it means the world to me that you believed in my success even when I couldn't see that for myself. Thank you for your unending love and support not only as an author, but as your daughter. You both shaped me into the independent woman I am today and I am forever grateful. The same goes for my grandparents. Nan and Pop, thank you for being supportive and being so incredibly excited for me during this entire process. Additionally, I would like to thank the team at Blue Mount Publishing. You guys made my clueless first-time self-publishing journey as smooth as possible and did an absolutely wonderful job. The book would not be complete without you guys, and it definitely would not look as good. I also want to thank my dogs. Yes, my dogs, it would not be an acknowledgement without mentioning them. Pippa, Levi and Koda, thank you for listening to me read my manuscript aloud thousands of times. Thank you for sitting with me while I write to keep me company and thank you for being the light of my life. Pretty sappy I know since they can't read but you best believe I will be reading this to them as well. Finally, I want to thank all the authors out there who got me interested in fantasy and fiction, who's characters built my personality, who's writing styles shaped my own and who made me believe this was possible. Sara J. Maas, Jennifer L. Armentrout, H.D Carlton, Rebecca Yarros and Carrissa Broadbent are a few of my idols that come to mind. You guys are the coolest ever and thank you for the universes you have created that give the nerds, like myself, a means of escape. I hope that one day my books will provide that comfort as well. Before I end off, I want to thank you, the reader. Thanks for picking up this book and deciding to read it. I appreciate you more than you'll ever know. Well maybe you will know. I don't know, just know that I am crying with gratitude while I write this haha. Follow your dreams and make them a reality. Thank you for making mine real.

Love,

Madi

About the Author

Madison L. Bailey is a first time author that lives in a rural community in Eastern Canada. When she's not reading or writing, she spends her time working as a Registered Nurse in a Emergency Room. She lives with her three dogs and two skinny pigs and is often found curled up on her couch with a smutty little fantasy book in her lap.

TO BE QUEEN OF SCORCHED ASHES

Madison L. Bailey